The Lives Of The Roman Poets: Containing A Critical And Historical Account Of Them And Their Writings, With Large Quotations Of Their Most Celebrated Passages, As Far As Was Necessary To Compare And Illustrate Their Several Excellencies, As Well As To Dis

Lewis Crusius

Nabu Public Domain Reprints:

You are holding a reproduction of an original work published before 1923 that is in the public domain in the United States of America, and possibly other countries. You may freely copy and distribute this work as no entity (individual or corporate) has a copyright on the body of the work. This book may contain prior copyright references, and library stamps (as most of these works were scanned from library copies). These have been scanned and retained as part of the historical artifact.

This book may have occasional imperfections such as missing or blurred pages, poor pictures, errant marks, etc. that were either part of the original artifact, or were introduced by the scanning process. We believe this work is culturally important, and despite the imperfections, have elected to bring it back into print as part of our continuing commitment to the preservation of printed works worldwide. We appreciate your understanding of the imperfections in the preservation process, and hope you enjoy this valuable book.

THE LIVES OF THE Roman POETS.

CONTAINING

A Critical and Historical Account of Them and their Writings, with large Quotations of their most celebrated Passages, as far as was necessary to compare and illustrate their several Excellencies, as well as to discover wherein they were deficient.

To which is added,

A Chronological Table, fitted to the Years before and after CHRIST, shewing the Times when they flourished and published their Works, and exhibiting the more remarkable Events coincident with them.

Together with

An INTRODUCTION concerning the Origin and Progress of POETRY in general; and an ESSAY on Dramatic POETRY in particular.

By *L. CRUSIUS*, late of St. JOHN's College, CAMBRIDGE.

―――― *Dulces ante omnia Musæ*
Quarum sacra fero ―――― Virg. Georg.

The THIRD EDITION.

In TWO VOLUMES.

VOL. II.

LONDON:

Printed for W. INNYS and J. RICHARDSON, J. CLARKE, R. MANBY, C. BATHURST, and H. SHUTE COX. 1753.

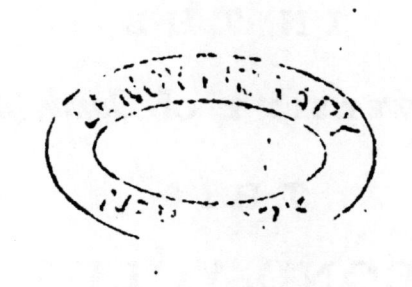

TO THE
Reverend and Learned
Dr. JOHN NEWCOME,
THE
Lady MARGARET's Profeſſor of Divinity
IN THE
UNIVERSITY of *Cambridge,*
THIS
SECOND VOLUME
OF THE
LIVES of the Roman POETS,
With due Reſpect and Gratitude,
Is humbly inſcribed
By his moſt obliged
And moſt obedient Servant,
LEWIS CRUSIUS.

THE LIFE OF Valerius Flaccus.

WE have very imperfect accounts left us of C. VALERIUS FLACCUS: We find him cotemporary with *Martial*; and *Quintilian*[*] says, he died very young, and left his Poem of the *Argonautic* expedition imperfect. There are many places that claim him, but *Setia*, now *Sezza*, a town of *Campania*, near *Velitre*, seems to have the best title, and he from thence bears the sirname SETINUS. *Martial* intimates, that he lived at *Padua*; if not, that he was born there, in the following Epigram, wherein he advises his friend to leave Poetry to practise at the Bar, as much the more profitable profession. But let us hear the Poet's own words:

O mihi curarum pretium non vile mearum
   Flacce, Antenorei spes & Alumne laris;
Pierios differ cantusque chorosque sororum;
   Æs dabit ex istis nulla puella tibi.
Quid possunt hederæ Bacchi dare? Palladis arbor
   Inclinat varias pondere nigra comas.
Præter aquas Helicon, & serta, lyrasque Deorum
   Nil habet & magnum semper inane Sophos.
Quid petis a Phœbo? nummos habet arca Minervæ,
   Hæc sapit, hæc omnes fœnerat una Deos.
Quid tibi cum Cirrha? quid cum Permessidos unda?
   Romanum propius, divitiusque forum est,

[*] *Inst. Orat. Lib.* 10. *C.* 1.

The LIFE of Valerius Flaccus.

Illic Æra sonant, at circum pulpita nostra,
Et steriles cathedras Basia sola crepant.
                                          Lib. 1. Ep. 77.

Dear FLACCUS, gentle partner of my care,
Thy country's glory, *Padua* the fair,
The fruitless song and starving Muses leave,
Nor *Clio* nor her sisters aught can give;
Why court *Apollo*, proud of laurel'd praise?
The well fill'd Chest is his whom *Pallas* sways,
Her's are the fruitful Olive's bending boughs,
Whilst useless Ivy for your *Bacchus* grows.
Clear waters *Helicon* indeed affords,
The Lyre, and Garland, and fine empty words,
What's *Cirrha*, or *Permessian* streams to you,
The *Forum*'s nearer, and is richer too:
There chinks the purse that swells with client's fee,
But where's the man that pays for Poetry?
A cold salute, a faint applause they give,
On this thin diet must we Poets live.

HAVING nothing to say of FLACCUS's life, let us look into his Poem. It is addressed to the Emperor *Vespasian*, and the Poet at the same time takes occasion to compliment *Domitian* upon his Poetry, and *Titus* on his conquest of *Judæa*. He has been blamed by the Critics for affecting too great a magnificence at the entrance into his Poem, which they would have like those of *Homer* and *Virgil*, more simple and unadorn'd. Here follow the invocation of *Apollo*, and the address to *Vespasian*:

Phœbe mone, si Cumeæ mihi conscia vatis
Stat castâ cortina domo, si laurea digna
Fronte viret. Tuque O pelagi cui major aperti
Fama, Caledonius postquam tua carbasa vexit
Oceanus, Phrygios prius indignatus Iulos,
Eripe me populis & habenti nubila terræ,
Sancte pater, veterumque fave veneranda canenti
Facta virum, versam proles tua pandit Idumen,

Namque

Namque potest, Solymo nigrantem pulvere fratrem,
Spargentemque faces, & in omni turre furentem.
Lib. 1. Ver. 5.

If conscious at *Cumæan* Rites I bend,
And at the hallow'd service pure attend;
If undefil'd thy laurel'd wreath I wear;
Phœbus, inspire my numbers, hear my pray'r.
And thou, whose glory from the ocean springs,
On which thy fleets successful spread their wings,
The Northern ocean, that indignant bore
The *Julian* ships back to the *Gallic* shore;
Deign, mighty Prince, the Poet's fame to raise
Above mean censure, and protect his lays;
Support the Muse aspiring to unfold
Heroic acts in antient story told.
The *Flavian* Bard a nobler theme pursues,
A brother's triumph o'er the vanquish'd *Jews*.
The smoaking towns of *Solyma* declare
The Hero's valour and their own despair.

THE learn'd world has been divided in their opinion of this Author: Some Commentators have not scrupled to exalt him above all the *Latin* Poets, *Virgil* only excepted; whilst other Critics have undervalued him as much. The Poem we are about to consider, is an imitation rather than a translation of *Apollonius* the *Greek* Poet, four books of whose Poem are yet extant. And this the learned reader will find, if he will be at the pains of making the comparison; and it has been observed, that the *Latin* Poet has succeeded best in those parts where he had not the *Greek* in view. In a word, he may pass for no mean writer; and the purity of his style and poetical turn of his expression, has absolutely set him above S. *Italicus*, if not above *Lucan*: As to the conduct of the Poem, he is even their inferior. *Statius* is his superior, both in Poetry and the execution of his Poem, in the *Thebaid*: Neither *Lucan*'s nor S. *Italicus*'s subjects would bear the several alterations, nor admit the many fictitious ornaments

ornaments neceſſary to make them a juſt Epic Poem. But the Story which *Flaccus* choſe for his ſubject, being of the greateſt antiquity as well as note, as bordering on the fabulous times, left room for his genius to exert itſelf with advantage; and having *Apollonius*'s work before him, by comparing it with thoſe of *Homer* and *Virgil*, he might have ſeen where it was deficient, and have ſupplied thoſe wants in laying out his own ſubject. But I am apt to believe that Poets ſeldom take any other guide than their own genius, which makes ſo many fail in the invention and diſpoſition of their Poems.

THE hiſtory of the *Argonautic* expedition, when clear'd from fable, ſeems only this. About the year 1268. before CHRIST, *Jaſon* with *Hercules, Theſeus, Caſtor, Pollux*, and ſome other *Greeks*, having got *Argus*, an able ſhipwright for thoſe times, to build them a veſſel of conſiderable burden, that bore the builder's name in honour of his art, undertook an expedition to *Colchos*, in a kind of piracy, which was not counted diſhonourable in thoſe early times, when mankind had not yet learnt the juſt arts of peace and civil ſociety between one nation and another. After many adventures, and having eſcaped great dangers, they ſucceeded in their attempt, and by the directions and aſſiſtance of the treacherous *Medea*, brought away the treaſures they went for; and at the end of four years returned to *Jolchos* a port in *Theſſaly*, from whence they firſt ſet out.

SUCH a ſubject would naturally admit all the ornaments that a good invention was capable of giving it. But indeed the beauty of a well regulated deſign ſeems to have been ſtudied by few either Antients or Moderns. The language of the Gods was what the former chiefly aim'd at; by this they meant the ornaments of ſtyle and numbers, for which our Author claims his ſhare of praiſe, and if he has not maintained the ſame ſpirit thro' the whole, we muſt make ſome allowances, ſince he did not live to correct and finiſh it. His admirers think he wanted neither genius nor

diligence

diligence to have made it an excellent Poem, had death spar'd him: That considering the disadvantage of the *Latin* to the *Greek*, *Apollonius* has been far from suffering where FLACCUS has seem'd to translate him: That none of the spirit has been lost in the transfusion; and that he may be placed in the number of those few Authors, whose copies have rival'd their originals.

As to his knowledge, FLACCUS is thought much superior to the *Greek*, who has many geographical errors, and some which might argue that he was little acquainted either with history or philosophy: Yet this *Apollonius* had the reputation of great learning. He was scholar to the Poet *Callimachus*, whom he succeeded in the care of the *Ptolomean* Library.

As this Poem of FLACCUS's is little known to the generality of readers, I shall here offer them the outlines of it, by which they will be better able to judge of the design and the disposition. But first I must observe, that if *Apollonius* had not treated this subject before FLACCUS, he would have passed for a writer of much learning and skill in antiquity; whereas now we can hardly question his owing the greatest part of his knowledge to the *Greek*. But to our sketch of the Poem:

PELIAS, after having dethroned his brother *Æson*, reigned in *Hæmonia* and *Thessaly*, but grew troubled in mind at many prodigies, which the Augurs said, portended his destruction by *Jason*, *Æson*'s son *Pelias* therefore studied all means to get rid of this object of his Fear: *Greece* was now at peace; *Hercules* had subdued all the monsters that infested it. *Pelias* therefore resolves to send his nephew upon an expedition to *Colchos*. The pretence of it, according to the Poet's legend, was this: *Athamas* the son of *Æolus*, and uncle to *Æson* and *Pelia*, had *Phrixus*, and *Helle* by his first wife *Nephele*: She being afterwards turn'd into a cloud, he married *Ino* the daughter of *Cadmus*; who like a true step-mother hating her husband's children, persuaded the women of the country (*Æolia*) to parch all the corn that had been laid up for seed.

The land being sown with this seed, was barren, and a great famine ensued. *Ino* sent some persons, whom she had bribed to her purposes, to consult the Oracle of *Apollo*; who, according to their instructions, reported, that the God required that *Phrixus* and *Helle* should be sacrificed. *Athamas* for a long time refused to comply with so cruel an order, but at length was forced to submit. Just as the children were going to be led to the altar, their own mother *Nephele* descending from the sky, bids them fly, and gives them a ram with a Golden Fleece, that would bear them over the sea: But *Helle* not sitting fast on the ram's back, was drowned in that part of the sea which was called after her name. *Phrixus* came to *Colchos*, where he sacrificed the ram in the temple of *Mars*, and not long after (as *Pelias* tells *Jason*) was treacherously murdered by *Æetes* King of *Colchos* and father of *Mædea*, in the height of a public entertainment. *Jason* soon perceived that his uncle's aim was his death, more than a desire of revenge: However, relying on the protection of *Juno* and *Minerva*, whom he devoutly invokes, he undertakes the voyage. The Goddesses hear and grant his prayer; and whilst *Juno* spreads the report of this bold adventure thro' the cities of *Greece*, to raise the ambition of other noble youths to accompany *Jason*; *Minerva* goes to *Argus*, whom she directs to build the famous ship that bore his name. Then follows a poetical account of the several heroes that came to make the voyage with *Jason*, who craftily engages *Acastus* his uncle's son to go along with him. The *Argonauts* ship was built of the inspired and prophetic oak of the *Dodonean* grove sacred to *Jupiter*. The circumstances of *Jason*'s taking his leave of his parents *Æson* and *Alcimeda*, is very pathetically described.

Now *Phœbus* begins to be in pain for the fate of the *Colchian* King his son, and addresses himself to *Jupiter* about him. That God's answer is fine and full of dignity. *Boreas* descrying the *Argonauts*, on their voyage, hastens to inform *Æolus*, whose abode is described, and prevails with him to let out the other winds,

winds, who all join and raise a furious storm, which Neptune at the intreaty of *Juno* and *Minerva* appeases. In the mean time, *Pelias* discovering that his son was gone with *Jason*, enters into a transport of rage, and resolves the death of *Æson* and *Alcimede*. She performs infernal rites for the safety of her son *Jason*, and at the same time devotes *Pelias* to the Furies, whose aid she invokes; and then drinking some of the blood of the victim with her husband; the guards, whom *Pelias* had sent to put them to death, find them both expiring: but not content with that, by the tyrant's order they murder their younger son before their eyes. Then the Poet describes the situation of Hell, in which part there are some lines lost. There is a description left of the two gates, the one leading to *Tartarus*, and the other to *Elyzium*. The shades of *Æson* and *Alcimede* are conveyed through the latter by *Mercury* to the regions of the blessed, who comforts them by the way with an account of the punishment that *Pelias* is doom'd to suffer for all his crimes. Here ends the first book; which I have been the longer about, as being obliged to explain some circumstances at large, to make the narration of those that follow clear and intelligible.

In the 2d book, the *Argonauts* are described sailing by Mount *Ossa* and *Pallene*, places famous for the battle of the Gods and Giants: thence they come to *Lemnos*. Here there is a long Episode of the *Lemnian* women, who murdered their husbands at their return from the *Thracian* war, in which they had been absent three years: only *Hypsipile* saved her father King *Thoas*'s life, and conveyed him away in the nighttime by sea in a small vessel. The Poet represents this cruel action as a contrivance of *Venus* to be revenged on *Vulcan*, to whom *Lemnos*, was sacred, for having caught her in his net and exposed her with *Mars*. That Goddess goes to *Fame*, and bids her inspire the *Lemnian* women with a jealous fury against their husbands; suggesting that they had brought home other wives from *Thrace*. Then the Goddess being disguised,

guised, speaks to the principal women, whom she fills with that belief. The whole Episode is well managed, and the incidents finely prepared: But the Poet should not have related it in his own person. But to proceed: The *Argonauts* land at *Lemnos*; *Hypsipile* falls in love with *Jason*, who answers her desires; and the rest of the *Argonauts* spend some time with the *Lemnian* women, 'till the stormy season is past. *Hercules*, who had no paramour among the *Lemnians*, awakens them from this lethargy of love, and bids them make haste to sea. They sail to *Troy*, where *Laomedon* reigned, and for his perjury to *Apollo* and *Neptune* was plagued by a sea monster: For to avert a plague that before afflicted the people, the Oracle of *Jupiter* had commanded that a virgin, by lot, should every year be exposed to the monster to be devoured, and it was now fallen on the King's daughter. *Hercules* delivers the Princess, and kills the monster; but the ungrateful *Laomedon* proposed to have murdered his guest and benefactor the same night. But the *Argonauts* pursued their voyage, and came to *Cyzicum*: which concludes the 2d book.

Cyzicus King of the country, after having kindly entertained the *Argonauts*, informs them that he was at war with the *Pelasgians*. The *Argonauts* set sail again, but by stress of weather are forced back in the night-time into the same port: so that the guards of the country mistaking them for their enemies, the *Pelasgians* begin a skirmish that proves fatal to both sides, but chiefly to King *Cyzicus* and his people. Day-light discovers the mistake, and the *Argonauts* celebrate with tears the funeral of the unfortunate King, and perform solemnn rites by the advice of the Prophet *Mopsus*, to appease the ghosts of their deceased friends and allies. In describing these rites and ceremonies, the Poet seems to have affected to imitate *Virgil*'s exactness, whom he has very often in his eye. From thence the *Argonauts* sail along the coast of *Mysia*, where *Hercules* and *Hylas* land. *Juno* here sends *Minerva* to prepare the *Colchians* to receive the *Argonauts*

nauts in a friendly manner; *Minerva* goes, though she knows, it is but a pretence to get her out of the way. Then *Juno* contrives the loss of *Hylas*, the favourite companion of *Hercules*: She tells *Dryope* a Wood Nymph, that a fine opportunity now offered of enjoying that lovely youth, which would make her the envy of all her sister Nymphs: then she raises a stag, that crosses the wood just before *Hercules* and *Hylas*; the youth eagerly pursues the sport, whilst *Hercules* himself encourages him to it. At length the stag takes the water, of a fountain, where *Hylas* being fatigued drops the chase to bathe: Here the Nymph steals him away. The *Argonauts*, after some stay for *Hercules*, who went in search of *Hylas*, are forced to sail away without him.

The 4th book opens with *Jupiter's* compassion for his son's sorrows; and after having reproved *Juno*, he pours out a rich dew upon *Hercules*, which composes the Heroe to rest. *Hylas* appears to him in a dream, and comforts him, and promises him immortality as the reward of his labours. At the request of *Latona*, *Diana*, and *Apollo*, *Iris* is sent to prevent *Hercules's* going to *Troy*, and to bid him make haste to deliver *Prometheus*, who had been so long confined and tormented on mount *Caucasus* for stealing fire from heaven. In the mean time the *Argonauts* come to the *Bebrycian* coast, where *Amycus* the son of *Neptune* reigned: He was a cruel and inhospitable Prince, and being a great boxer, used to force every stranger that entered his dominions to fight him with the *Cestus*, and he had hitherto slain all that had engaged him. This the *Argonauts* are informed of by some of their company whom they sent to discover the country, who had met with a stranger bewailing the loss of his friend *Otreus*, whom *Amycus* had lately fought with and killed. *Pollux*, as yet but a stripling, presents himself to fight the Tyrant, who insults his youth and beauty, but after some resistance is slain by the *Argonaut*. The ship now enters the *Bosphorus*, upon which the Poet takes occasion to relate the story of *Io*; who, being persecuted

persecuted by *Juno*, and passing over those seas, when she was transformed into a cow, had given them the name of *Bosphorus*. The *Argonauts* arrive at the *Thyanean* coast, where *Zethes* and *Calais* the sons of *Boreas* deliver *Phineus* from the persecution of the Harpies. Thence they sailed by the *Cyanean* rocks, so fatal to all that passed near them, but *Minerva* drives off the rocks, and saves the ship. Thence they proceed to the coast of the *Mariandyni*, where King *Lycus* of *Greek* original kindly entertains them, and congratulates them on their victory, over *Amycus*, who had slain his brother.

The 5th book begins with a melancholy scene of the death of *Idmon* and *Typhys*, two of the *Argonauts*, the latter was their Pilot: The prophetic ship names *Erginus* to succeed him. As they proceed on their voyage, they pass under the rock where *Prometheus* was chained, and whom *Hercules* was then delivering: They hear the *Titan*'s cries, and soon after see the bird, that used to prey upon his liver, expiring on the shore. At length they arrive at *Colchos*, and sail up the river *Phasis*, where they find the monument which *Phrixus* had erected in memory of his sister *Helle*. Here *Jason* casts anchor, and having sacrificed to them both, implores their assistance in his undertaking.

The *Colchian* King is warned by many prodigies to restore the Golden Fleece: *Perses* his brother and all his counsellors had advised him to it; but *Æetes* having no regard to the happiness of his people, obstinately refuses, punishes some of the boldest, and even attempts to kill his brother, who had gained the love of the people, and was suspected to aspire to the crown. He saves his life by flight, and returns not long after with a great army, which he had raised among the neighbouring nations, against *Æetes*, and had already attacked the city, but was repulsed with loss; and a truce was agreed on for two days between the contending parties to bury their dead, at the time when the *Argonauts* landed. *Juno* and *Pallas*, tho' they foresee *Æetes*'s treachery, agree that the *Argonauts*

nauts shall assist him against *Perses*, as being the weakest side.

MEDEA having had a frightful dream that night, went early the next morning to make the proper lustrations in the river; where she sees the *Argonauts*, and taking them for enemies, was going to fly back; Her Nurse assures her they are *Greeks*. *Juno* makes *Jason* appear with uncommon beauty and comeliness; and comes up to *Medea*, whom he addresses in a very engaging manner, desiring leave to speak to the King. *Medea* sends one of her attendants with *Jason*, to lead him to the court; They meet the King in the temple of *Apollo*, which the Poet describes. *Jason*, in imitation of *Æneas* in *Virgil*, is described entering the city and temple, covered with a cloud by *Juno*. He discovers himself, acquaints *Æetes* with his errand, and offers some rich presents to exchange for the Golden Fleece. The Tyrant conceals his rage at this request, and with dissembled friendship promises to give it, provided the *Argonauts* assist him first against the enemy that laid siege to the city.

ÆETES now invites them to an entertainment, where he informs *Jason* of the cause of the war, and the character of his allies there present. Then the Poet describes *Mars* in his progress from the northern regions, who is surprised to see the *Argonauts* at *Colchos*, and to hear that *Æetes* had promised to deliver them the Golden Fleece, which had been consecrated to him. The furious God hastens to complain to *Jupiter* of this wrong done him by *Minerva* and *Juno*; the former answers him. *Jupiter* puts an end to their dispute, by acquainting them with his and *Fate*'s decree, and allows them severally to take what side they pleased in the war. The book concludes with a description of the entertainment of the Gods, where the Muses sing to *Apollo*'s harp; After which the assembly breaks up, and all retire to rest.

THE 6th book begins with *Mars*, who could take no rest, but resolves to destroy the *Argonauts* and their ship. *Perses* being alarmed at the arrival of the *Greeks*, deputes some persons to assure them of his good intentions towards them, and of *Æetes*'s treacherous temper, and to try to persuade them to join their forces with his *Scythians* against the *Colchian* King: but this was in vain. Here the forces of *Perses* are described: A bloody battle ensues, which is related at large: *Æetes* gets the advantage, which is entirely owing to the valour of the *Greeks*.

Juno, fearing *Æetes*'s baseness, finds no other way to get the Fleece for *Jason*, but by the enchantments of *Medea*. To secure her, she goes to *Venus*, and desires the use of her girdle to regain *Jupiter*'s love. *Venus* soon perceived this was but a pretence; but as she hated the children of the Sun, she readily lends her girdle. Furnished with this, *Juno* disguises her self like *Chalciope*, *Medea*'s sister; and blaming her want of curiosity, carries out *Medea* on the walls of the city, to view the *Greek* heroes fighting for her father: Among the rest they perceive *Jason* signalizing his valour. *Juno* never lets *Medea* lose sight of him, who, pretending she did not know him, asks her counterfeit sister who that prodigy of valour was; *Juno* informs her of his quality and merit; Then bidding her observe him farther, the Goddess animates the Hero with unusual vigour. *Medea* feels a strange passion kindle in her, but is not able to resist the force of love. *Juno* now finding her sufficiently inflamed, leaves her alone; she grows very anxious for the success of *Jason*'s request to her Father. The battle goes against the *Scythians*, of whom the *Greeks* make a great slaughter. *Minerva* fearing *Jason* should kill *Perses*, whom *Jupiter* intended to set on the throne of *Colchos*, and thereby draw on him the indignation of that God, conveys *Perses* wrapp'd in a cloud, out of the battle to his camp; and *Medea* returns to the palace, never satisfied with beholding the *Thessalian* Hero; which ends the 6th book.

Medea spends the night in great anxiety; love and duty struggle and alternately prevail in her breast. The next morning the *Argonauts* begin to think of the Golden

den Fleece, for which they had undergone so many labours; but before *Jason* demanded it, the *Colchian* King in a haughty manner tells him the hard terms by which it was to be obtained; namely, to sow the field of *Mars* with the serpent's teeth, to charm the dragon that guarded the Fleece, and fight the men that would spring up from that seed. *Jason* resolves to undertake it; *Medea* pities him, but for some time struggles with her passion. *Juno*, to compleat her purpose, prevails with *Venus* to come to *Medea* in the disguise of her aunt *Circe*. By this means the Goddess insinuates herself into the secret of *Medea's* love, whom she prompts to give way to it by her own example, who having left the barren plains of *Colchos*, was now, by her marriage with *Picus*, become Sovereign of *Latium* in *Italy*. Afterwards she persuades *Medea* to walk out that night, under pretence of a sacrifice to *Diana*. She meets *Jason* in a grove, to which he went by *Juno's* direction; He implores her protection and assistance, which at length she grants him. Then *Medea* performs all the magical ceremonies necessary to arm him for the adventure, and gives him the proper instructions for his conduct, and then leads him to the field of *Mars*, which he sows: The armed Men spring up, and by her inchantments turn their arms against each other, every one mistaking his fellow for *Jason*.

The 8th book begins with *Medea's* last struggle between love, and duty, and remorse for what she had already done; but Love prevailing, she renews her enchantments, and meets her Heroe, whom *Juno* had made exceeding beautiful, in the place where the dragon guarded the Golden Fleece. Here the two lovers enter into solemn engagements of mutual fidelity, and *Medea* agrees to accompany *Jason*, whom she now calls her husband, into *Thessaly*. As they come near the tree, *Jason* is terrified by the fire which flashed from the dragon's eyes. *Medea* having in vain endeavoured to sooth him to rest, promising to watch the Fleece for him, has recourse to her spells, and charms him into a dead sleep; then bids *Jason* climb up by the dragon's back
into

into the tree where the Fleece hung; which he takes down, and haftens away in triumph with that and *Medea* to the ſhip. The *Argonauts* ſet ſail. *Æetes* is ſoon informed of his daughter's treachery and flight. *Abſyrtus* her brother, and *Styrus* a *Scythian* Prince, *Medea*'s deſtined huſband, fit out ſome ſhips, and purſue them, and overtake the *Argonauts* feaſting aſhore at the mouth of the *Danube*, and ſolemnizing the Nuptials of *Jaſon* and *Medea*. *Juno*, to deliver them from the preſent danger, raiſes a ſtorm, which ſeparates them; but *Styrus*, who being blinded by his love for *Medea* ſtrove to bear up againſt the ſtorm, is caſt away. When it was over, the *Argonauts* ſoon deſcried the enemy again: then they begin to murmur againſt *Medea*, and exhort *Jaſon* not to expoſe them all to ruin for her ſake. She ſoon diſcovers their deſign, and ſpeaks of it to *Jaſon* with indignation: juſt where *Jaſon* is deſcribed as ſtudying ſome dubious anſwer to gain time, as being yet irreſolute what to do, the Poem abruptly breaks off.

It is very probable the Author lived to go no farther. *Baptiſta Pius* an *Italian* has tranſlated the reſt from *Apollonius*, and added it to Flaccus's Poem; to which we muſt refer the Reader for the reſt of the ſtory, ſince it is proper this ſketch ſhould end where Flaccus breaks off, as being only intended to ſhew his manner of treating this ſubject.

I think we may allow him to have been maſter of ſome invention, and much ſpirit. Though his Poem is thus hiſtorically conducted, it is fuller of machinery than the *Æneis*. An affectation of the marvellous runs through the whole. The manners are not ill expreſſed, and the characters well diſtinguiſhed and various: They are not very moral indeed, nor polite; neither of which could be expected of ſo barbarous an age as that in which this event happened, which may partly excuſe the fabulous air and turn of the whole narration. All time before this in the *Greek* Hiſtory, is confeſſedly fabulous and obſcure! and this *Æpocha* bordering upon thoſe dark ages, has partaken of their

fate

fate so far, that the very Historians in treating of it, have inserted many seeming fables in their accounts.

But in order to discover *Flaccus*'s genius with regard to the style and sentiments, we must quote some passages of his Poem; and where he has *Virgil* in view, it may not be improper to subjoin those passages of the *Æneid*, which he has imitated. We shall find his style in the main noble and poetical, though not equally kept up, his descriptions strong and full, and his comparisons apt and lively. The first that offers is an elegant description of the *Æolian* Islands, the supposed seat of the Winds.

> *Æquore Trinacrio refugique a parte Pelori*
> *Stat rupes horrenda fretis, quot in æthera surgit*
> *Molibus, infernas totidem demissa sub undas:*
> *Nec scopulos aut antra minor juxta altera tellus*
> *Cernitur; illam Achamas habitat, nudusque Pyrag-*
>   *mon.*
> *Has Nimbi, ventique domos, & naufraga servat*
> *Tempestas: hinc in terras latumque profundum*
> *Est iter: hinc olim soliti miscere polumque*
> *Infelixque fretum (neque enim tunc Æolus illis*
> *Rector erat) Libyâ cum rumperet advena Calpen*
> *Oceanus, cum flens Siculos OEnotria fines*
> *Perderet, & mediis intrarent montibus undæ,*
> *Intonuit donec pavidis ex æthere Ventis*
> *Omnipotens, regemque dedit, quem jussa vereri*
> *Sæva cohors in monte; chalybs iterataque muris*
> *Saxa domant Euros. Cum jam prohibere frementum*
> *Ora nequit Rex, tunc aditus & claustra refringit,*
> *Ipse volens, placatque data fera murmura porta.*

Encompass'd by *Sicilian* Seas, appears
A rising rock, that to *Pelorus* bears;
Its bottom deep beneath the waves extends
Far as its summit to the clouds ascends:
Hard by another rears its craggy brow,
Whose cliffs and caves can equal horrors show.
In that *Pyracmon* feeds Vulcanian fires,
To this the stormy train of Winds retires:
Hence

Hence to the earth, and o'er the spreading deep
They wing their way, and with destruction sweep;
Hence unrestrain'd of old their fury wrought,
And to the skies the swelling billows brought.
No *Æolus* as yet controul'd their Pow'r;
Then *Calpe* rent from *Libya*'s parting shore,
Admitted the *Atlantic*'s pouring tide;
Then first *Trinacria* from *Italia*'s side
Dividing, felt the lashing surges bound,
'Till *Jove* impatient hurl'd his thunder round;
The Winds retir'd astonish'd and confin'd
Their King obey'd, whom he in wrath assign'd
Within their iron prison closely pent,
Where adamantine rocks restrain their vent.
When loud for liberty his subjects call,
The God himself unbars the gloomy Hall;
Then cease their murmurs, and they issue forth
Tempests and stormy winds, led by the furious
     North.   Lib. 1. Ver. 579.

Virgil had occasion, one would have thought, to have dwelt as largely on such a description of the Winds; and yet we find him thus contracting many great images into the compass of a few lines.

Nimborum in patriam, loca fœta furentibus Austris
Æoliam venit: hic vasto rex Æolus antro
Luctantes ventos, tempestatesque sonoras
Imperio premit, ac vinclis & carcere frœnat.
Illi indignantes magno cum murmure, montis
Circum claustra fremunt: Celsa sedet Æolus arce
Sceptra tenens, mollitque animos & temperat iras.
Ni faciat, maria ac terras cœlumque profundum
Quippe ferant rapidi secum, verrantque per auras:
Sed pater hoc metuens speluncis abdidit atris
Omnipotens; molemque & montes insuper altos
Imposuit, regemque dedit, qui fœdere certo
Et premere, & laxas sciret dare jussus habenas.
                      Lib. 1. Ver. 55.

The restless regions of the storms she sought;
Where in a spacious cave of living stone
The Tyrant *Æolus* from his airy throne,
With pow'r imperial curbs the struggling Winds,
And sounding Tempests in dark prisons binds;
This way and that th' impatient captives tend,
And pressing for release, the mountains rend;
High in his Hall th'undaunted Monarch stands,
And shakes his scepter, and their rage commands;
Which did he not, their unresisted sway
Would sweep the world before them in their way;
Earth, Air and Seas through empty space would roll,
And Heav'n would fly before the driving soul,
In fear of this, the Father of the Gods
Confin'd their fury to those dark abodes,
And lock'd 'em safe within, oppress'd with mountain loads;
Impos'd a King, with arbitrary sway,
To lose their fetters, or their force allay.
Dryden.

Alcimede's Imprecation against *Pelias* is very solemn, and a fine imitation of *Dido*'s against *Æneas* in *Virgil*. *Alcimede* speaks some lines before those here quoted; but as they seem rather introductory to, than a part of the Imprecation it self, I chose to omit them:

———*Tu Nuncia sontum*
Virgo Jovi, terras oculis quæ prospicis æquis;
Ultricesque Deæ: Fasque, & grandæva sororum
Pœna parens, meritis Regis succedite tectis,
Et sævas inserte faces. Sacer effera raptet
Corda pavor; nec sola mei gravia affore nati
Arma ratemque putet: classesque & Pontica signa
Atque indignatos temerato littore reges
Mente agitet, semperque metu deducat ad undas
Arma ciens; mors sera viam, tentataque claudat
Effugia, & nostras nequeat præcurrere diras.
Sed reduces jam jamque viros, auroque coruscum
Cernat iter: stabo insultans, & ovantia contra
Ora, manusque feram: Tum vobis siquid inausum
Arcanumque

*Arcanumque nefas, & adhuc incognita Leti
Sors superest, date fallaci pudibunda senectæ
Exitia, indecoresque obitus, non marte, nec armis,
Aut nati precor ille mei dignatus ut unquam
Ense cadat, quem fida manus, quem cura suorum
Diripiat laceretque senem: nec membra sepulchro
Contegat: hæc noster de rege piacula sanguis
Sumat, & heu cunctæ quas misit in æquora Gentes.*
                         Lib. 1. Ver. 794.

Just Goddess, whose impartial eye beholds,
Whose care, to *Jove* all human crimes unfolds;
Ye Deities of vengeance, and thou first
Parent of Furies, Punishment accurst,
On *Pelias*, arm'd with all your brands, attend,
And thro' his soul your quickest terrors send;
Nor let his mind distemper'd only fear
My Son's approach, or think his *Argo* near;
Th' assembled pow'rs of *Colchis* let him dread,
And *Pontic* Hosts stand threatening o'er his head.
His rest let wars alarms successive break,
Let death refuse that ease his torments seek.
These Curses may he not escape, but see
Jason return with Golden Victory.
Then will I stand insulting by his side,
His pain my joy, his misery my pride;
If any plagues untry'd remain in store,
On his curst head the plenteous anguish pour.
May want and infamy bring on his fate,
And Death most horrid his old age await,
Let him not fall by arms in Honour's field,
Or by my Son, but to black treason yield
His hated life, his corps deny'd a grave;
Such vengeance may our race on *Pelias* have.

Dido's Imprecation in the 4th book of the *Æneis* runs thus;

*Sol, qui terrarum flammis opera omnia lustras,
Tuque harum interpres curarum, & conscia Juno;
Nocturnisque Hecate trivijs ululata per urbes,*
                                      Et

*Diræ ultrices, & Dij morientis Elisæ;
Accipite hæc, meritumque malis advertite numen,
Et nostras audite preces: si tangere portus
Infandum caput, ac terris adnare necesse est;
Et, si fata Jovis poscunt, his terminus hæret.
At bello audacis populi vexatus & armis,
Finibus extorris, complexu avulsus Iuli
Auxilium imploret, videatque indigna suorum
Funera: nec, cum se sub leges pacis iniquæ
Tradiderit, regno aut optata luce fruatur.
Sed cadat ante diem, mediaque inhumatus arena.
Hæc precor, hanc vocem extremam cum sanguine fundo.
Tum vos, O Tyrij, stirpem & genus omne futurum,
Exercete odijs, cinerique hæc mittite nostro
Munera; nullus amor populis, nec fœdera sunto.
Exoriare aliquis nostris ex ossibus ultor
Qui face Dardanios, ferroque sequare Colonos,
Nunc, olim, quocunque dabunt se tempore vires;
Littora littoribus contraria, fluctibus undas
Imprecor, arma armis; pugnent ipsique nepotes.*

Ver. 607.

Thou Sun, who view'st at once the world below,
Thou *Juno*, guardian of the nuptial vow,
Thou *Hecat*, hearken from thy dark abodes;
Ye furies, fiends, and violated Gods,
All pow'rs invok'd with *Dido*'s dying breath,
Attend her curses, and avenge her death.
If so the *Fates* ordain and *Jove* commands,
Th' ungrateful wretch should find the *Latian* lands;
Yet let a race untam'd and haughty foes
His peaceful entrance with dire Arms oppose;
Oppress'd with numbers in th' unequal field,
His men discourag'd, and himself expell'd,
Let him for succour sue from place to place,
Torn from his subjects and his son's embrace:
First let him see his friends in battle slain,
And their untimely fate lament in vain:
And when at length the cruel war shall cease,
On hard conditions may he buy his peace.

Nor let him then enjoy supreme command,
But fall untimely by some hostile hand;
And lie unbury'd on the barren sand!
These are my pray'rs, and this my dying will,
And you, my *Tyrians*, every curse fulfil;
Perpetual hate and mortal wars proclaim
Against the prince, the people and the name:
These grateful off'rings on my grave bestow,
Nor league, nor love, the hostile nations know.
Now and from hence in every future age,
When rage excites your arms, and strength supplies the rage,
Rise some avenger of our *Libyan* blood,
With fire and sword pursue the perjur'd brood:
Our arms, our seas, our shores oppos'd to theirs,
And the same hate descend on all our heirs.
                                                            Dryden.

THE description FLACCUS gives of the two gates, one leading to *Tartarus*, the other to *Elyzium*, is very poetical. That seat of the blessed is likewise well described: both are imitated from the 6th book of the *Æneid*.

Stant geminæ æternum portæ, quarum altera dura
Semper lege patens, populus regesque receptat.
Ast aliam tentare nefas & tendere contra;
Rara & sponte patet, si quando pectore Ductor
Vulnera nota gerens galeis præfixa rotisque
Cui domus, aut studium, mortales pellere curas,
Culta fides, longe metus, atque ignota cupido:
Seu venit in vittis, castaque in veste sacerdos:
Quos omnes, lenis plantis & lampada quassans
Progenies Atlantis agit: lucet via late
Igne Dei, donec silvas & amœna piorum
Deveniat, camposque ubi Sol, totumque per annum
Durat aprica dies, thyasique chorique virorum,
Carminaque & quorum populis jam nulla cupido.
                                                    Lib. 1. Ver. 833.

Two different Gates lead to the realms below,
Kings and their subjects undistinguish'd go
                                                                Thro'

Thro' the wide portals of the common Gate;
The other opens not, unless by Fate
For some brave Shade ordain'd, who greatly dy'd
In Honour's cause, to ancestors ally'd
Of highest worth; one studious to appear
A friend to men, devoid of guilt or fear;
Or Priest unstain'd, with holy fillets bound;
Such *Hermes* leads; whose waving torch around
Spreads a clear light along the sacred way;
'Till to the regions of eternal day
They come descending, where thro' flow'ry plains
Or shady groves they pass to meet the swains,
Blest Choir! that singing with their wands advance,
And greeting bid him join the chearful dance,
And all the joys that in those realms abound;
But among mortals here can ne'er be found.

The two Ways are thus spoken of by the Sybil in *Virgil*:

Hic locus est, partes ubi se via finditur in ambas:
Dextra, quæ Ditis magni sub mœnia tendit,
Hâc iter Elyzium nobis; at læva malorum
Exercet pœnas, & ad impia tartara mittit.
Lib. 6. Ver. 638.

'Tis here in different Paths the Way divides;
The Right to *Pluto*'s golden Palace guides;
The Left to that unhappy Region tends,
Which to the depth of *Tartarus* descends
The seat of night profound, and punish'd fiends.

Elyzium he describes as follows, with the Pleasures of the Place;

Devenêre locos lætos, & amœna vireta
Fortunatorum nemorum, sedesque beatas.
Largior hic campos Æthæer, & lumine vestit
Purpureo: solemque suum, sua sidera norunt.
Pars in gramineis exercent membra palæstris;
Contendunt ludo, & fulva luctantur arena;
Pars pedibus plaudunt choreas, & carmina dicunt.
Lib. 6. Ver. 638.

These

These holy Rites perform'd, they took their way
Where long extended plains of pleasure lay;
The verdant fields with those of Heav'n may vie,
With Æther vested and a purple Sky:
The blissful seats of happy souls below,
Stars of their own, and their own suns they know.
Their airy limbs in sports they exercise,
And on the green contend the wrestler's prize;
Some in heroic verse divinely sing,
Others in artful measures lead the ring.

The Inhabitants are thus described by the same great Genius;

Hic manus, ob Patriam pugnando vulnera passi;
Quique sacerdotes casti dum vita manebat,
Quique pij vates, & Phœbo digna locuti,
Inventas aut qui vitam excoluere per artes,
Quique sui memores alios fecére merendo:
Omnibus his nivea cinguntur tempora Vitta.
Ver. 660.

Here Patriots live, who for their country's good
In fighting fields were prodigal of blood;
Priests of unblemish'd lives here make abode;
And Poets worthy their inspiring God;
And searching Wits of more mechanic parts,
Who grac'd their age with new invented arts;
Those who to worth their bounty did extend,
And those who knew that bounty to commend;
The heads of these with holy fillets bound,
And all their temples were with garlands crown'd.
Dryden.

Flaccus in the beginning of the second book gives a description of *Fame*, which languishes when compared with the fine original in the 4th book of the *Æneis*. *Juno* is represented as descending to *Fame*.

——*Dea se piceo per sudum turbida nimbo*
Præcipitat, Famamque vagam vestigat in umbra:
Quam

24 The LIFE of Valerius Flaccus.

Tot vigiles oculi subter, mirabile dictu,
Tot linguæ, totidem ora sonant, tot subrigit aures.
Nocte volat, cœli medio, terræque per umbram
Stridens, nec dulci declinat lumina somno.
Luce sedet custos, aut summi culmine tecti,
Turribus aut altis, & magnas territat urbes;
Tam ficti pravique tenax, quam nuncia veri.

Lib. 4. Ver. 174.

Fame, the great ill, from small beginning grows;
Swift from the first; and every moment brings
New vigour to her flights, new pinions to her wings.
Soon grows the pigmy to gigantic size,
Her feet on earth, her forehead in the skies:
Enrag'd against the Gods, revengeful Earth
Produc'd her, last of the *Titanean* birth.
Swift in her walk, more swift her winged haste;
A monstrous phantom, horrible and vast;
As many plumes, as raise her lofty flight,
So many piercing Eyes enlarge her sight;
Millions of opening mouths to *Fame* belong,
And ev'ry mouth is furnish'd with a tongue;
And round with list'ning ears the flying plague is hung.
She fills the peaceful universe with cries;
No slumbers ever close her wakeful eyes.
By day from lofty tow'rs her head she shews,
And spreads through trembling crowds disast'rous news;
With Court Informers haunts, and Royal Spies;
Things done relates, not done she feigns, and mingles truth with lies.
Talk is her business; and her chief delight
To tell of prodigies, and cause affright.

Dryden.

In the same book, the description of *Hypsipile*'s growing love for *Jason*, is formed upon the model of *Dido*'s for *Æneas*.

Præcipueque ducis casus mirata requirit
Hypsipile, quæ fata trahant, quæ regis agat vis:

Aut

perception after death, agreeably to the *Pythagorean* Philosophy.

> ——— *Non si mortalia membra*
> *Sortitusque breves, & parvi tempora fati*
> *Perpetimur, socius superi quondam ignis Olympi;*
> *Fas ideo miscere neces, ferroque morantes*
> *Exigere hinc animas, redituraque semina Cælo.*
> *Quippe nec in ventos, nec in ultima solvimur ossa.*
> *Ira manet, duratque dolor: cum deinde tremendi*
> *Ad solium venere Jovis, quæstuque nefandum*
> *Edocuere necem, patet illis janua leti,*
> *Atque iterum remeare licet: comes una sororum*
> *Additur, & pariter terras atque æquora lustrant.*
> *Quisque suos fontes inimicaque pectora pœnis*
> *Implicat, & varia meritos formidine pulsant.*
>
> Lib. 3. Ver. 378.

Tho' this frail body yielding soon decays,
And a short period terminates our days,
And souls immortal are to Heav'n ally'd;
Yet may we not with murd'ring hand divide
Souls from their Bodies; for the Souls aspire
To join their parent, pure ætherial fire.
They neither perish, nor disperse in Air;
But mindful of their wrongs, to *Jove* they bear
Their just complaint, at whose tremendous throne
Their death injurious, they aloud bemoan.
His leave earth to revisit they obtain,
The furies horrid sisters join the train,
There range about each guilty foe to find,
And fill with terrors his distracted mind.

In the 4th book, *Hylas*, after he had been stolen away from *Hercules*, appears to him in a dream, and after having satisfied him of his present condition, and encouraged him to continue his Labours, the fruits of which he should soon reap in a glorious immortality, disappears. The following comparison is finely introduced to illustrate the Hero's behaviour on this occasion.

Talibus

Talibus orantem dictis, visuque fruentem
Ille ultro petit, & vacuis amplexibus instat,
Languentisque movet frustra conamina dextræ;
Corpus hebet somno refugaque eluditur umbra
Tum lachrymis tum voce sequi, tum rumpere questus,
Dum sopor & vano spes mæsta resolvitur actu:
Fluctus ab undisoni ceu forte crepidine saxi
Cum rapit Alcyonis miseræ fœtumque laremque
It super ægra parens, queriturque, tumentibus undis,
Certa sequi quocunque ferant: audetque pavetque,
Icta fatiscit aquis donec domus, haustaque fluctu est.
Illa dolens vocem dedit & se sustulit alis.
                                Lib. 4. Ver. 38.

The shade thus speaking seem'd with joy to view
The Heroe, who with eager transport flew
To his embrace; his arms he stretch'd in vain
To clasp the phantom, that still mock'd his pains
By sleep o'erpower'd, the languid motion falls,
Hylas, with tears and soft complaints he calls.
At length the workings of his troubled breast
Join'd to those efforts, interrupt his rest.
So when the dashings of the cruel deep
Down from the rock the Halcyon's nestlings sweep.
Th' afflicted mother follows o'er the flood,
Now fearless, trembling now, her hapless brood;
'Till the frail nest admits the fatal wave,
It sinks; she leaves, lamenting, what she cannot save.

AT the feast of the *Argonauts*, after *Pollux* had slain *Amycus*, *Orpheus* sings the fable of *Io*. There are some circumstances in FLACCUS, which *Ovid* had not touch'd upon; Such is the following. As *Io* was coming for refuge into *Ægypt*, *Juno* sent *Tysiphone* to keep her from entering that country; but the River *Nile* swelling his stream overwhelms the *Fury*, and delivers *Io* from her persecution. This is nobly expressed by the Poet.

——*Erebi virgo ditem volat æthere Memphim*
Præripere, & Pharia venientem pellere terra
Contra Nilus adest, & toto gurgite torrens

Tysiphonen agit, atque imis illidit arenis;
Ditis opem & sævi clamantem numina Regni.
                              Lib. 4. Ver. 407.

Swift flew the Fiend to reach the *Memphian* strand,
Where *Io* she forbids the *Pharian* land.
The friendly *Nil*, now moved with pity, strove
In *Io*'s cause, with tide impetuous drove
The Fury down, and plung'd her in the deep;
Then dash'd the monster on the sandy sweep,
In vain Hell's pow'rs invoking to her aid.

THE description of the Harpies is happily imitated from *Virgil*. *Phineus*, whom they were sent to torment for his having discover'd the secrets of *Jupiter*, thus describes them to the *Argonauts*.

——*Harpyæ semper mea pabula servant,*
Fallere quas nunquam misero locus; ilicet omnes,
Deveniunt, niger intorto ceu turbine nimbus,
Jamque alis procul & sonitu mihi nota Celæno:
Diripiunt, verruntque dapes, fœdataque turbant
Pocula: sævit odor, surgitque miserrima pugna.
Parque mihi monstrisque fames. Sprevere quod omnes
Polluerintque manu, quodque unguibus excidit atris
Has mihi fert in luce moras.   Lib. 4. Ver. 450.

My daily food the Harpies watching spy,
No place, no art conceals it from their eye;
Swift as the whirlwind unexpected down
The monsters pour, and seize it as their own;
First dire *Celæno* flaps her sooty wings,
O'erturns the table, cups and dishes flings
All on a heap confus'd, then taints the air
With stench obscene, and kindles horrid war.
Our hunger seems alike, yet none I taste
But what their filthy talons drop thro' haste.
Such scraps a wretched life with pain support.

Virgil had thus described them and their dwelling;

——*Strophades Grajo stant nomine dictæ*
Insulæ in Ionio magno: quas dira Celæno,
                              Harpyiæque

The LIFE of Valerius Flaccus.

Harpyiæque colunt aliæ: Phineia postquam
Clausa domus, mensasque metu liquére priores,
Tristius haud illis monstrum, nec sævior ulla
Pestis, & ira Deûm Stygiis sese extulit undis.
Virginei volucrum vultus, fædissima ventris
Proluvies, uncæque manus, & pallida semper
Ora fame.——   Æneid. Lib. 3. Ver. 210.

Those Isles are compass'd by the *Ionian* main,
The dire abode where the foul Harpies reign:
Forc'd by the winged warriors to repair
To their old homes, and leave their costly fare.
Monsters more fierce offended Heav'n ne'er sent
From Hell's abyss for human punishment.
With virgin faces, but with wombs obscene,
Foul paunches, and with ordure still unclean;
With claws for hands, and looks for ever lean.
                                                    Dryden.

Their coming to disturb the *Trojans* and devour their meat, is as follows in the same book.

——Subitæ horrifico lapsu de montibus adsunt
Harpiæ, & magnis quatiunt clangoribus alas,
Diripiuntque dates, contactuque omnia fædant
Immundo, tum vox tetrum dira inter odorem.
                                        Lib. 4. Ver. 225.

When from the mountain tops, with hideous cry
And clatt'ring wings, the hungry Harpies fly;
They snatch the meat, defiling all they find,
And parting leave a loathsome stench behind.
                                                    Dryden.

And as *Helenus* in *Virgil* directs *Æneas* in his voyage by Prophecy, so here *Phineus* who was a Prophet, instructs the *Argonauts* in their course in gratitude to the sons of *Boreas*, who had delivered him from the Harpies.

The 5th and 6th books have not many passages that deserve to be distinguished from the rest; the speeches of the Gods, which are very frequent in this Poem and particularly in these books, cannot seem very entertaining

tertaining to us, who can never be brought to reconcile the tumultuous passions of weak Men to the character of Divinity. But we cannot blame FLACCUS for a fault chargeable on the Heathen Theology that could suppose such Absurdities, to call it by no worse a name.

As the antient Heroes were supposed to be descended from some God, not one of them can die, but some Deity must lament his death; and even *Jupiter* is afraid to save one of his descendants in the battle, lest the other Gods, who had already complained of the severity of his decrees, should murmur more at his partiality. It was *Colaxes* a *Scythian* Prince, for whom *Jupiter* is represented thus concerned; and whose bravery and success, 'till he meets *Jason* by whom he is destined to be slain, is very elegantly compared to a torrent that carries all before it, 'till it dashes with a precipitate fall down the side of a mountain, and turns into a river.

Hei mihi! si duræ natum subducere sorti
Molior, atque meis ausim confidere Regnis,
Frater adhuc Amyci mæret nece, cunctaque Divûm
Turba fremunt, quorum nati cecidere cadentque.
Quin habeat sua quemque dies, cunctisque negabo
Quæ mihi supremos misero sic fa'us honores
Congerit, atque animis moriturum ingentibus implet.
Ille volat campis, immensaque funera miscet
Per cuneos, velut hyberno proruptus ab arcu
Imber agens scopulos, nemorumque opacumque ruinas.
Donec ab ingenti bacchatus vertice montis
Frangitur, inque novum paullatim deficit amnem.
Lib. 6. Ver. 624.

Should I defer my son's impending fate,
And claim the pow'r of my almighty state,
Full many a valiant ghost reluctant dies,
And all the Gods with clamour rend the skies,
Whose race divine is here profusely slain,
And more shall yet lie bleeding on the plain.

But

But 'tis decreed, let Man his period have,
None shall defend whom *Jove* denies to save.
This said, he rais'd his son's collected fame,
And o'er his breast diffus'd a martial flame,
With full renown to grace his parting breath,
And urge him forward to a glorious death:
Fierce thro' the ranks the ardent warrior goes,
And rages wide amidst his slaughter'd foes.
Thus from the Rainbow with impetuous pow'r
Bursts the wild fury of some wint'ry show'r;
With wasteful noise descends the sweeping flood,
Drives the huge rocks, and tears the bending wood;
'Till rushing down some craggy mountain's side,
In a new river foams the rolling tide.

The first part of the comparison alludes to that of *Virgil*:

——Rapidus montano flumine torrens
Sternit agros, sternit sata læta, boumque labores,
Præcipitesque trahit silvas———

       Æneid. Lib. 2. Ver. 305.

Not with so fierce a rage the foaming flood
Roars when he finds his rapid course withstood;
Bears down the dams with unresisted sway,
A sweeps the Cattle and the Cots away.
         Dryden.

In the 7th book, *Juno* disguised like *Chalciope*, *Medea*'s sister, leads her out to the walls to see the battle. This is done in imitation of *Homer*, who brings out *Andromache* on the like occasion. Here FLACCUS seems very fond of machinery. *Juno* had borrowed the charms and enchanting girdle of *Venus* in order to inspire *Medea* with love for *Jason*: But then not satisfied with her own endeavours, she desires *Venus* to go in person to compleat the work and protect *Jason*. Why, as in *Virgil*, could not *Juno* at first have left it to *Venus*, as the fittest person to manage a Love Intrigue? To do more is superfluous; but this is not yet enough: *Iris* is charged to be obedient

dient to the orders of *Venus*, who sends her to *Jason* to bid him meet *Medea* at the temple of *Diana*. In the mean time *Juno* sits on mount *Caucasus* very sollicitous about the event, of which the Poet represents her as altogether ignorant.

——*Caucaseis speculatrix Juno resedit*
Rupibus, attonitos Æææ in mœnia vultus
Speque metuque tenens, & adhuc ignara futuri.
Lib. 7. Ver. 190.

On the high rock of *Caucasus* the Queen
Of Heav'n with hopes and fear perplex'd was seen
Watching, her eyes fixt on th' *Æean* gate,
As yet a stranger to the will of Fate.

I shall quote no more examples, the aforesaid may suffice to point out some of his beauties as well as his faults. It cannot be denied but that a spirit of true Poetry reigns thro' the whole, tho' not alike kept up in all the parts; to do which required the judgment of riper years than FLACCUS attained to, who is supposed not to have much out-lived thirty. If he is not so wise a man, he seems to be a better Poet than *Lucan*, and has more fire than *Silius Italicus*; and his stile, tho' not so magnificent, is more correct than that of *Statius*. He has professedly imitated *Virgil*, and often does it in a noble and happy manner; and is in general far from deserving to be so much neglected as he has been in comparison of other Poets no ways superior to him, either for their matter, stile, or versification.

THE LIFE OF Caius Silius Italicus.

CAIUS SILIUS ITALICUS descended of the antient and noble family of the *Silii*, and perhaps the grandson of that *C. Silius*, who was a third time Consul when *Augustus* made his will the year before his death, was born under *Tiberius*; but Authors are not agreed in the place of his nativity, nor is it to be determined from any passage in his works. Some are of opinion that he was born at *Italica* in *Spain*; but had he been a *Spaniard*, it is very unlikely that *Martial* who has often spoke in his praise, should forget to congratulate his country on having given birth to so illustrious a person. Others suppose he was born at *Confinium* in *Italy*, which place according to *Strabo*, had the Name *Italica* given it during the Social War; but *Velleius Paterculus*, who mentions something of a design that was in agitation during that war of changing the town's name, has no where said it was ever done: which is a good argument that this intended change did never take place. Besides, the Grammarian makes this objection to his birth at either of the aforesaid places; that if so, SILIUS must have been sirnam'd ITALICENSIS from *Italica*, and not ITALICUS as we find him constantly called. But let us pass on to something more certain concerning him.

Tho' Eloquence began to degenerate even under *Tiberius*, yet SILIUS, who had a great Genius to it, proposed the most likely means to restore it, by a careful imitation of *Cicero*; in which he so well succeeded, that soon after he came to the Bar, he got the character of the best Orator of his time. He pass'd with good applause thro' all those great offices, which lead to the Consulship; and became very remarkable by the death of *Nero*. *Pliny* the Younger, to whom we are beholden for most that we know of Silius, says, That it was reported, that he had at first laid out for *Nero*'s favour, which he acquired to a great degree, by accusing some great persons: a vile abuse of eloquence! but too frequent in those degenerate times. *Pliny* does not altogether free our author from this charge, but adds, that if he did so, he made ample amends for it afterwards by a long and uniform course of honour and virtue; and tho' he was likewise highly in favour with *Vitellius*, he had the art to gain the affection and esteem of the public, at the same time that he maintained himself in the good graces of that prince.

Under *Vespasian* he was sent Proconsul into *Asia*, from whence he returned to *Rome* with an unblemished character, his reputation still increasing with his employments. After having thus spent the better part of his life in his country's service, he bid adieu to public affairs, resolving to consecrate the remainder to a polite retirement and the *Muses*.

In order to this purpose, besides other fine seats, he purchased *Cicero*'s famous Villa at *Tusculum*, and an estate near *Naples*, which is said to have been *Virgil*'s, and in which was his tomb, which *Silius* very frequently visited; paying such great honour to that excellent Poet's memory, that he annually used to celebrate his birth-day with more solemnity than his own.

I must add one circumstance that seems to make very much for the honour of Silius. It appears from *Martial*, that his steady conduct had gained him among the *Romans* the Sirname of Perpetuus, that is *the constant*. *Martial* calls him twice by this name, once in a Poem written in his praise, *Lib.* 7. *Ep.* 62. and another time, when

when he only mentions him as one of those great men, who disdained not to give his Epigrams a place in their libraries, *Lib*. 6. *Ep*. 64. If the former may be understood as a compliment, the latter must be absurdly used, or prove that it was an appellation given him by the public voice.

Silius lived to see his eldest son Consul, and his other son was almost arrived to the age fit for obtaining it, which his merit already demanded, when an untimely death snatch'd him away from that and all his Father's hopes, *Martial*, Lib. 8. Ep. 66. As *Silius* grew old, he kept very close in his retirement, insomuch that he begged to be excused by reason of his advanced age from going to court to salute *Trajan* on his first coming to the Empire: and a few years after having been for some time afflicted with an incurable ulcer, after all remedies were found ineffectual for his relief, he put a period to his own life by a voluntary abstinence. This was a common practice among the *Romans*, and agreeably to the erroneous principles of the *Stoick* Philosophy, was counted an act of heroic bravery. *Atticus*, tho' an Epicurean in the latter part of his life, is remarkable for dying in the same manner. I cannot better conclude this account of Silius's life, than with *Martial*'s Epigram, wherein he mentions his possessing the two seats abovementioned, and pays him, who was his Patron, a fine compliment on this occasion.

Silius hæc magni celebrat monumenta Maronis,
Jugera facundi qui Ciceronis habet:
Hæredem Dominumque sui tumulique larisque
Non alium mallet nec Maro nec Cicero.
                                Lib. 11. *Ep*. 49.

Of *Tully*'s seat my Silius is possest,
And his the tomb where *Virgil*'s ashes rest:
Could those great shades return to choose their heir,
The present owner they would both prefer.

It was *Pliny*'s opinion, that Silius owed his success in Poetry more to his application than to any strong genius for it. He was on the decline of life before he
applied.

applied himself to it; so that, had Poetry been his talent, it is thought he would have found and followed the bent of his Genius sooner. Thus *Ovid*, though a man of great eloquence in pleading, soon left the Bar for the Muses; for Nature is seldom at a loss to find means to exert herself agreeably to her bent, and we find the greatest impediments generally too weak to stop the force of inclination:

Naturam expellas furca licet usque recurret.

WE may therefore conclude that some genius added to much leisure and the greatest admiration of *Virgil*, were the motives that prevailed with SILIUS to turn Poet in his old age: At least, ambition and the thirst of glory in public life got the better of his other inclinations.

HOWEVER it must still be granted, that he had a great and universal genius, that rendered him very capable to succeed in some degree in whatever he applied himself to, though he has fallen much short of his great pattern *Virgil* in Poetry.

BUT *Martial*, agreeably to his friendship for SILIUS, and perhaps in acknowledgment for favours received, has addressed him as the glory of the Muses in his time:

SILI, Castalidum decus sororum,
Qui perjuria barbari furoris
Ingenti premis ore, perfidosque
Fastus Hannibalis, levesque Pœnos
Magnis cedere cogis Africanis;
Paulum seposita severitate
Dum blanda vagus alea December
Incertis sonat hinc & hinc fritillis,
Et ludit rota nequiore talo
Nostris otia commoda Camœnis.
Nec torva lege fronte, sed remissa
Lascivis madidos jocis libellos.
Sic forsan tener ausus est Catullus
Magno mittere passerem Maroni.

SILIUS,

38 *The* LIFE *of* C. Silius Italicus.

which was now so nearly confined to truth, that it durst not launch out into those agreeable fictions that give a life to the narration of the *Ilias* and *Æneis*.

It is in this respect, that I cannot forbear calling Silius's judgment in question, who is too often tempted to imitate *Virgil*'s machinery, without a proper consideration of the many objections he was liable to for so doing. I think *Lucan*'s conduct in his *Pharsalia* more commendable, for having introduced but few of these ornaments into his Poem, which like that of Silius, being altogether historical, could not with any propriety receive them.

I need not detain the Reader, by giving him a sketch of the Poem: None, but those who are strangers to the *Roman* History, need such an illustration; and they may be informed of all at large in a translation of our Author by one *Ross*, which tho' far from doing justice to him, has yet kept pretty close to the original. But if the *Latin* wants fire and spirit sometimes, the *English* is so heavy, and the numbers are so rude and untuneable, that I could not offer them to the *English* reader in the quotations that are hereafter made out of this Poem.

Therefore I think it sufficient to make such occasional observations upon Silius's management of his subject in several parts of the Poem, as may shew his genius and point out a character to the reader.

After a short prosecution of his subject, Silius makes *Juno*, who still kept up her resentment against the *Romans* as the descendants of the *Trojans*, and sought to make her favourite *Carthaginians* the sovereigns of the world, declare, when he saw the bad success of her party in the first *Punic* war, that she should in time have a complete revenge by the terrible overthrows that her darling *Hannibal* would give the *Romans*. This machine is in imitation of *Virgil's* in the first book of the *Æneis*. But *Juno*'s impending storm improves on *Virgil*'s, meeting with following, Juno *Hannibal*'s father to continue him in the same implacable enmity to
the

passages out of Silius's Poem, I cannot begin by a nobler than *Jupiter*'s answer to *Venus*, in which the Poet has happily introduced a fine compliment to the *Vespasians* Father and Son, and particularly to *Domitian*, who reigned at the time of Silius's writing this book. Hence we may infer, that he retired from public affairs at least soon after the death of *Titus Vespasian*. But let us hear *Jupiter* speak.

Pelle metus, neu te Tyriæ coxanima gentis
Turbarint Cytherea; tenet, longumque tenebit
Tarpeias arces sanguis tuus: hâc ego Martis
Mole vires spectare paro atque expendere Bello.
Gens ferri patiens, ac læta domare labores
Paullatim antiquo patrum desuescit honori.
Atque ille haud unquam parcus pro laude cruoris,
Et semper famæ sitiens obscura sedendo
Tempora agit, multum volvens inglorius ævum.
Desidiæ virtus paullatim victa senescit:
Magnæ molis opus, multoque labore parandum
Tot populos inter soli sibi poscere regna.
Jamque tibi eveniet tempus, quo maxima rerum
Nobilior sit Roma malis; hinc nomina nostro
Non indigna polo referet labor, hinc tibi Paullus,
Hinc Fabius, gratusque mihi Marcellus opimis,
Hi tantum parient Latio per vulnera Regnum
Quod luxu & multum mutata mente Nepotes,
Non tamen evertisse queant: jamque ipse creatus
Qui Pœnum revocet Patriæ, Latioque repulsum.
Ante suæ muros Carthaginis exuat armis.
Hinc, Cytherea, tuis longo regnabitur ævo.
Exin se Curibus virtus cælestis ad astra
Efferet, & sacris augebit nomen Iülis.
Bellatrix gens baccifero nutrita Sabino;
Hinc pater ignotam donabit vincere Thulen,
Inque Caledonios primus trahet agmina lucos.
Compescet ripis Rhenum, reget impiger Afros,
Palmiferamque senex bello domitabit Idumen,
Nec Stygis ille lacus, viduataque numine regna
Sed superum sedes, nostrosque tenebit honores.

Tum

Contending pow'rs reduce, extensive sway
O'er all assume, and make a world obey:
And yet the time's at hand, when you'll confess
Rome's tow'ring glory founded on distress:
Calamity shall teach her to aspire,
As purest gold refines in quickest fire.
Her sons great acts new stars unto the skies,
New names shall add. Hence *Paulus* will arise.
Great *Fabius*, and *Marcellus*, glorious made
By noblest spoils; a sure foundation laid
Of Empire, by their valour rais'd shall stand
Unhurt, by Luxury's destroying hand,
To *Rome* already is the Heroe born,
Who shall th' insulting *Tyrian*'s pride o'erturn;
Fierce *Hannibal* from *Italy* recall,
And conqu'ring him, make envious *Carthage* fall.
Then shall thy race long flourish in command,
And spread their conquests wide thro' ev'ry land:
A race divine from *Cures* then shall spring
That will new glories to thy *Julius* bring:
The father of the Warrior *Sabine* breed
His hardy legions shall to *Thule* lead;
Thro' *Caledonian* woods first cut his way,
And teach the *Rhine* and *Afric* to obey.
Palm-bearing *Idumea* last shall yield
Him trophies, when grown old in Honour's field:
Nor shall he to the *Stygian* lake descend,
Such worth to Heav'n may justly recommend.
  To him succeeds a youth of active mind
Equal to that high pow'r for him design'd:
Palestine vanquish'd shall his temples crown.
Domitian next, brave chief of high renown!
A beardless youth he'll make the *Belgian* fly,
Tarpeian fires his courage will defy:
Thy sacred head the lambent flames shall spare,
I'll make thee mine, as thou mankind thy care:
The subject world thy presence long shall bless;
Ganges with bow unbent will thee confess
His Lord, and *Bactria* quell'd, submissive lay
Her empty quivers in her victor's way,

Triumphant

Triumphant from the North thy Car shall come,
And from the vanquish'd East bring Laurels home.
To thee great *Bacchus* yields; the *Ister* bears
Thy troops reluctant to *Sarmatic* wars:
When the *Barbarians* thou shalt close confine
To their own limits, and just bounds assign;
A *Tully*'s eloquence shall yield to thine:
Such harmony's admir'd by all the Nine;
And *Orpheus* would his Lyre submissive lend,
Orpheus for whom the rivers did suspend
Their course, and mountains with attention bend.
See! where the Capitol sinks in decay,
Sacred of old to me; soon comes the day,
By him renew'd its radiant roof shall rise,
And with his golden tow'rs invade the skies.
But thou, O born of Gods, that shall give birth
To future Deities, the happy earth
Rule with a father's power, retiring late
To these bright mansions of cælestial state:
Quirinus pleas'd for thee will quit his throne
Betwixt thy brother and thy father's crown,
And near thee fix'd shall shine thy starry son.

I shall now subjoin that fine passage in the first book of the *Æneis*, which Silius had in his eye when he wrote the foregoing lines, which I think may serve as an example of a fine Imitation. *Jupiter* comforts *Venus*, as follows.

Illi subridens hominum sator atque Deorum,
Vultu, quo cœlum, tempestatesque serenat,
Oscula libavit natæ; dehinc talia fatur:
Parce metu, Cytherea; manent immota tuorum
Fata tibi: cernes urbem, & promissa Lavini
Mœnia, sublimemque feres ad sidera cœli
Magnanimum Æneam: neque me sententia vertit.
Hic (tibi fabor enim, quando hæc te cura remordet,
Longius & volvens fatorum arcana movebo)
Bellum ingens geret Italia, populosque feroces
Contundet, moresque viris, & mœnia ponet,
Tertia dum Latio regnantem viderit æstas,

Ternaque

Ternaque transferint Rutulis hyberna subactis.
At puer Ascanius, cui nunc cognomen Iülo
Additur (Ilus erat, dum res stetit Ilia regno)
Triginta magnus volvendis mensibus orbes
Imperio explebit, regnumque à sede Lavini
Transferet, & longam multa vi muniet Albam.
Hic jam ter centum totos regnabitur annos
Gente sub Hectorea; donec regina sacerdos,
Marte gravis, geminum partu dabit Ilia prolem.
Inde lupæ fulvo nutricis tegmine lætus
Romulus, excipiet gentem, & mavortia condet
Mœnia, Romanosque suo de nomine dicet.
His ego nec metas rerum, nec tempora pono:
Imperium sine fine dedi: quin aspera Juno,
Quæ mare nunc, terrasque metu, cœlumque fatigat,
Consilia in melius referet, mecúmque fovebit
Romanos rerum Dominos, gentemque togatam.
Sic placitum; veniet lustris labentibus ætas
Cum domus Assaràci Phthiam, clarasque Mycenas
Servitio premet, ac victis dominabitur Argis.
Nascetur pulchra Trojanus origine Cæsar,
(Imperium Oceano, famam qui terminet astris)
Julius, à magno demissum nomen Iülo.
Hunc tu olim cœlo spoliis orientis onustum
Accipies secura; vocabitur hic quoque votis.
Aspera tùm positis mitescent sæcula bellis;
Cana fides, & Vesta, Remo cum fratre Quirinus
Jura dabunt: diræ ferro, & compagibus arctis
Claudentur belli portæ. Furor impius intùs
Sæva sedens super arma, & centum vinctus ahenis
Post tergum nodis, fremit horridus ore cruento.

Lib. 1. Ver. 258.

To whom the father of immortal race
Smiling with that serene indulgent face
With which he drives the clouds and clears the skies,
First gave a holy kiss, then thus replies:
Daughter, dismiss thy fears; to thy desire
The fates of thine are fix'd and stand entire.
Thou shalt behold thy wish'd *Lavinian* walls,
And ripe for Heav'n, when Fate *Æneas* calls,

Then shalt thou bear him up sublime to me;
No councils have revers'd my firm decree.
And left new fears disturb thy happy state,
Know I have search'd the mystic rolls of Fate:
Thy Son (nor is th' appointed season far)
In *Italy* shall wage successful war.
Shall tame fierce nations in the bloody field,
And sovereign laws impose, and cities build;
Till after ev'ry foe subdued, the Sun
Thrice thro' the Signs his annual race shall run:
This is the time prefix'd. *Ascanius* then,
Now call'd *Iülus*, shall begin his reign.
He thirty rowling years the crown shall wear:
Then from *Lavinium* shall the seat transfer,
And with hard labour *Alba Longa* build:
The throne with his succession shall be fill'd
Three hundred circuits more: Then shall be seen
Ia the fair, a Priestess and a Queen;
Who full of *Mars*, in time, with kindly throws
Shall at a birth two goodly boys disclose.
The royal babes a tawny wolf shall drain:
Then *Romulus* his Grandsire's throne shall gain;
Of martial tow'rs the founder shall become,
The people *Romans* call, the City *Rome*.
To them no bounds of empire I assign,
Nor term of years to their immortal line.
Ev'n haughty *Juno*, who with endless broils
Earth, seas and heav'n, and *Jove* himself turmoils,
At length aton'd, her friendly pow'r shall join,
To cherish and advance the *Trojan* line.
The subject world shall *Rome*'s dominion own,
And prostrate shall adore the nation of the Gown.
An age is rip'ning in revolving fate,
When *Troy* shall overturn the *Grœcian* state;
And sweet revenge her conqu'ring sons shall call
To crush the people that conspir'd her fall.
Then *Cæsar* from the *Julian* stock shall rise,
Whose empire ocean, and whose fame the skies
Alone shall bound: whom fraught with eastern spoil
Our heav'n, the just reward of human toil.

Securely

Securely shall repay with rites divine;
And incense shall ascend before his sacred shrine
Then dire Debate, and impious war shall cease,
And the stern age be soften'd into peace.
Then banish'd Faith shall once again return,
And vestal fires in hallow'd temples burn:
And *Remus* with *Quirinus* shall sustain
The righteous laws, and fraud and force restrain.
Janus himself before his *Fane* shall wait,
And keep the dreadful issues of his gate.
With bolts and iron bars: within remains
Imprison'd, Fury, bound in brazen chains:
High on a trophy rais'd of useless arms
He sits, and threats the world with vain alarms.
                                        Dryden

I hope none of my readers, but such as are insensibl
of the fine strokes of poetry, will be angry at the lengt
of these two quotations, or at my thus setting then
together; which I think the readiest way to shew th
beauties of both Authors, at least it is most useful fo
the instruction of the young Student, for whose be
nefit this work was chiefly undertaken. I now pro
ceed to transcribe some other passages from SILIUS
The following account of the origin of the Templ
of *Jupiter-Ammon* is very curious and entertaining.

Nam cui Dona Jovis non divulgata per orbem.
In Gremio Thebes geminas sedisse Columbas?
Quarum Chaonias pennis quæ contigit oras
Implet fatidico Dodonida murmure quercum.
At quæ Carpathium super æquor vecta, per auras
In Libyen niveis tranavit concolor alis,
Hanc sedem primo Cythereia condidit ales;
Hic ubi nunc aras lucosque videtis opacos
Ductore electo gregis, (admirabile dictu)
Lanigeri capitis media inter cornua perstans,
Marmaricis ales populis responsa canebat:
Mox subitum nemus atque annoso robore lucus
Exsiluit, qualesque premunt nunc sidera quercus

A prima venere die, prisca inde pavore
Arbor numen habet, coliturque tepentibus aris.
                                Lib. 3. Ver. 678.

To whom on earth are *Jove*'s fam'd gifts unknown,
The sacred doves that first at *Thebes* were shown?
To the *Chaonian* coast one steer'd her flight,
Inspiring oaks with her prophetic light;
But she, whom snowy wings high soaring bore
O'er seas *Carpathian*, reach'd the *Libyan* shore.
Here *Cytherea*'s bird first chose to dwell,
And singling out the Ram, alighting fell
Betwixt his horns, and thence instructive taught
Those oracles, the wondring people sought.
Where now these altars and the shady wood
Delightful you behold, there first she stood;
Men saw amaz'd at once a grove arise
Of these tall oaks, and sudden reach the skies.
Hence antient rev'rence to this Grove is paid,
And smoaking altars are with victims fed.

THE Description of the *Alps* in the same book is very just and poetical:

Cuncta gelu, canaque æternum grandine tecta
Atque ævi glaciem cohibent, regit ardua montis
Ætherei facies, surgentique obvia Phœbo
Duratas nescit flammis mollire pruinas.
Quantum Tartareus regni pallentis hiatus
Ad manes imos, atque atræ stagna Paludis
A supera tellure patet: tam longa per auras
Erigitur tellus & cælum intercipit umbra.
Nullum ver usquam, nulliques æstatis honores:
Sola jugis habitat diris, sedesque tuetur
Perpetuas deformis hyems; illa undique nubes
Huc atras agit, & mixtos cum grandine nimbos.
Jam cuncti flatus, ventique furentia regna
Alpina posuere domo, caligat in altis
Obtutus saxis, abeuntque in nubila montes.
Mixtus Athos Tauro: Rhodope adjuncta Mimanti,
Ossaque cum Pindo, tamque Hæmo conferit Othrys.
                                Lib. 3. Ver. 478.

In every part eternally prevail
The growing frost, and undissolving hail;
The aged ice endures: each lofty brow
Of these aerial hills is crown'd with snow:
Tho' *Phœbus* rising on their Summit play,
The solid frost defies his fiercest ray:
Far as the gloomy dwellings sink below
Our surface, where the *Stygian* waters flow,
So high above the vale the mountains rise,
And with their shadow intercept the skies.
Nor Spring, nor Summer knows the gloomy year:
Winter deform'd for ever fix'd dwells here,
And on these dreary cliffs her seat defends;
Whence all around she storms dispensing sends.
Mad *Boreas* here and all his boist'rous Train
Have chose their home, hence scour the earth and
    main.
The weaken'd eye grows dim to take the height,
Which piercing thro' the clouds eludes the dazled
    sight.

THE scene of the soldiers consternation to see one mountain rising above the other is happily illustrated by the comparison of a traveller at sea, who can only see the water.

> *Quoque magis subiere jugo atque evadere nisi*
> *Erexere gradum, crescit labor, ardua supra*
> *Sese aperit fessis, & nascitur altera moles.*
> *Unde nec edomitos, exsudatosque labores*
> *Respexisse libet, tanta formidine plena*
> *Exterrent repetita oculis, atque una pruinæ*
> *Canentis, quacunque datur permittere visus*
> *Ingeritur facies: medio sic navita ponto*
> *Quum dulces liquit terras, & inania nullos*
> *Inveniunt ventos securo carbasa malo*
> *Immensas prospectat aquas, ac victa profundis*
> *Æquoribus, fessus renovat sua lumina cælo.*
>   Lib 7. Ver. 190.

The higher they ascend, and seek to ease
Their wearied steps, their labours still increase:

To one great height a greater doth succeed,
And every ill another seems to breed.
Hence all their toils and labours, which before
They had o'ercome, they tremble to explore.
Objects repeated, terrors new present,
Which ever way their trembling eyes are bent.
The horrid face of winter hoary white
Appearing, gives sad limits to their sight.
So when the unskil'd sailor vent'rous leaves
His sweet abode, for which too late he grieves,
And the brisk gale no longer swells the sails,
Far as his view extends, the sea prevails:
Tir'd with the boundless prospect, then he tries
To ease his sight, and upward cast his eyes.

The description of the river *Ticinus* is as beautiful as those of the celebrated fountain in *Ovid*, where *Salmacis* and *Hermaphroditus* bathed, and *Narcissus* admired his own beauty.

Cæruleas Ticinus aquas & stagna vadoso
Perspicuus servat turbari nescia fundo,
Ac nitidum viridi lente trahit amne liquorem;
Vix credas labi, ripis tam mitis opacis
Argutos inter volucrum certamina cantus,
Somniferam ducit lucenti gurgite lympham.
Lib. 4. Ver. 82.

Ticinus in a shallow channel flows;
Yet gently glides the limpid stream along
The shady banks, where feather'd warblers throng;
From spray to spray the wanton songsters skip:
The tide transparent scarce is seen to creep,
And with low murmurs soft invites to sleep.

Before I quote the following passage, I cannot forbear condemning Silius for an absurd imitation of *Virgil*. The Consul *Scipio* is introduced speaking to his horse *Garganus;* to whom he promises the fine trappings of *Chryxus*'s horse. This *Chryxus* was a prince of the *Gauls* of great stature and fierceness, whom the Consul was going to attack. *Mezentius* is indeed

indeed made to speak to his horse *Rhætus* in the *Æneis*; but he was agitated by the extremity of grief and despair: and those violent passions make men address their discourse to the most inanimate parts of nature. *Scipio* was cool, and wanted only to encourage his horse to ride up against the *Gaul*. Besides, what might be supposed a beautiful image in those early times, when fine horses were uncommon, and made the delight as well as the reward of the greatest Heroes; is absurd to be imitated in the second *Punic* War by a grave and illustrious *Roman*, such as this elder *Scipio* was. But the Poet has succeeded better in his comparison of *Chryxus*'s fall when slain by the Consul, with that of a great pile cast into the sea.

Haud aliter structo Tyrrhena ad littora saxo
Pugnatura fretis subter cæcisque procellis,
Pila immane sonans, impingitur ardua ponto:
Immugit Nereus, divisaque cærula pulsu
Illisum accipiunt irata sub æquora montem. Lib. 4.

So where a mound is raising on the strand
To quell the billows that insult the land
A mighty pile is cast, that falling rives
The foaming surges, and resounding drives
With shock impetuous; they with angry roar
Admit the dashing rock, and yield the shore.

The imitation Silius makes of the battle of the *Horatii* and *Curiatii* in the *Roman* story, by an engagement of three *Romans* with as many *Carthaginians*, is agreeably related, though too like *Livy*'s account in the circumstances of the combat. When *Mars* is made to descend with his train to instruct young *Scipio* in his first campaign, who afterwards saves his Father's life, and bears him wounded to his tent; I must confess, that I think this machinery needless, and of little advantage to a circumstance which is so beautiful in History. The Poet represents the God of war as admiring the heroic conduct of *Scipio*, who, according to *Livy*, was but sixteen years old, when he behaved with so much gallantry. *Mars* foretells *Scipio*'s *pio*'s victory over *Hannibal* afterwards, and then returns to Heaven. This seems but a poor expedition for a God; and to mend the matter, it is *Jupiter* himself, who out of concern for the Consul's life, sends him to his relief, when he was encompassed and attacked by a body of *Carthaginians*.

This happens at the battle of *Trebia*: that river swells with the number of the slain, that stop'd the course of his stream, so that the Consul *Scipio* is again in danger of his life. Silius here makes him expostulate with the river for favouring the *Carthaginians*, which at last he threatens to destroy, by letting out his waters by several cuts. The River-God full of resentment at this insult, swells higher, and lifting up his oozy head, reproves *Scipio* for his unjust menaces. *Venus* as she lay in the embraces of *Vulcan*, saw and heard their dispute; and being in pain for *Scipio*, throws some of her husband's fires into the river, which soon sink the waters; but after the river's submission, and at his humble request, he is allowed to flow in his usual banks.

Were it not an ungrateful task to be thus forced to censure and expose my Author's failings, which I must do as they come in my way, unless I would leave the less skilful reader to be often misled by seeming beauties, I might proceed farther in this examination: But it is enough to have shewn some of his beauties, and some of his errors; into the latter of which he often falls, by a too great affectation of adorning his subject.

To prevent which in others, I shall venture to lay down the following rule of *Lucretius*, though somewhat differently applied.

Ornari res ipsa negat contenta doceri.

A great subject is so far incapable of receiving additional ornaments from fiction, as it is above them, and so will shine most in the beautiful and sublime simplicity of the narration; like fine figures in sculpture to which the most elegant drapery would not only be an incumbrance, but conceal some of the greatest beauties that appear to advantage in the nudity.

This leads me to consider in what cases a judicious Poet will introduce a machine. I know but two; either to set off a little circumstance that would appear mean without it, as *Virgil* has done, where *Æneas* meets his Mother *Venus* in the wood and asks her the way, not knowing who it was he spoke to; or secondly to compass some important event, for which the reader is to be prepared, and yet is as it were to be surprized at the manner of its being brought about; as where *Juno* in the same book goes to *Æolus* to get him to raise a storm that should unexpectedly drive the *Trojan* Fleet into the port of *Africa* near *Carthage*, which was to be the scene of that fine episode of his amour with *Dido*. When Poets have been willing to introduce machines into their subject without some such like view, as the two above mentioned instances, they are not only needless but often prove disadvantageous to the Poem they were intended to grace.

To sum up the character of Silius in a few words: He was not a stranger to some of those great qualities required to form a great Poet; he was inferior to none of them in learning, both historical, moral, and natural; he had the judgment to chuse a subject equally interesting and illustrious. His characters are noble and just, and the sentiments great and beautiful. We have seen that his descriptions are bold and well circumstantiated, and the images very poetical, but the expression, the colouring, is weak and often spiritless. He is master of many excellencies, but often loses the influence of the ætherial particle, that enthusiastic fire, which strengthens every figure, and animates every line in *Homer* and *Virgil*. Though Silius does not always creep; he can sometimes rise with dignity and gracefulness: but he weaken'd his fire by attempting to imitate *Virgil's* correctness. *Homer's* fire as more fierce and blazing, would have warmed his flagging Muse. A less intelligent reader is often apt to mistake
the

the close exactness of *Virgil* for coldness: You lose the beauty of some of his truest images for want of due attention to the labour'd correctness of his expression, which like a curious figure encompassed by a strong shade does not strike every common eye. SILIUS by attempting to do the same, has sometimes left his figures without life, and his stile spiritless. But, however *Statius* modestly said of himself, that he follow'd *Virgil* at a distance, yet his fire made him often run out of the course, as SILIUS's caution kept him behind. So hard is it to observe the golden mean in Poetry as well as in other things. But though I have not failed observing SILIUS's faults, I think he has many more excellencies; so that he justly deserves the character of a good Poet, who would be much more esteemed were he more known.

THE LIFE OF MARTIAL.

MARCUS VALERIUS MARTIALIS was a native of *Bilbilis* now *Bilboa*, the capital of the province of *Biscay* in *Spain*. In his youth he was sent to prosecute his studies at *Rome*, being intended for the Law; but finding in himself no great talent that way, he left the Bar and applied himself to Poetry, to which his genius led him. He was so fortunate in the exercise of that easy vein of writing in which he excelled, that it soon got him the acquaintance and friendship of many of the first rank at *Rome*; and particularly of *Silius Italicus, Stella* and *Pliny* the Younger; the latter of whom speaks very handsomely of him in his Epistles. Three succeeding Emperors became his patrons, *Domitian, Nerva,* and *Trajan*; the former made him a *Roman* Knight, and granted him the privileges of a Citizen that had three children. *Stertinius* a *Roman* Nobleman hrd so great an esteem for him, that he placed his statue in his library, whilst the Poet was yet living; an honour generally paid to the memory of the illustrious dead only. The emperor *Verus*, who reigned with *Antoninus* the Philosopher, used to call MARTIAL his *Virgil*, thereby sufficiently intimating the esteem he had for his works.

TOWARDS the middle of *Trajan*'s reign, MARTIAL grew desirous of retiring to his native country, after having

Sum fateor semperque fui, Callistrate, pauper,
Sed non obscurus, nec male notus eques.
Sed toto legor orbe frequens, & dicitur hic est;
Quodque cinis paucis, hoc mihi vita dedit.
Lib. 5. Ep. 13.

Low is my fortune, yet not quite so mean
 But in the rank of *Roman* Knights I'm seen.
My Works with pleasure thro' the world are read;
 The praise few dead obtain, is to me living paid.

WE have no other helps to determine the time of our Poet's birth and death, than what his works can afford, which still make it conjectural. He says he liv'd at *Rome* thirty four years, and was grey-haired when he retired to *Bilboa*; where he married *Marcella*, I think his second wife, and after three years silence publish'd his 12th book of Epigrams: we hear no more of him after this, and so may suppose he did not long survive this publication. If we knew the date of *Pliny*'s letter about his death, which is addressed to *Cornelius Priscus*, and very probably the same person to whom the Poet has dedicated his 12th book, we might determine it, and thereby pretty nearly fix his birth. All that can be gathered from what has been said, is that supposing him twenty two at his first coming to *Rome*, where he lived thirty four years, he must be fifty nine when he publish'd his last book; for the 13th and 14th books seem to have been written long before it. He was born the 1st of *March*, as he tells us, *Lib.* 10. *Ep.* 24. which might happen about the tenth year of *Claudian*, and so his coming to *Rome* will fall in with the beginning of *Vespasian*'s reign; and his death, supposing it to have happened within a year after the 12th book was published, about the 15th of *Trajan*.

BEFORE we examine his works, it may not be improper to enquire a little into the nature of Epigrammatic Poetry.

ORIGINALLY the word *Epigram* signified only an Inscription; which being often comprehended in a
few

few lines or verses, came afterwards to signify more particularly certain short Poems.

The Critics have defined the Epigram to be a short Poem containing a clear exposition of some thing, or character, or action. It is distinguished into the Pointed and not Pointed: The Pointed Epigram is that which has a turn or sting in the conclusion, and if well done, is generally reckoned the best; though there are many good Epigrams which are of the second sort, unpointed, that have no turn at all. *Navagerius* a learned *Italian* and great admirer of *Catullus*, who excells in the unpointed Epigram, used on his birth day every year to burn a certain number of MARTIAL's books, in honour to the other Poet's memory: But besides that this savour'd too much of vanity, MARTIAL has many excellent Epigrams of the unpointed sort.

True Wit seems likewise in a peculiar manner to be the Epigrammatist's province, at least he should go on no other foundation than that which is just and beautiful. Some have defined the Beautiful in writing to be that which truly and properly, to which I add, and elegantly describes the mutual relation and agreement between the nature of things and our ideas of them. This happy talent more particularly concerns the Epigrammatist, whose compositions being short and confined to a single subject, make themselves easy to be understood and censured by almost every reader, who may with little labour discern the beauties or blemishes that lye in a small compass.

But as true Wit and just thoughts are not always at a Writer's command, the Epigrammatist is very liable to run into false wit. If there be a mixture of truth and falshood in the thought, it may sometimes be allowed in a good Epigram; but if that thought on which the turn depends should prove false the whole Epigram is bad.

To shew himself a master, the Poet should not only invent a happy turn, but let his expression be concise and clear; for a good thought is sometimes spoiled by adding to, or enlarging it, or at least becomes ambiguous and obscure. As true beauty is most comely in a plain dress, so a fine thougt shines most in its genuine simplicity, without any additional ornaments from the Poet's fancy.

To begin with examining some of MARTIAL's Epigrams by the rules aforesaid, I shall instance in that on the celebrated story of *Pætus* and *Arria*. Almost every reader knows, that *Nero* having ordered *Pætus* to die, *Arria* that noble *Roman's* wife, took a generous resolution to die with him, with whom she had lived many years in all the endearments of the most tender conjugal affection, so that this happy couple were become the admiration of the Age. In order to let her husband see how easy it was to die, she stabbed her self in his presence, and drawing the dagger all bloody out of her bosom, and presenting it to him, with an air full of heroic constancy mingled with the sweetest affection, said, *Pætus*, it is not painful.

MARTIAL, imagining that by some addition of his own, he could give a new grace to this heroic lady's action and expression, makes her say besides the words above; believe me, *Pætus*, it is the wound you are going to give your self that gives me pain. By this indiscreet addition the chief beauty of the action and thought is destroyed; for *Arria*, by saying to her husband, *Non dolet Pæte*, *Pætus*, it is not painful, encouraged him to plunge the Dagger to his heart, with the same indifference and resolution that he had just seen her do it: But the Poet's addition makes the poor Lady kill her self to no purpose, by that unseasonable expression of tenderness for him, which must discourage him from killing himself, because she says that would give her pain though her own death gave her none. Though that excellent Lady might naturally be supposed full of such tender sentiments, yet she had too much of the noble *Roman* in her to increase his agonies by such a declaration, and therefore this additional thought, tho' natural and beautiful in it self, is in this place very improper. The Epigram is as follows. *Casta*

Casta suo gladium cum traderet Arria Pæto,
  Quem de visceribus traxerat ipsa suis,
Crede mihi, vulnus quod feci, non dolet, inquit ;
  Sed, quod tu facies, hoc mihi, Pæte, dolet.
                              Lib. 1. Ep. 4.

The virtuous *Arria* drawing from her breast
The reeking dagger, *Pætus* thus addrest ;
This does not pain me, *Pætus*, but I rue
The wound you'll make and doubly die in you.

THIS instance wherein MARTIAL has failed, may shew that it is no easy manner to write a good Epigram upon a known subject, especially where the thought, and even the expression of the turn are already made to the Poet's hand.

I shall next proceed to shew by the example of MARTIAL, how an Epigrammatist may treat the same subject well and ill at different times.

IN the following Epigram the subject is nobly executed, and the turn just and well pointed.

Antoni Phario nil objecture Photino,
  Et levius tabula quam Cicerone nocens :
Quid gladium demens Romana stringis in ora?
  Hoc admisisset nec Catilina nefas.
Impius infando miles corrumpitur auro,
  Et tantis opibus vox tacet una tibi.
Quid profunt sacræ pretiosa silentia Linguæ ?
  Incipient omnes pro Cicerone loqui. Lib. 5. Ep. 50.

Photinus' Crime shew'd not more cruel will,
O *Antony*, than thy proscription bill.
But *Cicero*'s death did far exceed the rest,
Ev'n *Catiline* would spare his sacred breast.
A soldier's avarice brib'd by heaps of gold,
To thy Revenge the dear bought silence sold ;
But what avails the silence of one tongue,
Whilst thousands in its stead proclaim the wrong ?

THE reader may observe, that *Antony* is here made as criminal for proscribing *Cicero* as *Photi-*

nus for having *Pompey* assassinated, when he fled, after the battle of *Pharsalia*, to *Ptolemy* in *Ægypt*. MARTIAL, who seems full of indignation against the memory of *Antony*, and perhaps was willing to compliment *S. Italicus*, who was one of his Patrons, and a great admirer of *Cicero*'s, as it were correcting his former assertion, which is however repeated in the first verse of the following Epigram, undertakes to shew, that *Antony* was more criminal in putting *Cicero* to Death, than *Photinus* in murdering *Pompey*; and uses this argument, that what *Photinus* did was for his Prince's service, whereas *Antony* kill'd *Cicero* to gratify his own revenge. But the Poet was not aware, that the converse of this proposition is equally true, *viz.* that *Antony* is more excusable than *Photinus*, because the latter assassinated *Pompey* without any provocation, merely to satisfy his own and his master's timorous policy, in doing which they were guilty of the highest ingratitude to *Pompey*, who had been a benefactor to *Ægypt* and them: whereas *Antony* had, as he thought, received the most injurious treatment imaginable from *Cicero*, whose eloquent harangues in the Senate, had caused him to be declared a traitor and the enemy of his Country. But let us see the Epigram.

> *Par scelus admisit Phariis Antonius armis;*
> *Abscidit vultus ensis uterque sacros*
> *Illud laurigeros ageret cum læta triumphos*
> *Hoc tibi, Roma, caput, cum loquereris, erat.*
> *Antoni tamen est pejor quam causa Photini;*
> *Hic facinus Domino præstitit, ille sibi.*
>
> Lib. 3. Ep. 65.

Alike was *Antony*'s and *Ægypt*'s guilt;
Each *Rome*'s best blood in her two Heroes spilt.
Pompey the *Roman* arms to triumphs led,
Rome, when she spoke, bid *Tully* be her head.
Yet he a victim to resentment falls,
When *Antony* provok'd for vengeance calls.
The *Pharian* to the *Roman* yields the Prize,
Photinus but obeys when *Pompey* dies.

At the same time that I condemn the turn of this Epigram as ambiguous at best, it is but justice to the Poet to say, that the expressions are noble and very poetical.

The following Epigram is an instance of a turn made upon a false thought, which may impose upon us at first by an air of the sublime.

Sextantes, Calliste, duos infunde Falerni;
　Tu super æstivas, Alcime, funde nives.
Pinguescat nimio modidus mihi crinis amomo,
　Lassenturque rosis tempora sutilibus.
Jam vicina jubent nos vivere Mausolæa,
　Cum doceant ipsos posse perire Deos.

　　　　　　　　　　　　Lib. 5. Ep. 65.

Boy, fill with gen'rous wine the swelling bowl,
Temper'd with summer's snow to make it cool:
With ointments rich perfume my hair, my head
Crown with full Garlands of wreath'd roses made:
Yon *Mausoleum* bids us life enjoy,
Which shews, that death can even Gods destroy.

The Latin word *vivere* emphatically signifies to be merry and enjoy the pleasures of Life. The Poet here supposes himself sitting in sight of the Tombs of the Emperors, who by the gross flattery of the times used to be stiled Gods even in their life time. Martial therefore recommends the present enjoyment of life from this Consideration, that the Gods themselves had but a short time to live. The Gods as meaning the Emperors had indeed but a short time to live, they were subject to death as well as other men: But the general notion of Gods implying immortal Beings, makes the thought false, unless some epithet were added to soften the expression, and then the turn it self would be lost.

I shall give another example where the Poet has lessened the greatness of the thought and action, by making some addition to it; which generally happens when we give our fancy way and so forget the strict propriety of the person's character, whose actions or sentiments are made the subject of an Epigram. The Character of *Portia*, that illustrious daughter of *Cato* of *Utica* and wife of *Brutus*, is well known, as well as the trial she made of her own constancy and secrecy, when she found *Brutus*, scrupled to trust her with a secret. The following Epigram introduces her as killing her self by swallowing live coals; and speaking to those about her, she reminds them of what her Father had said a little before his death to those, who out of Zeal for his safety had taken his sword away: Do not you know, said that great *Roman*, that a man resolved to die, can stop his breath, or run his head against the wall? *Portia* hereby intimated that she was a true daughter of *Cato*, and so all their endeavours to prevent her death were to no purpose; having said that, she swallowed the burning coals. But MARTIAL, after she had done that makes her say, by way of triumph, now, what signifies your depriving me of a sword? It would be unbecoming her steady virtue to insult the zealous affections of her attendants, and at best this addition is superfluous.

Conjugis audisset fatum cum Porci Bruti,
  Et subtracta sibi quæreret arma dolor:
Nondum scitis, ait, mortem non posse negari?
  Credideram satis hoc vos docuisse patrem.
Dixit, & ardéntes avido bibit ore favillas:
  I nunc, & ferrum turba molesta nega.
                                    Lib. 1. Ep. 43.

When *Porcia* heard of *Brutus*' death, her woes
She sought the readiest way with life to close:
The weapon gone, she said, Death to restrain
I thought my Father's fate had shewn was vain.
Then hastily the burning coals devour'd;
Now keep, she cries, officious friends, the sword.

THERE are other Epigrams that seem faulty, because the Poet has been deceived in the choice of his subject, by the seeming dignity and excellency of it. In this light I consider that of MARTIAL on *Mucius Scævola*,

Scævola. The Story is finely told by the Poet; but I see only baseness and falshood at the bottom of it, though related at large in all the pomp of *Livy*'s eloquence. If indeed, as *Virgil* says, all is fair against an enemy.

Dolus an virtus, quis in hoste requirat?

I shall acquit the Poet's judgment, as carried away in this particular by the public voice, which seemed to lay it down as a maxim, by their admiring what *Mucius* did, That the greatest crimes become acts of virtue when committed for the service of our country. But I think the *Romans* have in many instances shewn their abhorrence of such principles, and allowed that there were laws and rights of war; however, they forgot themselves in the case of *Mucius*. The turn MARTIAL has made in the last lines is very fine and just, for *Porsena*'s making peace with the *Romans*, whom he had reduced to great distress by a long and close siege, was partly owing to his amazement and admiration of the desperate courage of young *Mucius*, and partly to that lie by which that prince was made to believe that there were many others who had entered with *Mucius* into a combination to attack his life, if he did not save it by speedily putting an end to the war, and abandoning the interests of the banished *Tarquins*.

Cum peteret regem decepta satellite dextra,
  Injecit sacris se peritura focis:
Sed tam sæva pius miracula non tulit hostis,
  Et raptum flammis jussit abire virum.
Urere quam potuit contempto Mucius igne,
  Hanc spectare manum Porsena non potuit:
Major deceptæ fama est & gloria dextræ;
  Si non erraset fecerat illa minus. Lib. 1. Ep. 22.

The hand that meant the King, but slew his Guard,
Atones its errour in the flames; so hard
Is *Mucius* to condemn, so much he dares
What to behold the *Tuscan* monarch fears.

Such

Such cruel courage that good prince admires,
Dismiss'd with safety the bold youth retires.
Happy the hand whose praise from errour grown
Had from success inferior honour known.

There is a noble kind of Epigram that concludes with a moral sentence fitly applied to some action. Martial sometimes excels that way. The reader will see a beautiful instance of it in the following Epigram.

Quod magni Thraseæ consummatique Catonis
   Dogmata sic sequeris, salvus ut esse velis,
Pectore nec nudo strictos incurris in enses
   Quod fecisse velim te, Deciane, facis.
Nolo virum facili redimit qui sanguine famam;
   Hunc volo laudari qui sine morte potest.
Lib. 1. Ep. 9.

Cato and *Thrasea*'s virtues that you dare
Nobly to follow, yet of life take care,
Nor desp'rate on the pointed weapon fall;
This conduct, *Decianus*, pleases all.
I like not him who dies to purchase name,
But him whose conduct guards both life and fame.

Having thus examined several kinds of Epigrams of a serious turn, I shall proceed in the same manner with some that are enlivened by a more pleasant vein of wit.

There are some, in which an elegant enumeration of circustances preparatory to the turn, is sometimes requisite to make the Epigram compleat. The parts ought here to be agreeably distributed, the expression easy, clear, and lively: This may make a low subject shine. The following Epigram will shew Martial's success this way.

Occurrit tibi nemo quod libenter,
Quod quacunque venis fuga est, & ingens
Circa te, Ligurine, solitudo;
Quid sit, scire cupis? nimis poeta es:
Hoc valde vitium periculosum.

Nam tantos rogo quis ferat labores?
Et stanti legis, & legis sedenti,
Currenti legis, & legis canenti;
In Thermas fugio, sonas ad aurem:
Piscinam peto, non licet natare;
Ad cœnam propero, tenes euntem:
Ad cœnam venio, fugas sedentem:
Lassus dormio, suscitas jacentem.
Vis quantum mali facias videre,
Vir justus, probus, innocens, timeris. Lib. 3. Ep. 44.

That you should no kind welcome meet,
Nor any friend your coming greet;
That all men your approaches fly,
Surpriz'd you ask the reason why;
The reason! too much Poetry,
A dang'rous fault, big with offence;
For who can bear th' impertinence?
Whether I fit, stand, run, or sing,
Your verses in my ears must ring.
When I go bathe, the Poet's there,
And sounds heroics in my ear.
By friends invited would I go,
I'm stop'd to mark thy numbers flow.
To take a dinner if I come,
Your verses drive me fasting home:
When wearied I lie down to rest,
That with rehearsals you molest.
By this one folly see what mischief's done!
The just, good man we for the Poet shun.

This next is of the same kind, and though shorter, equally beautiful for the neat distribution of the parts, and the humour of the turn.

Ne valeam si non totis, Deciane, diebus,
  Et tecum totis noctibus esse velim:
Sed duo sunt, quæ nos distinguunt, millia passûm,
  Quatuor hæc fiunt cum rediturus eam.
Sæpe domi non es; cum sis quoque sæpe negaris;
  Vel tantum caussis, vel tibi sæpe vacas.

Te tamen ut videam duo millia non piget ire;
  Ut te non videam quatuor ire piget. Lib. 2. Ep. 5.

Both day and night with pleasure I could spend
To have the company of such a friend:
But 'tis two miles from me to you, two more
In walking home, which makes the journey four.
You're oft abroad, and when at home deny'd
For bus'ness, health, and God knows what beside.
Two miles I'd go to see a friend like you,
But four miles not to see you! Sir, adieu.

THERE are some Epigrams of this sort, which MARTIAL has brought within the compass of one Distich, including the narration and the turn. The following is a pleasant instance of it, but I could not preserve the conciseness of the Original in the translation.

Omnia promittis cum tota nocte bibisti:
  Mane nihil præstas, Posthume, mane bibas.
                              Lib. 12. Ep. 12.

After drinking all night, in a maudlin kind fit,
You promise me fair, but next morning forget.
To make you keep true to your word, the best way
Is to get you well drunk against break of day.

I shall add another of this kind, which Mr. *Addison* has translated in the Spectator, and pleasantly applied to the good old Knight Sir *Roger*, who was sometimes as full of his beautiful widow as the Person *Martial* describes was of his *Nævia*.

Quicquid agit Rufus, nihil est nisi Nævia Rufo:
  Si gaudet, si flet, si tacet, hanc loquitur.
Cœnat, propinat, poscit, negat, annuit, una est
  Nævia, si non sit Nævia, mutus erit.
Scriberet hesterna patri cum luce salutem,
  Nævia lux, inquit, Nævia, numen, ave.
                              Lib. 1. Eb. 69.

Let *Rufus* weep, rejoice, stand, sit, or walk,
Still he can nothing but of *Nævia* talk:

Let him eat, drink, ask questions, or dispute,
Still he must speak of *Nævia*, or be mute,
He wrote to's Father ending with this line,
I am my lovely *Nævia* ever thine.

MARTIAL has succeeded in such Epigrams as are properly speaking without any turn, being after the manner of that simplicity which is so beautiful in some of *Catullus*'s. The following is one instance out of several, and I think perfect in its kind.

Non donec tibi cur meos libellos,
Oranti toties & exigenti
Mararis Theodore? magna caussa est;
Dones tu mihi ne tuos libellos. Lib. 5. Ep. 73.

Cease, *Theodorus*, to admire,
Tho' often you my works admire,
That I them still refuse to give:
'Tis that I may not yours receive.

BUT there are some of these which by the too frequent use of the *Antithesis*, lose that character of humour in which the beauty of these Epigrams seems chiefly to consist.

Insequeris, fugio; fugis, insequar, hoc mihi mens est,
Velle tuum nolo Dyndime, nolle volo. Lib. 5. Ep. 84.

This *Dyndimus*, is my design, to fly
What you pursue, what you decline to try;
What you commend my humor disapproves,
But what you hate my wanton fancy loves.

AN excellent Epigram of this kind is that celebrated distich of *Virgil*'s, wherein he has paid the finest compliment to *Augustus*, that ever Poet did to his Patron in two lines, and upon so inconsiderable a circumstance as that on which the thought is founded. This little performance was the dawn of a great Genius.

Nocte pluit tota redeunt spectacula mane:
Divisum Imperium cum Jove Cæsar habet.

All

All night it rains, with day the show return;
Thus *Jove* and *Cæsar* rule the world by turns.

It would be time lost to take notice of the many little witticisms and false turns to be met with among Martial's Epigrams. I shall observe in general, that all meer allusions to words, equivocations and obscene hints are vitious, however they met with a toleration and even countenance among the ancients. His own necessity and the corrupt taste of the public are the best apology that can be made for him; as he lived chiefly by his wits, he was often obliged to compose to please the taste of the ill judging many, and that this was the case of his Epigrams in general he has the modesty to acknowledge himself.

Sunt bona, sunt quædam mediocria, sunt mala plura,
  Quæ legis hic: Aliter non fit, avite, liber.

Reader to books of Epigrams be kind:
Few good, indifferent some, more bad you'll find.

I hope the aforesaid remarks and examples will assist the less knowing reader in forming a right judgment of Epigrams in general, as well as of Martial's in particular. Upon the whole, it appears that his Genius was extensive and lively; no subject came amiss to him, and he was certainly capable, had the good taste of the age encouraged him to it, to keep up the spirit of this kind of Poetry, without the poor helps of false wit and obscenity. As for his stile it is various, according to the subject; he does not often rise to the sublime, and his expression is neither so pure nor so correct as that of *Catullus*. It is evident from several of Martial's Epigrams, that his works were received with applause in most parts of the *Roman* Empire: This he is allowed to declare himself by an indulgence peculiarly allowed to Poets of praising themselves.

Hic est quem legis, ille quem requiris,
Toto notus in orbe Martialis,
Argutis Epigrammaton Libellis, &c.   Lib. 1. Ep. 1.

But

But for fear the reader should refuse to admit the Poet as a sufficient witness in his own cause, I will produce a letter of *Pliny*'s, addressed to *Cornelius Priscus*, whom I take to be the same *Priscus*, that the Poet has dedicated his 12th book to, and was his friend and patron, and a man of Consular dignity. It is the 21st of the 3d book.

" I hear MARTIAL is dead, and am very sorry for
" it. He was a man of an easy, agreeable, and likely
" wit, who knew very well how to temper the seve-
" rity of Satire with the pleasantry of Wit, without
" a mixture of ill nature. Upon his leaving *Rome*, I
" made him a present towards the expences of his
" journey. This I owed to the friendship I had for
" him, as well as to the verses he had addressed to me.
" It was customary with our ancestors handsomely to
" requite all those whose writings had contributed
" to the glory of particular places or persons. But
" this among other good customs is now laid aside:
" For since we have ceased doing what is praise-wor-
" thy, we are grown careless of praise. Perhaps you
" have a curiosity to know what these verses were,
" which I thought so deserving of acknowledgment.
" I would send you to his book, if I did not remem-
" ber some of them. If you like these, the rest you
" may find in the collection of his works. Speaking
" to his Muse, the Poet charges her to wait on me at
" my house on the *Esquiline* hill, and address her self
" to me in a very respectful manner.

Sed ne tempore non tuo disertam
Pulses ebria januam, videto;
Totos dat tetricæ dies Minervæ,
Dum centum studet auribus virorum,
Hoc quod sæcula, posterique possint
Arpinis quoque comparare chartis:
Seras tutior ibis ad lucernas.
Hæc hora est tua, quum furit Liæus
Quum regnat rosa, quum madent Capilli:
Tunc me vel rigidi legant Catones. Lib. 10. Ep. 19.

Whilst *Pliny* studies that persuasive art
Which moves the rigid wondring magistrate;
Ages to come, like ours, will all confess,
His Eloquence does *Tully*'s best express.
Forbear, rash Muse, to interrupt his time,
So well employ'd, with thy intruding Rhime:
Observe the hour, soon as the sun's decline
Invites to mirth, to supper and to wine:
That season's yours, when rosy garlands crown
Each brow, and *Cato*'s stern forget to frown.

" Are you not of my opinion, that he, who spoke of
" me in this manner, deserved to receive some small
" marks of my affection at his departure from *Rome*,
" and of my sorrow for his death? He gave me as
" much as was in his power to give: and indeed what
" greater gift can a man receive from his friend, than
" immortal glory? But perhaps MARTIAL's Poems
" may not be immortal; should I grant it, yet you
" must allow that he wrote them with this view."
Thus far *Pliny*.

IF that great man's generous nature made him sensible of his obligation to the Poet, and prompted him to be liberal to him in return, nothing but MARTIAL's real merit could induce a man of his sincerity to speak so advantageously of him after his death. The Verses above are part of a kind of Epistle Dedicatory to *Pliny*, to whom MARTIAL sent a volume of his Epigrams.

BUT before I close this writer's life, it may be expected that I should say something more particularly concerning the looser part of his works.

THOUGH it is true, as has been already observed in the life of *Catullus*, that some of the gravest and best men among the Ancients did sometimes indulge a loose vein of Poetry, and particularly about the time of their *Saturnalia*, a festival among them that fell out about the time of our Christmas; yet one is still at a loss to conceive how they could reconcile this Practice with their own excellent notions of moral virtue and public decency. MARTIAL alludes in one of his Epigrams to the following story.

At the time the Games in honour of *Flora* were celebrating on the theatre at *Rome*, upon *Cato*'s coming in there, the obscene dances ceased for a while; the very Actors being as it were ashamed to proceed in the presence of that virtuous man. The Historian observes, that *Cato* was surprized at the discontinuance of the entertainment, but being told the reason by a friend of his that sate by him, he went out of the theatre; the people shewed their applause by a loud clap, and then the diversion went on. Is it not almost unaccountable, if we did not consider the force of custom, that a great and wise nation should not be ashamed of a religious entertaiment and solemnity, for in this light the *Romans* considered these lewd Games called the *Floralia*, which they were ashamed to perform in the presence of *Cato!* MARTIAL only laughs at *Cato*'s absurdity in coming into the theatre on this occasion.

Nosses jocosæ dulce cum sacrum Floræ,
Festosque lusus & licentiam vulgi;
Cur in theatrum, Cato severe, venisti?
An ideo tantum veneras, ut exires? Lib. 1. Ep. 3.

Knowing what jocund sports and lewd delights
Attend the stage at *Flora*'s sacred rites,
The wanton vulgar's joy: why didst thou come,
Stern *Cato*, there? to go thence faster home?

Could one imagine that they who frequented these representations were the same people, among whom the nicer rules of decency were so rigorously observed, that a Senator was fined for saluting his wife before his son! But when we look into the history of their Gods, every thing there presents us with a scene of lewdness and infamy; and the greatest vices might from thence borrow their sanction and recommendation. Surely were their virtuous men to have reflected impartially on the inconsistency of their own
conduct

conduct and principles, and how their reason and religion were as it were in open contradiction, they would have abolished such infamous diversions: But this is too serious an enquiry for me to make; I leave their public lewdness and MARTIAL's obscenity, as things no less abominable than unaccountable, to the just detestation of all those who profess to have any regard, I need not say to religion, but to common decency and good breeding.

THE LIFE OF JUVENAL.

WITHOUT entering into a tedious examination of the different opinions of commentators about the birth and age of JUVENAL, I shall endeavour to settle both as near as I can, by such scattered hints as I have collected from his own writings. The account of his life, by some attributed to *Suetonius*, but more probably to *Probus* the Grammarian, is found in different manuscripts with considerable variations; and *Suidas* is not always to be depended upon in his. However, such points as both these writers of antiquity are agreed in, we may make use of, as having an appearance of truth, especially where we can get no better information.

JUVENAL was born, about the beginning of *Claudius*'s reign, at *Aquinum*, a town belonging to the territory of the antient *Volci* in *Campania*, and since celebrated for having given birth to *Thomas* sirnamed *Aquinas*, the famous father of scholastic philosophy. Our Poet's father was a rich freed man, who gave him a liberal education, and agreeably to the taste of the age, bred him up to the study of eloquence, in which he made great progress, first under *Fronto* the Grammarian, and afterwards, as it is generally conjectured, under *Quintilian*, who is thought to have seen some of his first satires, and to commend them, though he does not name the Poet; where he says,

74   The LIFE of Juvenal.

says, speaking of the *Roman* satire, *Sunt clare hodie quoque & qui olim nominabuntur* *.

JUVENAL contracted an early friendship with *Martial* the Poet, who addresses three several Epigrams to him, *Lib*. 7. *Ep*. 23. and 91. where he gives him the title of *the Eloquent*, and proves that JUVENAL follow'd the Bar, and the 18th *Ep*. of *Lib*. 12. The last being written by *Martial* after he was retired to *Bilboa*, which was under *Trajan*, and speaks of JUVENAL as a man yet in full vigour, seems to argue that JUVENAL had written but few satires yet; or why should he not have mentioned them in a private epistle to so intimate a friend, when *Domitian*, JUVENAL's enemy, was dead, and *Martial* himself had now no more measures to keep with any other great men that might think themselves attacked by the Satirist. This circumstance of *Martial's* silence convinces me, that JUVENAL never professed Poetry, and that his Satires were written very late; that he had distinguished himself many [...] by his eloquence at the Bar, and had improved [...] and interest at *Rome* before he thought [...] the very title of which in his Satires speaks [...] ing; *Subastum redolent decla*[...] of his Satires: And we are [...] first essay, which he made [...] small audience of [...] friends [...] by their applau[...] which reachi[...] favourite at th[...] whom the Sat[...] that *Misium* m[...] sent the offen[...] pretence of gi[...] that was to be[...] was not idle d[...] observations of [...] differences of [...]

—————

The LIFE of Juvenal

...ought up into a Satire, which is the 15th in the order they are commonly published. But let us see his passage for which the Satirist was thus disgraced: This perhaps with other favourite passages he has preserved, by inserting them into some of those Satires which we now have, and seem to have been all written since his return from *Ægypt*.

Carritur ad vocem jucundam, & carmen amicæ
Thebaidos, lætam fecit cum Statius urbem,
Promissistque diem: tanta dulcedine captos
Afficit ille animos, tantaque libidine vulgi
Auditur! sed cum fregit subsellia versu,
Esurit, intactam Paridi nisi vendit Agaven.
Ille & militiæ multis largitur honorem,
Semestri vatum digitos circumligat auro.
Quod non dant proceres, dabit histrio—Sat. 7. Ver 82.

All *Rome* is pleas'd when *Statius* will rehearse,
And longing crowds expect the promis'd verse.
His lofty numbers with so great a gust
They hear, and swallow with such eager lust:
But while the common suffrage crowns his cause,
And broke the benches with their loud applause,
His Muse had starv'd, had not a piece unread,
And by a Player bought, supply'd her bread.
...can dispose of honours and commands,
...pow'r of *Rome* is in an Actor's hands;
...ceful gown and military
...com Play'r outgives... ing Lord.
Dryden.

says, speaking of the *Roman* satire, *Sunt clare hodie quoque & qui olim nominabuntur* *.

JUVENAL contracted an early friendship with *Martial* the Poet, who addresses three several Epigrams to him, *Lib.* 7. *Ep.* 23. and 91. where he gives him the title of *the Eloquent*, and proves that JUVENAL follow'd the Bar, and the 18th *Ep.* of *Lib.* 12. The last being written by *Martial* after he was retired to *Bilboa*, which was under *Trajan*, and speaks of JUVENAL as a man yet in full vigour, seems to argue that JUVENAL had written but few satires yet; or why should he not have mentioned them in a private epistle to so intimate a friend, when *Domitian*, JUVENAL's enemy, was dead, and *Martial* himself had now no more measures to keep with any other great men that might think themselves attacked by the Satirist. This circumstance of *Martial's* silence convinces me, that JUVENAL never professed Poetry, and that his Satires were written very late; that he had distinguished himself many years by his eloquence at the Bar, and had improved his fortune and interest at *Rome* before he thought of Poetry, the very stile of which in his Satires speaks a long habit of declaiming; *Subactum redolent declamatorem*, say the Critics of his Satires: And we are told that he recited his first essay, which he made being above forty, to a small audience of his friends: but being encouraged by their applause, he hazarded a greater publication; which reaching the ears of *Paris*, *Domitian's* chief favourite at that time, though but a *Pantomime* Player, whom the Satirist had severely insulted in the Satire, that *Minion* made his complaint to the Emperor, who sent the offending Poet into banishment, under the pretence of giving him the Prefecture of a cohort that was to be quartered in that city of *Egypt*. He was not idle during his stay there, but made such observations of the ridiculous superstition and religious differences of that blind people, as he afterwards

---

* *Inst. Orat.* Lib. 10. Cap. 1.

wrought

wrought up into a Satire, which is the 15th in the order they are commonly published. But let us see this passage for which the Satirist was thus disgraced: This perhaps with other favourite passages he has preserved, by inserting them into some of those Satires which we now have, and seem to have been all written since his return from *Ægypt.*

> *Curritur ad vocem jucundam, & carmen amicæ*
> *Thebaidos, lætam fecit cum Statius urbem,*
> *Promisitque diem: tanta dulcedine captos*
> *Afficit ille animos, tantaque libidine vulgi*
> *Auditur! sed cum fregit subsellia versu,*
> *Esurit, intactam Paridi nisi vendit Agaven.*
> *Ille & militiæ multis largitur honorem,*
> *Semestri vatum digitos circumligat auro.*
> *Quod non dant proceres, dabit histrio*—Sat. 7. Ver. 81.

All *Rome* is pleas'd when *Statius* will rehearse,
And longing crowds expect the promis'd verse.
His lofty numbers with so great a gust
They hear, and swallow with such eager lust:
But while the common suffrage crown'd his cause,
And broke the benches with their loud applause,
His Muse had starv'd, had not a piece unread,
And by a Player bought, supply'd her bread.
He can dispose of honours and commands,
The pow'r of *Rome* is in an Actor's hands;
The peaceful gown and military sword:
The bounteous Play'r outgives the pinching Lord.
Dryden.

AFTER *Domitian*'s death, JUVENAL returned to *Rome,* sufficiently cautioned not only against attacking the characters of those in power under arbitrary princes, but against all personal reflections upon the great men living; and therefore he thus wisely concludes the debate he is supposed to have maintained with a friend of his on this head, in the first Satire, which seems the first that he wrote after his being recalled from banishment.

——Experiar quid concedatur in illos
Quorum Flaminia tegitur cinis atque Latina:
Since none the living villains dare implead,
Arraign them in the persons of the dead. *Dryden.*

Mr. *Dryden* has very imperfectly rendered his Author's meaning: JUVENAL, after having heard the danger which his friend assures him will attend his attacking the great men then living, closes the conference with this resolution, " Then I will try what " liberties I may be allowed with those whose ashes " lye under the *Flaminian* and *Latin* ways." All along those two famous roads the *Romans* of the first quality used to be buried. The *English* reader must excuse it, if in many other places the *Latin* is not truly rendered; let him read Lord *Roscommon*'s excellent Poem on translated verse, and then he will be able to judge how difficult it is, not to say often impossible, strictly to give the sense, and at the same time preserve the spirit of the original. I thought myself obliged to make this digression in justice to the memory of *Dryden*, who has given us excellent translations of *Juvenal, Virgil,* and other *Latin* Poets;—though he is in general much inferior to his originals, and often mistakes their meaning, or renders it in a loose manner. Far be it from me to have the vanity to think I have not failed where that great genius could not help erring. As I have only translated some quotations out of such Poets as had never been translated by others, or at least not by any of our great masters, I might, though no Poet, be able in a few rhimes to give the sense of my author more exactly than they who translated a whole Poem. But to return to JUVENAL.

In his 4th Satire, where he exposes the infamous debaucheries and luxury of *Domitian*'s court, he speaks of him as dead some time before the writing of that Satire.

Atque utinam his potius nugis tota illa dedisset
Tempora sævitiæ, claras quibus abstulit urbi
Illustresque

Illuſtreſque animas impune, & vindice nullo:
Sed periit poſtquam cerdonibus eſſe timendus
Cœperat, hoc nocuit Lamiarum cæde madenti.
                              Sat. 4. Ver. 150.

The 13th Satire is addreſſed to his friend *Calvinus*, who he ſays was born under the Conſulſhip of *Fonteius Capito*:

——— *Qui jam poſt terga reliquit*
Sexaginta annos, Fonteio conſule natus.

(Which anſwers to the year of *Rome* 811, and the 6th of *Nero*'s reign); and was ſixty years old at the time of the Poet's writing this Satire, which therefore was the year of *Rome* 871, and anſwers to the beginning of the 3d year of *Adrian*'s reign. From all which I infer, that Juvenal was at this time above ſeventy: for ſince he is on all hands ſaid to be born under *Claudian*, we may fix it to the middle or 6th year of that Emperor's reign; and ſuppoſing, with all Authors that ſpeak of his death, that he attained to eighty, he died about the 11th year of *Adrian*'s reign.

As to his perſon, we are told that he was of a large ſtature, which made ſome think him to be of *Gallic* extraction. We meet with nothing relating to his moral character or way of life, but both from the manner of his puniſhment by *Domitian*, and the whole tenour of his writings, he ſeems to have been a friend to ſobriety and virtue.

As to what I have ſaid of his writing all the Satires now extant after his return from *Egypt*, ſome make this objection, That what is alledged from the laſt lines of the 1ſt Satire above quoted, is not a full proof of the matter: For it may be ſuppoſed, ſay they, that the Satiriſt made this declaration the better to cover his real deſign: for by this means he might hope with ſecurity and under feigned names to expoſe the vices of *Domitian*'s court in ſome Satires which he publiſhed in *Domitian*'s life time; and ſuch a Satire they will have the 7th to be, out of which I have produced the paſſage that is ſuppoſed to have been the occasion of his banishment. But I think it evident, that *Trajan* is the generous Prince that is said by JUVENAL to be the only encourager of learning; but that, according to the plan laid down in his 1st Satire, he brings instances of a discouragement from a late reign namely *Domitian*'s: and taking them in this light, we shall find all that is said in that Satire to be very properly introduced, and among the rest the famous one above-mentioned about *Paris*, who, though at first but an Actor when he became the Emperor's favourite, was the only patron the learned could find at that Prince's court. But I leave this dispute to the reader's discretion, who, upon examining the reasons on both sides, will readily see which opinion is the most probable.

As Satire seems to have arrived to its highest perfection in JUVENAL, it will not be foreign to the present purpose to premise some observations on its rise and progress, before we come to treat of JUVENAL's Satires in particular.

THE *Latin* word *Satira*, whence comes our *Satire*, has nothing in its original signification like that which the moderns have affixed to it. Learned men are now agreed, that *Satira* or *Satura* is an adjective depending on the substantive *Lanx* understood, which signify together, a basket filled with all sorts of Fruit. It was afterwards applied to signify other different things mixed together. Thus those laws were called *Suturæ leges*, which had several heads or titles, and a collection of various histories was called *Historia satura*; and when the Senators gave their votes promiscuously together, they were said *per saturam ferre sententias*; and when applied to Poetry, the word retained its signification, such Poems as were composed on miscellaneous subjects being by the old *Romans* called *Satires*.

As to that kind of Poetry properly so called, it was long before it came to any considerable Improvement, taking its rude beginning from the coarse wit and raillery of the people when assembled at their harvest feasts;

feasts: and something like was for a long time after kept up among the *Romans* at the time of their celebrating the *Saturnalia*. These rustic jests were in time improved into their *Fescennine* verses; and now there began to be something like Poetry produced on these occasions. They took their name from a town in *Tuscany*, whose natives first introduced them among the *Romans*. They were in the nature of dialogues, intermixed with songs and dances.

Fescennina per hunc inventa licentia morem,
Versibus alternis opprobria rustica fudit.

Hence those loose dialogues at solemn feasts;
Yet still they were but mirth and country jests.
Creech.

Not long after these Dialogues the first use of Satire came in, which was borrowed from the *Greek* satirical plays, and were a low kind of Tragi-comedy, but had yet arrive to no exactness. From the medley of subjects which generally composed these dramatic pieces, they were called *Satiræ*; but the lewdness of the *Fescennine* verses was excluded. They were the first theatrical representations at *Rome*, and continued in vogue till *Livius Andronicus* set himself, after the manner of the *Greeks*, to write regular plays. This new improvement of his made the Satires fall into contempt and disuse for a long time; *Nævius* and others pursuing the same method with *Livius* in imitating and translating the *Greek* plays; and *Ennius* did the same, but he having a genius to all kinds of Poetry, and an inclination to the old satiric pieces, imagined, that if the same spirit and variety were preserved in Poems not calculated for the stage, it would meet with the public approbation: Accordingly he published some Poems of this sort, and called them Satires, allowing himself the liberty of all kinds of measure, as appears from the fragments. *Horace* found some things in them worthy of imitation, as *Virgil* did in his Poem on the second *Punic* war. *Pacuvius* who flourished a little after *Ennius*,

followed

followed his method in writing Satires as well as Plays. *Lucilius* who succeeded *Pacuvius*, applied himself entirely to this kind of Poetry, which he very much improved, by confining himself to the Hexameter verse, and imitating entirely the *Greek* Iambic writers and the old *Greek* comic Poets in the sharpness of his invectives and censures. But in *Horace*'s opinion his numbers were rough, his stile incorrect, and corrupted by an affectation of mixing *Greek* with *Latin*. But *Quintilian* is of opinion that *Horace* has censured him too severely, and sets him as much above those severe censures, as he thinks him beneath that applause some admirers of the old Poets still gave him in his time.

Horace succeeded and corrected all his faults, and gave Satire all the perfection that was consistent with his own design, which was to be agreeable rather than bitter, to be familiar, insinuating and instructive, and therefore affected a style that should be plain, witty and elegant. *Persius*, agreeably to the dignity of the *Stoic* philosophy, which he professed, chose to instruct and reform, rather than please, and wrote in a higher stile: But his severity is too great, and his character is so serious, that wit misbecomes him, where-ever he seems to aim at it. JUVENAL has undoubtedly improved on both: He is elegant and witty with *Horace*, grave and sublime with *Persius*, and to both their characters has added the pomp of his own eloquence, which makes him the most entertaining, as well as the clearest writer of the three. But in this he differs from *Horace*, that as he used a low, comic stile, JUVENAL raises his to the height of tragedy, as he says himself; which no Satirist before him had yet attempted.

Fingimus hæc altum Satira sumente Cothurnum,
Scilicet & finem aggressi, legemque priorum
Grande Sophocleo carmen bacchamur hiatu
Montibus ignotum Rutulis cæloque Latino.

BUT this the Poet does not say out of vanity, but
led

led to it from the nature of his subject; so elsewhere he undervalues his Poetry, where he would insinuate that the wickedness of the times would provoke a man to write Satires, even though he had no genius for Poetry.

Si natura negat, facit indignatio versum
Qualemcunque potest; quales ego vel Cluvienus.

It has very justly been observed, that there never was a greater fall in stile, than from the Odes of *Horace* to his Satires; and though he did it with design, the indolence of his temper might be one motive to his doing so. The same indolence made him decline celebrating the praises of *Augustus* in some considerable Poem, notwithstanding the many instances that Prince made him to undertake such a work. But this negligence of his should by no means be misunderstood as a rule for the stile of Satire: And we find the best modern Poets among the *Italians*, the *French* and Us, have chosen to imitate JUVENAL in this particular rather than *Horace*: for surely the magnificence of stile and the beauty of numbers will adorn the thoughts, and lively turns and bold figures will add weight and energy to the expressions. As to the purity of diction's being on *Horace*'s side, that was the fault of the times, not of JUVENAL, who seems to have been an accomplished Orator before he applied himself to Poetry. This was *Ovid*'s excellency likewise, and yet he was never thought the worse Poet for it; so that they who pretend to find the declamatory stile in his writings shew their prejudice more than their understanding. *Lucan*'s stile has more of this vehemence in it, yet I think he is very far from having a prosaic stile as well as JUVENAL. 'Tis a coldness of fancy destitute of spirit and genius that makes a Poet loyter into Prose.

It may be convenient in this place to obviate an objection commonly made to the licentious boldness of JUVENAL's expressions, which is of two kinds; the one, of exposing men's persons and names, as we well as their vices; the other, of running into subjects not decent to be mentioned, and calling some things too plainly by their common names.

In answer to the first, it may be said, that those he has exposed, by naming them, were either dead for the most part, or persons so lost to all honour and virtue, that it was a piece of justice to lay open their characters; if possible, thereby to deter the rest of the world from imitating their abominable vices: not but that he has often suppressed their real names, and been content to make them known by describing them, which he took care to do by such distinguishing marks, that you could not but know who was pointed at.

As to the other point, if he be found guilty of it, he is not to be vindicated nor excused for so doing: But before it is given against him we are to consider first, whether the licentiousness of the times was not such, as might make it necessary to censure the most enormous vices; and secondly, whether he has been altogether as broad in his expressions as is commonly imagined.

With regard to the first, it is evident, no age of the world more openly gloried in the most infamous debauchery than that he lived in the former part of his life: And if the end of Satire is a reformation of manners, it were an idle attempt to think to effect it, by Innuendo's and a few general hints. Such men were to be stung home and cut to the quick to make their callous minds the least sensible of the vileness of their manners. But when all the monstrous circumstances of the lewd scene were strongly painted and exposed to public view in the blackest colours, then guilt must surely fly in their faces for what they had committed, and their consciences must awake from that lethargy in which they had been laid; as he says it happened to the great men at *Rome*, whom *Lucilius* had exposed some ages before.

Ense velut stricto quoties Lucilius ardens

Infremuit,

*Infremuit, rubet auditer, cui frigida mens est
Criminibus, tacita sudant præcordia culpa.* Sat. 1.

But when *Lucilius* brandishes his pen,
And flashes in the face of guilty men,
A cold sweat stands in drops on ev'ry part.
Dryden.

As to his expressions, it does not appear that he has not avoided the more gross expressions, though the general practice of the antients was too licentious in this particular.: But I might justify the Satirist much better, by urging the authority of some of the Fathers, who thought themselves obliged in direct terms many times to expose the obscene ceremonies and lewd mythology of the Heathens: as in a lethargy the strongest and most offensive smells are sometimes applied to provoke the patient to sneeze. And what other way was sufficient to discountenance the enormities that were become almost the common practice, by the detestable example and encouragement of *Nero*'s and *Domitian*'s court. *Lucilius* had practised this method before successfully in much better times; and the liberty of the old *Greek* Comedy had been found useful to the public at *Athens*, or it would not have continued 'till the thirty tyrants set up by the *Lacedemonians* thought fit to restrain it, that their oppressions might not be made public and exposed on the theatre. That *Lucilius* imitated this liberty of the *Greek* Poets, we are assured by *Horace*.

*Eupolis, atque Cratinus, Aristophanesque Poetæ,
Atque alii quorum Comœdia prisca virorum est.
Si quis erat dignus describi quod malus, aut fur,
Quod mæchus foret, aut sicarius, aut alioqui
Famosus, multa cum libertate notabant,
Hinc omnis pendet Lucilius, hosce secutus.*
Lib. 1. Sat. 4. Ver. 1.

Cratin and *Eupolis* that lash'd the age,
Those old Comedian Furies of the Stage,
If they were to describe a vile, unjust,
And cheating knave, or scourge a lawless lust,

Or other crimes; regardless of his fame
They show'd the man, and boldly told his name.
- This is *Lucilius'* way, he follows those.   *Creech.*

AFTER all that has been alledged, this licentious stile is not justifiable, even in the best light we can place it, and is what no polite writer, to say no more, will attempt to imitate.

BUT let us now look into some passages of JUVENAL's Satires, which will naturally help us to discover his principles and genius: for a man of his impetuous spirit seems hardly capable of disguising his real sentiments. In this view he will appear a true generous spirited *Roman*, a friend to liberty and virtue. How finely does he enforce the necessity, as well as shew the advantage of moderation, with respect to the desire of riches! yet in the midst of the severest precepts he discovers a rational regard for the weakness of human nature, which cannot content it self with the meer necessaries of life.

> ——————— *Mensura tamen quæ*
> *Sufficiat census, si quis me consulit, edam:*
> *In quantum sitis atque fames & frigora poscunt,*
> *Quantum, Epicure, tibi parvis suffecit in hortis,*
> *Quantum Socratici ceperunt ante Penates.*
> *Nunquam aliud natura, aliud sapientia dicit:*
> *Acribus exemplis videor te claudere: misce*
> *Ergo aliquid nostris de moribus; effice summam*
> *Bis septem ordinibus quam lex dignatur Othonis.*
> *Hæc quoque si rugam trahit, extenditque labellum,*
> *Sume duos equites; fac tertia quadringenta.*
> *Si nondum implevi gremium, si panditur ultra*
> *Nec Cræsi fortuna unquam, nec Persica regna*
> *Sufficient animo, nec divitiæ Narcissi.*
> Sat. 14. Ver. 317.

Upon mentioning *Narcissus* that wicked and overgrown favourite of the Emperor *Claudius*, he cannot forbear adding two lines to shew the weakness of the Prince, and to what monstrous degree the favourite abused it.

Indulsit

Indulsit Cæsar cui Claudius omnia, cujus
Paruit imperiis uxorem occidere jussus.

If any ask me what would satisfy,
To make life easy, I would thus reply:
As much as keeps out hunger, thirst, and cold,
Or what contented *Socrates* of old;
As much as made wise *Epicurus* blest,
Who in small gardens spacious realms possest.
This is what Nature's wants may well suffice,
He that wou'd more, is covetous, not wise,
But since among mankind so few there are,
Who will conform to Philosophic fare;
Thus much I will indulge thee for thy ease,
And mingle something of our times to please:
Therefore enjoy a plentiful estate,
As much as will a Knight of *Rome* create,
By *Roscian* law: and if that will not do,
Double, and take as much as will make two;
Nay, three, to satisfy thy last desire:
But if to more than this thou dost aspire,
Believe me, all the riches of the East,
The wealth of *Cræsus* cannot make thee blest.
The treasure *Claudius* to *Narcissus* gave
Would make thee, *Claudius* like, an arrant slave,
Who to obey his mighty Minion's will
Did his lov'd Empress *Messalina* kill.   *Dryden.*

Such unexpected strokes of Satire as this on *Claudius* and *Narcissus* are frequent in this Poet, and always happily introduced. I know none of them of a more agreeable turn than the following, where he seems only to use that common figure among Poets, when they would make the reader conceive how impossible it is for them to describe some extraordinary circumstance, as it deserves. *Boileau* in his *Lutrin*, *Garth* in his *Dispensary*, and Mr. *Pope* in his *Dunciad*, have very successfully imitated this as well as many other of Juvenal's beauties.

——*Circumsilet agmine facto*
Morborum omne genus, quorum si nomina quæras,
                                        Promptius

Promptius expediam; quot amaverit Hippia mæchos;
Quot Themison ægros autumno occiderit uno;
Quot Basilus socios; quot circumscripserit Hirrus
Pupillos, &c. ——————   Sat. 10. Ver. 218.

In fine, he wears no limb about him sound,
With sores and sicknesses beleaguer'd round:
Ask me their names, I sooner could relate
How many drudges on salt *Hippia* wait;
What crowds of patients the Town-Doctor kills;
Or how last Fall he rais'd the weekly Bills:
What provinces by *Basilus* were spoil'd;
What hords of heirs by guardians are beguil'd.
                                                Dryden.

THE uncommon severity and impartiality of his Satire is well worth our notice in JUVENAL. So where he has occasion to censure the profane abuse of the most solemn oaths among the *Romans*, who had formerly paid so religious a regard to them, he at the same time exposes some of the absurd and ridiculous forms of swearing then in use among them. The translator was forced to omit them, as not being able to render them without such circumlocutions as would have been both dull and tedious.

——————*Aspice quanta*
Voce negat, quæ sit ficti constantia vultus!
Per Solis radios, Tarpeïaque fulmina jurat,
Et Martis frameam, & Cyrrhæi spicula vatis.
Per calamos venatrices pharetramque Puellæ,
Perque tuum, pater Ægei Neptune, Tridentem;
Addit & Herculeos arcus, hastamque Minervæ:
Quicquid habent telorum armamentaria Cœli.
                                    Sat. 13. Ver. 76.

Observe the wretch who has his faith forsook,
How clear his voice, and how assur'd his look
Like Innocence, and as serenely bold
As Truth; how loudly he forswears his gold!
By *Neptune*'s Trident, by the Bolt of *Jove*,
And all the magazine of wrath above! *Dryden.*

IN the same Satire, whereas according to the heathen opinion *Jupiter* was wont to express his indignation at the wickedness of men, by a loud voice, as *Homer* tells us; JUVENAL very boldly ridicules this notion, and the folly of worshipping so many useless and senseless images of the Gods. At *Rome* it is to be observed that their number was almost infinite; for the *Romans* very politically adopted the Gods of all the conquered nations for their own.

———————————*Audis*
*Jupiter hæc, nec labra moves? cum mittere vocem
Debueris, vel marmoreus, vel æneus; aut cur
In carbone tuo charta pia thura soluta
Ponimus, & sectum vituli jecur, albaque porci
Omenta? ut vides, nullum discrimen habendum est,
Effigies inter vestras statuamque Bathylli.*
Sat. 13. Ver. 113.

Jove dost thou hear, and is thy thunder tame?
Wert thou all brass, thy brazen arm should rage
And fix the wretch a sign to future age;
Else why should mortals to thy feast repair,
Spend useless incense, and more useless pray'r?
Bathillus' statue at this rate may prove
Thy equal rival; or a greater *Jove*. *Dryden.*

A little before in the same Satire, the Poet, speaking of the innocence of the golden age, gives a ludicrous account of the many Deities, with whose worship the world had not yet been troubled, and concludes his description with this severe reflection on their numbers in his time.

———————*Nec turba Deorum
Talis ut est hodie, contentaque sidera paucis
Numinibus, miserum urgebant Atlanta minore
Pondere*——— Sat. 13. Ver. 46.

E'er Gods grew numerous, and the heav'nly crowd
Press'd wretched *Atlas* with a lighter load.
Dryden.

And the Poet has elsewhere no less truly than severely

verely exposed the infamous character of the greatest of those Deities.

> *Quis tamen affirmat nihil actum in montibus, aut in Speluncis? adeo senuerunt Jupiter & Mars?*
>
> Sat. 6. Ver. 58.

> And yet some lustful God might there make bold;
> Are *Jove* and *Mars* grown impotent and old?
>
> *Dryden.*

SHALL I call it art, or a happy genius, that though he generally rails, and is full of the sharpest invectives, yet JUVENAL is as witty and perhaps more diverting than *Horace*, who studied to be so? It is certain he seldom fails to provoke your laughter, even whilst he is raising your indignation; which talent of his is evidently seen in the three last quotations.

BUT when he is wholly bent upon moving his reader, his colours are so strong, and his figures so bold, that you are soon wrought up to the same pitch of indignation with him. Such as the following passage.

> *Cum tener uxorem ducat spado, Mævia Tuscum*
> *Figat aprum, & nuda teneat venabula mamma;*
> *Patricios omnes opibus cum provocet unus,*
> *Quò tondente gravis juveni mihi barba cadebat:*
> *Cum pars Niliacæ plebis, cum verna Canopi*
> *Crispinus, Tyrias humero revocante lacernas,*
> *Ventilet æstivum digitis sudantibus aurum,*
> *Nec sufferre queat majoris pondera gemmæ;*
> *Difficile est Satiram non scribere: nam quis iniquæ*
> *Tam patiens urbis, tam ferreus, ut teneat se?*
>
> Sat. 1. Ver. 22.

When sapless Eunuchs mount the marriage bed,
When mannish *Mævia*, that two-handed whore,
Astride on horse-back hunts the *Tuscan* boar,
When all our lords are by his wealth outvy'd,
Whose rasor on my callow beard was try'd;
When I behold the spawn of conquer'd *Nile*
Crispinus, both in birth and manners vile,

Pacing

Pacing in pomp with cloak of *Tyrian* die
Chang'd oft a day for needless luxury,
And finding oft occasion to be fan'd,
Ambitious to produce his Lady-hand:
Charg'd with light summer rings his fingers sweat,
Unable to support a Gem of weight.
Such fulsome objects meeting ev'ry where.
To view so lewd a town, and to refrain,
What hoops of Iron could my spleen contain!
Dryden.

THO' I am contending all this while for JUVENAL's superiority in Satire among the *Romans*, yet I confess it seems easier for a man to give a loose to his just indignation, and stir up the passions by the bitterest strokes of Satire, than with *Horace* genteely to reprove and artfully blame the fault, without so much as alarming the offender; as it is easier to cut off than restore a corrupted limb. At the same time it seems to me, that the first way is most natural, and with the profligate and vicious most effectual, as the latter is more artful, and fittest to be practised in a civil society. In short, had *Horace* been a worse courtier, he would have been more severe, and JUVENAL might have been more moderate had he lived in better times. Men were not very virtuous in the reign of *Augustas*, nor was the sanctity of his or *Mecænas*'s manners so very remarkable: They had their vices and failings like other men, but what they acted in private they discountenanced in public, thereby avoiding that scandal, which was the reproach of *Nero*'s and *Domitians*'s government. Accordingly *Horace*'s Satires are fitter to form the discreet and well bred man than the good and virtuous. But JUVENAL's writings at least recommend the noblest virtues, and pursue vice through all its shapes and disguises. He betrays no partial indulgence to himself or his friends, but keeping strictly to the business of Satire, censures the whole compass of human actions that deviate from the rules of honour and virtue.

Quicquid

Quicquid agunt homines, votum, timor, ira, voluptas,
Gaudia, discursus, nostri ferrago libelli. Sat. 186.
What human kind desires, and what they shun,
Rage, passions, pleasures, impotence of will,
Shall this satirical collection fill. **Dryden.**

As what has been already quoted is sufficient to show his talent for Satire, we may proceed to give some instances of that sublime moral and greatness of sentiments, that adorn his writings. *Persius* is his rival in this, but wants his graceful manner of recommending virtue. His tenth Satire is inimitable for the excellency of its morality and sublime sentiments. In the beginning of it, having displayed the great vanity of our desires, in answer to such as might enquire of him what wishes men might innocently make, he thus expresses himself, in the conclusion of the Satire, like an Oracle. How magnificently as well as rationally does he speak of the Divine Goodness!

―――――*Si consilium vis,*
Permittes ipsis expendere numinibus, quid
Conveniat nobis, rebusque sit utile nostris.
Nam pro jucundis aptissima quæque dabunt Dii.
Carior est illis homo, quam sibi : nos animorum
Impulsu, & cæca magnaque cupidine ducti
Conjugium petimus, partumque uxoris ; at illis
Notum, qui pueri, qualisque futura sit uxor.
Ut tamen & poscas aliquid, voveasque sacellis
Exta, & candiduli divina tomacula Porci :
Orandum est, ut sit mens sana in corpore sano :
Fortem posce animum, & mortis terrore carentem ;
Qui spatium vitæ extremum inter munera ponat
Naturæ, qui ferre queat quoscunque labores ;
Nesciat irasci, cupiat nihil, & potiores
Hærculis ærumnas credat sævosque labores,
Et Venere, & cænis, & plumis Sardinapali.
Monstro quod ipse tibi possis dare : semita certe
Tranquillæ per virtutem patet unica vitæ.
Nullum numen abest, si sit prudentia, sed te

Nos facimus Fortuna Deam, cœloque locamus.
                              Sat. 10. Ver. 346.

Receive my counsel, and securely move;
Intrust thy fortune to the pow'rs above;
Leave them to manage for thee, and to grant
What their unerring wisdom sees thee want:
In goodness as in greatness they excell;
Ah! that we lov'd our selves but half so well!
We blindly, by our headstrong passions led,
Are hot for action, and desire to wed;
Then wish for heirs; but to the Gods alone
Our future offspring and our wives are known.
Yet not to rob the Priests of pious gain,
That altars be not wholly built in vain;
Forgive the Gods the rest, and stand confin'd
To health of body and content of mind:
A soul, that can securely death defy,
And count it nature's privilege to die;
Serene and manly, harden'd to sustain
The load of life, and exercis'd in pain:
Guiltless of hate, and proof against desire;
That all thing weighs, and nothing can admire:
That dares prefer the toils of *Hercules*
To dalliance, banquets, and ignoble ease.
The path to peace is virtue: what I show,
Thy self may freely on thy self bestow. DRYDEN.

 In the preceding part of this Satire he had shewn the uncertainty of human greatness, and the cruel inconstancy of the public hatred or favour in the fall of *Sejanus*, that overgrown favourite of *Tiberius*.

*Jam stridunt ignes, jam follibus atque caminis
Ardet adoratum populo caput, & crepat ingens
Sejanus, deinde ex facie toto orbe secunda
Fiunt urceoli, pelves, sartago, Patellæ.
Pone domi laurus, duc in Capitolia magnum
Cretatumque bovem: Sejanus ducitur unco
Spectandus; gaudent omnes: quæ labra! quis illi
Vultus erat? nunquam (si quid mihi credis) amavi
Hunc hominem: sed quo cecidit sub crimine? quisquam*
           Delator?

Delator? quibus indiciis! quo teste probavit?
Nil horum: verbosa & grandis epistola venit
A Capreis: bene habet, nil plus interrogo: sed quid
Turba Remi? sequitur fortunam, ut semper, & odit
Damnatos——   Sat. 10. Ver. 51.

Sejanus almost first of *Roman* Names,
The great *Sejanus* crackles in the flames.
Form'd in the forge, the pliant brass is laid
On anvils, and of head and limbs are made,
Pans, cans, and piss-pots, a whole kitchen trade.
Adorn your doors with lawrels, and a bull
Milk-white and large lead to the Capitol;
Sejanus with a rope is drag'd along,
The sport and laughter of the giddy throng.
Good Lord! they cry, what Æthiops lips he has!
How foul a snout, and what a hanging face!
By Heav'n, I never could endure his sight:
But say, how came his monstrous crimes to light?
What is the charge? and who the evidence,
The saviour of the Nation and the Prince?
Nothing of this: but our old *Cæsar* sent
A noisy letter to his parliament.
Nay, Sirs, if *Cæsar* wrote, I ask no more,
He's guilty, and the question's out of door.
How goes the mob, for that's a mighty thing?
When the King's trump, the mob are for the King;
They follow fortune; and the common cry
Is still against the rogue condemn'd to die.
                                      Dryden.

THE Poet proceeding to shew the insatiableness of human desires, instances in the vain ambition of *Hannibal* and *Alexander.*

Expende Hannibalem: quot libras in duce summo
Invenies? hic est, quem non capit Africa Mauro
Perfusa oceano, Niloque admota tepenti.
Rursus ad Æthiopas populos, altosque Elephantos,
Additur imperiis Hispania: Pyrenæum
Transilit; opposuit natura Alpemque, nivemque.
                                      Diduxit

The LIFE of Juvenal.

Diduxit scopulos, & montem rupit aceto.
Jam tenet Italiam; tamen ultra tendere pergit;
Actum, inquit, nihil est, nisi Pœno milite portas
Frangimus, & media vexillum pono Suburra.
O qualis facies, & quali digna tabella,
Cum Getula ducem portaret bellua luscum!
Exitus ergo quis est? O Gloria! vincitur idem
Nempe & in exilium præceps fugit, atque ibi magnus
Mirandusque cliens sedet ad Tentoria regis,
Donec Bythino libeat vigilare Tyranno.
Finem animæ, quæ res humanas miscuit olim,
Non gladii, non saxa dabunt, non tela; sed ille
Cannarum vindex, & tanti sanguinis auctor
Annulus: I demens, & sævas curre per Alpes
Ut pueris placeas & declamatio fias.
Unus Pellæo juveni non sufficit orbis.
Æstuat infelix angusto limite mundi,
Ut Gyaræ clausus scopulis, parvoque Seripho.
Cum tamen a figulis munitam intraverit urbem
Sarcophago contentus erit. Mors sola fatetur
Quantula sint hominum cupuscula——
Sat. 10. Ver. 147.

Great *Hannibal* within the balance lay,
And tell how many pounds his ashes weigh;
Whom *Afric* was not able to contain,
Whose length runs level to th' *Atlantic* main,
And wearies fruitful *Nilus* to convey
The sun-beat waters by so long a way;
Which *Æthiopia*'s double clime divides,
And elephants in other mountains hides.
Spain first he won, the *Pyreneans* past,
And steepy *Alps*, the mounds that nature cast;
And with corroding juices, as he went,
A passage thro' the living rocks he rent.
Then like a torrent rolling from on high
He pours his headlong rage on *Italy*,
In three victorious battles over-run;
Yet still uneasy, cries, There's nothing done,
'Till level with the ground their gates are laid,
And *Punic* flags on *Roman* tow'rs display'd.

Ask what a face belong'd to his high fame,
His picture scarcely would deserve a frame:
A sign-post dawber would disdain to paint
The one-ey'd Heroe on his Elephant.
Now what's his end, O charming glory, say,
What rare first act to crown his huffing play?
In one deciding battle overcome,
He flies, is banish'd from his native home:
Begs refuge in a foreign court, and there
Attends his mean petition to prefer,
Repuls'd by surly grooms, who wait before
The sleeping tyrant's interdicted door.
What wondrous sort of death has heav'n design'd
Distinguish'd from the rest of human-kind
For so untam'd, so turbulent a mind!
Nor swords at hand, nor hissing darts afar;
But poison drawn thro' a ring's hollow plate
Must finish him; a sucking infant's fate.
Go, climb the *Alps*, ambitious fool,
To please the boys, and be a theme at school.
   One world suffic'd not *Alexander*'s mind,
Coop'd up he seem'd in earth and seas confin'd;
And struggling, stretch'd his restless limbs about
The narrow Globe, to find a passage out.
Yet enter'd in the Brick-built town, he try'd
The tomb, and found the streight dimensions wide.
Death only this mysterious truth unfolds,
The mighty soul how small a body holds. *Dryden.*

WERE I resolved to take notice of all the fine passages to be found in JUVENAL, I must transcribe the greater part of his Satires. I will conclude all with that fine observation in the 13th Satire on the danger of vicious courses, because of the very great difficulty of leaving off any ill habits once contracted.

Mobilis & varia est ferme natura malorum,
Cum scelus admittunt superest constantia, quid fas,
Atque nefas, tandem incipiunt sentire, peractis
Criminibus; tamen ad mores natura recurrit
Damnatos, fixa, & mutari nescia; nam quis
                                                   Peccandi

THE LIFE OF AUSONIUS.

DECIMUS MAGNUS AUSONIUS PÆONIUS was a native of *Bourdeaux* in *France*. His Father *Julius Ausonius* was a man no less celebrated for his skill in Physic than for his eloquence in the *Greek* language, to which he had so closely applied himself, that he had almost neglected the *Latin*. He lived thirty six years with his wife *Æmilia Æonia*, by whom he had two sons and a daughter. Our author was the second son. His elder brother got considerable preferment, having at different times been Governour of *Gaul*, *Africa*, and *Italy*. And even his father, whose great moderation rather inclined him to a retired life, was some years before his death made Governour of *Illyricum*. He lived to eighty eight years of age, still healthy and vigorous to such a degree, as to be able to discharge all the duties of publick life. This *Julius Ausonius*, together with *Cæcilius Argicius Arboreus* our Athor's wife's father, had been forced to fly their country, being Christians, upon a cruel persecution and proscription under the tyrant *Tetricus*.

Arboreus is said to have been a man of profound learning, and particularly well versed in Astrology, which had engaged him to cast his Grandson's nativity, but never discovered it to his family. Some

years

years after his death, his daughter accidentally found it among his papers; in which he expressed himself as having been much comforted for the loss of his only son, who died at thirty years of age, by the glorious prospect which the happy conjunction of young AUSONIUS's Planets gave him, of his future advancement and dignity.

These and many other particulars relating to some of his family are to be met with in AUSONIUS's book of *Parentalia*, a Poem, so called because he therein has gratefully commemorated the virtues and characters of his Relations; and it is in one of these Poems, in honour of his Grandfather *Arboreus*, that the Poet mentions his having cast his Nativity.

Tu cæli numeros & conscia sidera fati
  Callebas, studium dissimulanter agens.
Non ignota tibi nostræ quoque formula Vitæ,
  Signatis quam tu condideras tabulis.
Prodita non unquam; sed matris cura retexit
  Sedula, quam timidi cura tegebat avi.
Dicebas sed te solatia longa fovere,
  Quod mea præcipuus fata maneret honos:
Et modo consilijs animarum mixte piorum
  Fata tui certe nota nepotis habes.
Sentis quod quæstor, quod te Præfectus, & idem
  Consul, honorifico munere commemoro.

How Stars in various aspects when combin'd
Explain the destiny of human kind,
Was thine to know, and knowing, to conceal
That Science, others would with pride reveal.
My Horoscope became thy care, which show'd
What Fates hereafter for thy Grandson flow'd.
A Mother's fondness found, and durst unfold
That secret scheme, for thee ev'n now untold.
The tablets, when unseal'd, betray'd thy mind,
Thy joy, for what my happy fates design'd;
O thou, who, 'midst the blessed choir above,
Thy art confirm'd, may'st now secure approve;
Receive these honours which thy Grandson pays,
Who Quæstor, Præfect, Consul, sings thy praise.

We have no sufficient authority exactly to fix the time of Ausonius's birth, but without much fear of error we may place it about the year of Christ 320. At thirty years of age he was called to teach Grammar in the public schools at *Bourdeaux*, he behaved so much to the general satisfaction in this employ, that a few years after he was elected Professor of Rhetoric there; and after some years spent in promoting these studies, during which he had acquired an universal reputation, he was sent for by the Emperor *Valentinian* the Elder to instruct his Son *Gratian*, whom he associated with him in the Empire in the year 369. Ausonius wanted neither merit nor address to ingratiate himself with the Emperor and his royal pupils; for he soon afterwards had the care of *Gratian*'s brother *Valentinian* II. that he not only obtained the highest dignities for himself, but had credit enough to prefer all his Relations to the most honourable posts in the Empire. *Valentinian* made him *Quæstor*, and *Gratian* had not been long associated, before he made him Præfect, first of *Italy*, and then of *Gaul* in the year 376, and in 381, he was created Consul. Ausonius lived to a happy old age. Some years before his death he had retired to *Bourdeaux* his native City, probably not till after his Patron the Emperor *Gratian* was murdered by the tyrant *Maximus*, which happened in the year 385.

Juvenal in one of his Satires thought he had advanced a very improbable instance of the most extravagant power of Fortune, when he said,

Si Fortuna volet, fies de Rhetore Consul.

Sat. 7. Ver. 197.

I leave it to the reader to judge, whether it would have provoked his laughter or indignation most to see his prediction verified in the person of Ausonius, who from an obscure Professor of Rhetoric, was raised to the Consulship.

Before we enter upon the character of our Author as a Poet, it may be proper to obviate what *Vossius* and some other Critics have advanced, to prove that

Ausonius

Ausonius was a Heathen. He pretends to shew this from the Epistles of *Paulinus* to him: But I think the following lines, wherein that holy man justifies his retirement to his friend AUSONIUS, is a good argument of the contrary.

Non reor hoc sancto sic displicuisse parenti,
Mentis ut errorem credat sic vivere Christo.

Where *Paulinus*'s words mean that he cannot think his holy friend (whom as having been his instructor he calls *Parens* Father) could think an error of understanding to live so to Christ, that is, condemn his retirement from the world, which he did, the better to discharge, as he thought, the great duties of Christianity. *Paulinus* urges this motive of his retirement, as what he thinks will justify him to AUSONIUS, who condemned his quitting a public life. But AUSONIUS still persisted in his opinion, which surely he might do without derogating to his respect for Christianity, which being then supported and encouraged by Christian Princes, could not furnish *Paulinus* with those reasons for his retreat, which had induced the primitive Christians to embrace the anchoret and monastic life, namely to shelter themselves from persecution and avoid the fiery trial. But the following lines of the same *Paulinus* positively assert, that such was the tenderness of their mutual affection, speaking of himself and of *Ausonius*, that they were as unanimous in all other things as they were in their zeal for Christianity.

Inque tuo tantus nobis consensus amore est
Quantus & in Christo connexa mentis colendo.

I might use other arguments to prove his being a Christian, as from his education under two Aunts remarkable for their Christian Piety, and from his educating *Gratian* a Christian Prince of great piety.

In his old age and at the request of the Emperor *Theodosius* the Great, AUSONIUS published a compleat collection of his Poems. That Prince's letter to him on this occasion is yet extant, which I am willing to produce,

produce, as an instance of the great credit in which AUSONIUS lived, and of the politeness of that Emperor's taste, though he had been bred a soldier from his infancy. The language indeed is not very elegant, which could not be expected in a *Spanish* Officer in the fourth century. But we shall see by his letter, that by a long and faithful service he had learned to govern well and command with a good grace.

THEODOSIUS AUGUSTUS, AUSONIO Parenti, *Salutem.*

AMOR meus qui in te est, & admiratio ingenii atque eruditionis tuæ, quæ multo maxima sunt, fecit, parens jucundissime, ut morem aliis principibus solitum sequestrarem; familiaremque sermonem autographum ad te transmitterem, postulans, pro jure, non quidem regio, sed illius privatæ inter nos charitatis, ne fraudari me scriptorum tuorum lectione patiaris, quæ olim mihi cognita, & jam per tempus oblita, rursum desidero; non solum ut quæ sunt nota recolantur, sed ut ea, quæ fama celebri adjecta memorantur, accipiam. Quæ tu de promptuario Scriniorum, qui me amas, libens impertiare, secutus exempla auctorum optimorum, quibus par esse meruisti, qui Octaviano Augusto *rerum potienti, certatim opera sua tradebant, nullo fine in ejus honorem multa condentes. Qui, illi haud sciam, an æqualiter, ac ego te, admiratus sit, certe non amplius diligebat.* Vale Parens.

IT was common among the Ancients to compliment the person who had educated them with the title of *Father,* and the Master took the same pleasure in calling his Pupil *Son:* But I cannot see why *Theodosius* called *Ausonius* Father, unless in respect to his Collegue the Emperor *Gratian;* for *Theodosius* was General under *Valentinian* before *Ausonius* was made Præceptor to *Gratian.*

" *The Emperor* Theodosius, *to* Ausonius *his Father greeting.*

" THE love I bear you, added to the great opi-
" nion I have of your fine genius and learn-

'ing, have induced me, dear father, to lay aside the
'state of a Sovereign, and to send you a familiar let-
'ter of my own hand writing, to desire you as a
'pledge of our private friendship, not out of any
'regard to my dignity, to deprive me no longer of
'the pleasure of reading your works. I have for-
'merly seen some of them, and am now desirous
'to renew my knowledge of them; but you must
'likewise send me those other pieces of yours, which,
'as being of a later date, are only known to me by
'their reputation in the world. I flatter my self
'with your ready compliance with this request, in
'imitation of those excellent writers, to whom
'you are deservedly compared, who sought all occa-
'sions of presenting their compositions to *Augustus
'Octavianus*, and were continually publishing some-
'thing new in his praise. I cannot say whether he
'valued them as much as I do you; I am sure he
'could not have more affection for them, than I
'have for you. Farewell.

It is easy to discover the true occasion of this letter
o Ausonius; It was not meerly to have his works,
which having been published already, he might have
had elsewhere; nor was it a bare compliment: It was
o engage Ausonius, who perhaps was esteemed the
est Poet of the age, to write something that would
convey his name with honour to posterity; and that
Prince used the most powerful argument to prevail
with him, by comparing him with the excellent Poets
of the *Augustan* age, who strove to surpass each other
in celebrating the praises of *Augustus*. Whether *Theodosius* succceded is uncertain, since we find nothing
among Ausonius's works immediately addressed to
him, but the Poem prefixed by way of Dedication to
the rest of the Poems, which he sent as that Prince
had desired; in which there might seem an obscure
promise of the Poet to gratify some time or other the
Emperor's desire.

Agricolam si flava Ceres dare semina terræ,
Gradivus jubeat si capere arma ducem.

F 3 *Solvere*

Solvere de portu classem Neptunus inermem;
 Fidere tam fas est, quam dubitare nefas.
Insanum quamvis hyemet mare, crudaque tellus
 Seminibus, bello nec sit aperta manus.
Nil dubites autore bono: mortalia quærunt
 Consilium; certus jussa capesse Dei.
Scribere me Augustus jubet, & mea carmina poscit.
 Pene rogans, blando vis latet imperio.
Non habeo id genii: Cæsar sed jussit, habebo:
 Cur me posse negem, posse quod ille putat?
Invalidas vires ipse excitat, & juvat, idem
 Qui jubet: obsequium sufficit esse meum.
Non tutum. renuisse Deo: laudata pudoris
 Sæpe mora est, quoties contra parem dubitat.
Quin etiam non jussa parant erumpere dudum
 Carmina: quis nolit Cæsaris esse liber?
Ne ferat indignum Vatem, centumque lituras
 Mutandus semper deteriore nota.
Tu modo te jussisse, pater Romane, memento;
 Inque tuis culpis da tibi tu veniam.

Though AUSONIUS was very old when he sent this with his other Poems, he shews he had not lost his fire, which if it never blazed out with great brightness, had this advantage, that it maintained its vigour to the last; which was the reason I chose to quote it at length. Here follows the translation.

Tho' bad the season, yet at *Ceres'* will
Th' obedient hind prepares his lands to till.
If *Neptune* bid the Master spread his sails,
He soon obeys, nor dreads the wintry gales.
At *Mars'* command the Chief leads on to fight,
Nor doubts success; for Gods must order right.
So when great *Cæsar* asks the Muse to sing,
Such condescension must obedience bring.
In vain she pleads her want of tuneful art,
The Prince requesting shall enough impart:
His good opinion may the Muse suffice,
What he has once approv'd who dare despise?
When equals ask, 'tis modest to deny;
But duty bids us with the Gods comply.

My

My works, which had before essay'd to fly
The Poet's alt'ring hand and Critic eye,
Now grown ambitious liberty proclaim
Aloud, and in excuse plead *Cæsar*'s name.
Then mighty Prince with just indulgence view
Such faults as partly owe their birth to you.

Though Ausonius's works do not appear so excellent to us, it is certain *Theodosius* was not the only one who admired his Poetry, and compared him to the writers of the *Augustan* Age. Not to mention his favourite scholar *Paulinus*, some of whose letters, very much in his praise, are extant among his works, *Symmachus*, a person of the highest quality and learning, as well as integrity and worth, has said the same of Ausonius, on occasion of his excellent Poem on the *Moselle*, a famous River that runs through part of *France* and *Flanders*. His letter to Ausonius about this Poem is commonly placed before it as a kind of Preface, and is as follows.

SYMMACHUS, AUSONIO suo, *Salutem.*

Petis a me literas longiores: est hoc in nostri amoris indicium; sed ego qui sum pauperrimi mei ingenij conscius, Laconicæ malo studere brevitati, quam multijugis paginis infantiæ meæ maciem publicare. Nec mirum si eloquij nostri vena tenuata est, quam dudum neque ullius poematis tui, neque pedestrium voluminum lectione juvisti. Unde igitur sermonis mei largam poscis usuram cui nihil literati fœnoris credidisti? Volitat Mosella tuus per manus sinusque multorum divinis a te versibus consecratus. Sed tantum nostra ora prælabitur. Cur memet istius libelli quæso exortem esse voluisti? aut Ἀμουσότερος *tibi videbar, qui judicare non possem, aut certe malignus, qui laudare nescirem. Itaque vel ingenio meo plurimum, vel moribus derogasti: Et tamen contra interdictum tuum vix ad illius operis arcana perveni. Velim tacere quid sentiam: Velim justo de te Silentio vindicari; sed admiratio scriptorum sensum frangit injuriæ. Novi ego istum fluvium, cum æter-*

norum principum jampridem signa comitarer, parem multis, imparem maximis. Hunc tu mihi improviso clarorum versuum dignitate Ægyptio Nilo majorem, frigidiorem Scythico Tanai, clarioremque hoc nostro populari Tiberi reddidisti. Nequaquam tibi crederem de Mosellæ ortu ac meatu magna narranti, ni scirem quod nec in poemate mentiaris. Unde illa amnicorum piscium examina reperisti? quam nominibus varia tam coloribus, ut magnitudine distantia, sic sapore, quæ tu pigmentis istius carminis supra naturæ dona fucasti. Atqui in tuis mensis sæpe versatus, cum pleraque alia quæ tunc in pretio erant, esui objecta mirarer, nunquam hoc genus piscium deprehendi. Quando tibi bi pisces in libro nati sunt: Qui in ferculis non fuerint. Jocari me putas, atque agere nugas. Ita dominus probabilem me præstet, ut ego tuum carmen libris Maronis adjungo: Sed jam mei oblitus doloris, inhæreo laudibus tuis: Ne hoc quoque ad gloriam tuam trahas, quod te miramur offensi? Spargas licet volumina tua, & me semper excipias: fruimur tamen tuo opere, sed aliorum benignitate. Vale.

SYMMACHUS to AUSONIUS.

"YOU desire me to write you a long Letter: This
"is a proof of your affection to me. But I,
"who am sensible of my own weakness, chuse the
"*Laconic* brevity, rather than expose the poverty of
"my stile in many pages. And it is no wonder if the
"vein of my eloquence is impoverished, which has
"been kept so long without the supply either of your
"verse or prose. With what conscience then can
"you expect much from me, when you have sent me
"nothing? Your Poem on the *Moselle*, which you
"have immortalized in your excellent verses, is read
"and admired by many persons, but I was left out
"of the number. And why was I to be excluded?
"either you questioned my ability to discern its beauties,
"or mistrusted my inclination to commend it:
"either you wrong my understanding or character
"very much. Yet notwithstanding your opposition,

"I

"I have at last had your Poem in my hands. I could
"have a mind to hide my opinion of it, and by a just
"silence be in some sort revenged of you: But my
"admiration of it has made me forget your injurious
"behaviour. I knew the *Moselle*, when I served in
"the wars under our Emperors, that it was equal to
"many rivers, but much inferior to the greater of
"them. But you, by the charm of your excellent
"Poetry, have at once made it bigger than the *Nile*,
"cooler than the *Scythian Tanais*, and more renown-
"ed than our own *Tiber*. However, I shall hardly
"credit the strange things you say of its spring and
"course, but that I know you scorn to advance an
"untruth even in Poetry. But where could you find
"those swarms of river fish, of such various colours,
"so different in size and taste, which almost exceed
"nature in your beautiful description of them? As
"often as I dined at your table, and admired the rari-
"ties that covered it, I never met with any of these
"fish. How come you to give them place in your
"book, which could not obtain it at your table? But
"now you will imagine I begin to rally and trifle; but
"I solemnly protest that I put this Poem of yours in the
"same rank with the works of *Virgil*. Before I was
"aware, I have launched out into your praise; but
"do not let this add to your vanity that I admire you,
"though you have disobliged me. You may distribute
"your books as often as you please, and except me;
"I shall nevertheless enjoy your works, though I am
"beholden to others for the favour. Farewell."

As this Poem is the most considerable of any that AUSONIUS wrote, I thought this character which *Symmachus* has given of it, might not be disagreeable to the curious reader, who cannot suppose that this great man's friendship for AUSONIUS had so blinded his judgment as to make him launch out so far in praise of a bad Poem.

The rest of AUSONIUS's works do not come up to this; many of them were composed occasionally for the instruction of youth. Some were almost extempore

F 5 trials

trials of wit; of this sort was the *Cento Nuptialis* a Poem, which perhaps had been less taken notice of, if on another subject, or if the Parody had been made from the works of a more licentious Poet than *Virgil*. As I am far from approving the Poet's conduct in this respect, so I think it is but common justice to let him speak for himself, and quote part of his letter which he sent with the *Cento* to his religious friend and favourite scholar *Paulinus*.

AUSONIUS PAULINO, S.

Perlege hoc etiam, si operæ est, frivolum, & nullius pretij opusculum, quod nec labor excudit; nec cura limavit, sine ingenij acumine, & moræ maturitate. Centonem vocant, qui primi hac concinnatione luserunt. Solæ memoriæ negotium sparsa colligere, & integrare lacerata, quod ridere magis quam laudare possis. Piget Virgiliani carminis dignitatem tam joculari dehonestasse materia. Sed quid facerem? jussum erat; quodque est potentissimum imperandi genus, rogabat, qui jubere poterat: scilicet Imperator Valentinianus, vir meo judicio eruditus, qui nuptias quondam ejusmodi ludo descripserat, aptis equidem versibus & compositione festivâ. Experiri deinde volens quantum nostra contentione præcelleret, simile nos de eodem concinnare præcepit. Quam scrupulosum hoc mihi fuerit, intellige. Neque anteferri volebam neque posthaberi; cum aliorum quoque judicio detegenda esset adulatio inepta si cederem, insolentia, si, ut æmulus eminerem. Suscepi igitur similis recusanti, feliciterque & obnoxius gratiam tenui: nec victor offendi. Hoc die uno, & addita lucubratione properatum. Tanta mihi candoris tui & amoris fiducia est, ut severitati tuæ nec ridenda subtraherem, &c.

AUSONIUS to PAULINUS.

"I Send you a little trifling composition of mine,
" which was neither the product of labour, nor
" corrected with care, nor the offspring of genius,
" nor could be ripened by time to perfection. They
" who first amused themselves this way, called it a
" Cento

"*Cento.* The chief burden lies on the memory to
"collect what had been dispersed, and to put the se-
"veral scraps together, and when that is done, it de-
"serves to be laughed at, rather than commended. I
"was sorry too that I dishonoured the dignity of *Vir-
"gil*'s Poetry by so ludicrous a subject. But how
"could I avoid it? I was ordered to do it; and what
"laid the greater obligation upon me, he who had a
"right to command, requested it of me as a favour.
"In a word, it was the Emperor *Valentinian* himself,
"a Prince of excellent learning in my opinion; who,
"having formerly diverted himself by writing a Nup-
"tial Poem of this sort, that wanted neither art nor
"proper numbers to recommend it, had a mind to see
"how I should succeed in the like attempt. How
"nice a point this was, I leave you to judge. I did
"not desire to obtain the preference, and at the same
"time was unwilling to fall short of him; for had I
"yielded the prize, the world would have discovered
"the sordid adulation, as they would have condemned
"my insolence, had I strove as a rival to outshine him.
"I undertook it therefore with some shew of reluc-
"tancy, and had the happiness to succeed without dis-
"pleasing, and to conquer without offence. It was
"hurried up in one day and night's time. But I have
"some confidence in your candour and affection, that
"I was unwilling to conceal even so ridiculous a trifle
"from you, *&c.*

Perhaps some of the most rigid Censors of Ausonius would have been unwilling to forfeit their Prince's
favour, by an affectation of severity in a case when the
Prince himself had first set the example he required
them to follow.

As for the apology he makes for the obscene part of
it afterwards, I think it is trifling, and the conclusion
worst of all; for tho' we know the business of the wedding night, decency forbids us to describe it as he did;
and if he found himself under a necessity of writing in
this manner in obedience to *Valentinian*, nothing but
his vanity could put him upon publishing it afterwards.

What he has elsewhere said in a jocular manner to his son *Gregorius* (when he sent him the poem on *Cupid*'s being fastened to a cross by several female lovers, and which he has very happily executed) that we are apt to be fond even of our blemishes and scars, and not content to do amiss ourselves, would have others, approve our so doing; *Nævos nostros & cicatrices amamus, nec soli nostro vitio peccasse contenti, affectamus ut amentur*: This I think is really Ausonius's character in some measure, finding himself prefer'd from an inconsiderable Professor to the highest dignities in the Empire; his vanity made him still find a merit in trifles unbecoming his character.

Thus in his old age he continued to delight in the instructing of youth, for whom he would often compose little Poems suited to their capacity. The instruction of youth is certainly a commendable employment, but a *Roman* Consul, a Prefect of *Italy* and *Gaul*, one would imagine, might have found other business. I am ready to allow, that many of these compositions were for the use of his own grandchildren, or those of some of his friends of the first rank; and that they were the amusements of his leisure hours. Yet this will hardly excuse the carelessness with which he wrote them, who pretended to the glory of being a good Poet, or that self-liking which he betrays wherever he has occasion to mention himself in them.

But we may see by some other Poems, that his genius led him to trifle with his muse and to applaud himself for it afterwards. Such is that on the number Three and the letter that he sent with it to his friend *Symmachus* about it. "But (says the Poet) it was "composed over a glass of wine between dinner and "supper." But what need then of an apology about it, or, in answer to some ill-natured Critic's objection, that he had left out several things concerning the number Three, to shew the contrary by a long enumeration of many other particulars relating to that mysterious number, which his mentioning there does not

prove

prove that he thought of them all, as he would infinuate he had, when he composed the Poem.

I would not be understood, by what I have said, to undervalue AUSONIUS, who had a fine genius, a ready wit, and a great compass of learning and eloquence; but having attained the highest honours by his learning, he neglected to cultivate his genius, or to apply it to some noble subject. And as I think most of his lesser compositions are so many abuses of a fine genius, and only so much time and labour lost, it may be proper to caution such of my readers as may happen to be poetically given, from imitating so bad an example. His success in some of these trifles, carries his condemnation with it. Of this nature is his foolish, though ingenious Poem, where each verse begins and ends with a monosyllable. This was a fine present to his friend *Paulinus*, and is accompanied with a letter setting forth the difficulties he had to encounter in this arduous task; and being in a quibbling humour, he cannot help shewing it even in the letter, which he concludes saying, "In short it is what you will " rather pity than admire, or desire to imitate: for " if you should, you would find more torture of the " brain and injury to the eloquence of your stile, than " satisfaction from success in the attempt." *Ad summam, non est quod mereris, sed paucis literis additis, est cujus miserearis, neque æmulari velis: Et si quoque descenderis, majorem molestiam capias ingenii & facundiæ detrimento, quam oblectationem imitationis affectu.*

I cannot say much in praise of his Epigrams, many of them are translations from the *Greek*, and have but little spirit or elegance: Those of his own composition have a better turn, but are scarce worth imitation. His Poem on the Rose has some beauties in the Elegiac way, and had been put in the number of *Virgil*'s Juvenile Poems, till proved to be AUSONIUS's by *Alexander* from the authority of an antient Manuscript of this Poet's work.

His love Poems on *Bissula*, a fair *Suabian* captive, whom

whom he loved and afterwards set at liberty, are imperfect; and when he sent them entire to *Paulus*, a person of great Quality, he says, he never wrote them for public view; but could not refuse them to his pressing instances.

> *Ut voluisti, Paule, cunctos Bissulæ versus habes,*
> *Lusimus quos in Suevæ gratiam Virgunculæ:*
> *Otium magis foventes quam studentes gloriæ.*
> *Tu molestus flagitator lege molesta carmina;*
> *Tibi quod intristi exedendum est. Sic vetus verbum*
>   *jubet,*
> *Compedes, quas ipse fecit, ipsus ut gestus Faber.*

He wrote the Poem of the seven Wise Men, when he was Consul, and inscribed it to his friend *Drepanus* the Proconsul. He has also composed a collection of short Poems in praise of the principal Cities of the *Roman* Empire. He likewise abridged the lives of the twelve *Cæsars* from *Suetonius*, and of the other Emperors down to *Heliogabalus*; and wrote the Contents of *Homer*'s *Iliads* and *Odyssee*, partly in verse and partly prose.

Whilst he had the care of *Gratian*'s instruction, he translated some fables from the *Greek*, but they are lost.

There are several of his Epistles extant, both in verse and prose; those to *Paulinus* seem most laboured, and abound with the most tender expressions of friendship to that excellent man, whose answers are as ingenious as they are devout.

His *Idyllia* are miscellaneous Poems; two of them are on religious subjects, and savour of the true spirit of Christianity. There is nothing worth dwelling upon in particular of any of these Poems. He also wrote a Poem of the *Roman Fasti* or *Annals*, from the building of *Rome* down to his own time, including the space of 1118 years: but this work, which might have been very useful, is lost through the injuries of time. It was addressed to *Proculus*, who according to Ausonius was Consul four years after him; but I do

THE LIFE OF CLAUDIAN.

CLAUDIUS CLAUDIANUS was born at *Alexandria* in *Ægypt*, as we may suppose about the year of CHRIST 365, in the beginning of the reign of *Valentinian* I. I can find nothing particular relating to his birth, parentage, or education. But as *Alexandria* was then in its highest glory for learning, and contended even with *Athens* for the education of youth, we find from CLAUDIAN's own account, that he had made such progress in *Greek* learning, as to have indulged his poetic vein in that language, before he attempted any thing in the *Latin* Tongue. The same passage informs us when he came first to *Rome*, which was in the year of CHRIST 395. when *Olybrius* and *Probinus* were Consuls. We have a panegyrical Poem of his extant on that occasion, which perhaps was the first *Latin* Poem that he published; and he seems to insinuate as much in an Epistle addressed to *Probinus*, one of the Consuls, who probably was his first Patron. But hear him give this account himself.

Romanos bibimus primum te Consule fontes,
  Et Latiæ cessit Graia Thalia Togæ:
Incipiensque tuis a fascibus omina cepi,
  Fataque debebo posteriora tibi.

Of *Greece* and her *Parnassus* weary grown,
I sought the beauties of the *Roman* Gown;
Whose sacred springs I first presum'd to taste,
The Consul's *fasces* when *Probinus* grac'd:
His honours prov'd auspicious to my Muse,
His praise she for her latest theme will chuse.

From this passage it appears that *Claudian* could not be less than thirty when he first came to *Rome*, or at least when he wrote his first Latin Poem; and I have fixt the date of his birth accordingly. After having compleated his studies, he must have spent some time in acquainting himself with the excellencies of the *Latin*, as he had before of the *Greek*.

Petrarch and *Politian* claimed him as a *Florentine*, or at least that his father was a native of *Florence*: but *Giraldus* and the best Critics follow the authority of *Suidas*, and of *Sidonius Apollinaris*, and say, he was a native of *Alexandria* in *Ægypt*. There are some little Poems on sacred subjects, which through mistake have been ascribed by some Critics to Claudian; and so have made him be thought a Christian. But St. *Austin*, who was partly cotemporary with him, expressly says he was a Heathen; where he quotes some of his Verses in praise of *Theodosius, De Civit. Dei.* Lib. 1. Cap. 26. and *Paulus Orosius* the Historian, who likewise flourished about the same time, says the same, Lib. 7. Cap. 35. *Giraldus* therefore justly blames the ignorant credulity of *Barthius* and those Critics in this matter, and attributes these sacred Poems to *Claudius Mamercus* a Christian Poet of *Vienne* in *Gaul*, and cotemporary with *Sidonius Apollinaris*, who commends him at large, *Lib.* 4. *Epist.* 3. But to return to Claudian.

Not long after his coming to *Rome*, he insinuated himself into *Stilico*'s favour, who being a person of great abilities both for peace and war, though a *Goth* by birth, was now become so considerable under *Honorius*, that he may be said for many years to have governed the Western Empire.

He had so distinguished himself by his valour and conduct

conduct under the Emperor *Theodosius*, that he gave him the command of his forces, and as a farther reward of his services, bestowed his favourite Niece and adopted daughter the Princess *Serena* upon him, and on his death-bed recommended the Empire and his Sons to his care and protection.

Honorius was so fond of him that he made a fresh alliance with him, by marrying *Maria*, *Stilico*'s daughter by *Serena*. Being thus doubly related to the Emperor, and having destroyed all his rivals in the Eastern, where his influence reached, as well as the Western Empire, he wanted but the title of Emperor: and this his ambition put him upon endeavours of obtaining, at least for his Son *Eucherius*; but the plot being timely discovered, they were both put to death.

CLAUDIAN was probably involved in his Patron's disgrace, and severely persecuted both in his family, in his person and fortunes by *Hadrian*, an *Ægyptian* by birth, who was Captain of the Guards to *Honorius*, and seems to have succeeded *Stilico*, whose plot he had discovered, in the administration. There is an expostulatory Epistle of the Poet's extant addressed to this *Hadrian*, which seems to be one of the last of his writing, so that we may conclude that he obtained no redress from the Minister, whom he had likewise personally affronted in the following Epigram.

Mallius indulget somno noctesque diesque,
  Insomnis Pharius sacra profana rapit.
Omnibus hoc, Italæ gentes, exposcite votis,
  Mallius ut vigilet, dormiat ut Pharius.

Whilst *Mallius* day and night in sleep is lost,
By restless *Hadrian*'s plunders th' Empire's tost:
This change, O *Romans*, of great *Jove* implore,
That *Mallius* may sleep less, and *Hadrian* more.

THE poor Poet thus heavily vents his sorrows, complaining of *Hadrian*'s cruelty and unforgiving temper, in his Epistle to that Minister.

Audiat hoc commune solum, longeque carinis
Nota Pharos, flentemque attollens gurgite vultum,
Nostra gemat Nilus numerosis funera ripis.

                                              Which

Which passage, by the bye, proves the Poet to have been a native of *Alexandria* in *Egypt*.

> Let *Pharos* thro' the world by trade renown'd,
> Thy Rage, let *Ægypt* hear, our mother ground;
> To mourn my sorrows, from each oozy bed
> Let weeping *Nilus* raise his drooping head.

It appears from another part of this Epistle, that CLAUDIAN had formerly been in *Hadrian*'s favour, which he had now suddenly changed into hatred; and he insinuates as if the Minister had too easily lent an ear to false reports and malignant rumours; he begs pardon for his fault, which his grief for *Stilico*'s fall perhaps, or his vanity, or a heat of passion had betrayed him into, and beseeches him not to continue his violent indignation and anger against him: His house was now made desolate, and he driven to want and necessity, being robbed of all his friends, of some by death and tortures, of others by banishment. But all this and many more particulars of his complaint, leave us still to guess the true cause of his disgrace, nor can we tell how long he survived it.

But setting aside his abusing *Hadrian*, he seems to have behaved as a true Court Poet: nor was the Prince ungrateful to his Panegyrist; he obtained, as he mentions in his Epistle above-mentioned, several honours both civil and military, though they are not there particularly specified. But *Arcadius* and *Honorius* in conjunction with the *Roman* Senate, granted him an honour that seems to exceed any that ever had been bestowed on any Poet before; which *Gyraldus* says was discovered by a marble that was found in his time, and carefully examined by *Pomponius Lætus* and other able Antiquaries, who judged it to be the pedestal of CLAUDIAN's Statue in brass, which the Emperors at the Senate's request had ordered to be erected for him in *Trajan's Forum*, with the following most honourable inscription on the marble above mentioned.

CL. CLAUDIANO, V. C.

CL. CLAUDIANO, *V. C. Tribuno & Notario, inter cæteras ingentes artes, præglorosissimo Poetarum, licet ad memoriam sempiternam carmina ab eodem scripta sufficiant, attamen testimonij gratia, ob judicij sui fidem DD. NN. Arcadius & Honorius felicissimi & doctissimi Imperatores, Senatu petente, statuam in foro divi Trajani erigi, collocarique jusserunt.*

Under the Inscription was put the following *Greek* Epigram.

Ἐν ἑνὶ Βιργιλίοιο νόον ᾗ μῦσαν Ὁμήρου
Κλαυδιανὸν Ῥώμη ᾗ Βασιλεῖς ἔθεσαν.

"To CLAUDIUS CLAUDIANUS, Tribune
"and Notary, and among other great qualifications,
"the most excellent of Poets, though his own
"works are sufficient to make his name immortal,
"yet as a testimony of their approbation, the most
"learned and most happy Emperors *Arcadius* and
"*Honorius*, at the request of the Senate, have or-
"dered this statue to be erected and placed in the
"Forum of *Trajan*."

The Epigram underneath was no less glorious to the Poet.

" *Rome* and the *Cæsars* here his Statue raise,
" Who *Virgil*'s genius join'd to *Homer*'s lays.

In the Preface to his Poem on the *Getic* war, CLAUDIAN attributes this honour as owing to his Poems on the Consulship of *Honorius*.

Post resides annos longo velut excita somno
 Romanis fruitur nostra Thalia choris.
Optatos renovant eadem mihi culmina cœtus,
 Personat & noto Pythia vate domus.
Consulis hic fasces cecini, Libyamque receptam,
 Hic mihi prostratis bella canenda Getis:
Sed prior effigiem tribuit successus aënam,
 Oraque Patricius nostra dicavit honos.
Adnuit hunc titulum princeps, poscente Senatu.

After

The LIFE of Claudian.

After some years repose the slothful Muse,
The *Roman* towers, once more, awaken'd views.
Th' inspiring powers to all my bosom throng,
The vanquish'd *Getæ* shall adorn my song.
Th' imperial *Consul* first I strove to sing,
And *Libyan* rebels in subjection bring;
The former Theme a brazen statue crown'd,
Patrician honours thus my numbers found:
The Senate's voice that title did request
With which the *Cæsars* have their Poet grac'd.

I suppose that this absence of the Poet from *Rome*, was when the Princess *Serena*, who had a great esteem for Claudian, recommended and married him to a Lady of great quality and fortune in *Libya*, as he acknowledges very gratefully in an Epistle which he addresses to *Serena* from thence, a little before the wedding-day.

Non ego, cum peterem, solenni more procorum,
  Promisi gregibus pascua plena meis:
Nec quod mille mihi lateant sub palmite colles,
  Fluctuet & glauca pinguis oliva coma:
Nec quod nostra Ceres numerosa falce laboret,
  Aurataeque ferant culmina celsa trabes.
Suffecit mandasse deam; tua littera nobis,
  Et pecus, & segetes, & domus ampla fuit.
Inflexit soceros, & majestate petendi
  Texit pauperiem nominis umbra tui.

No spreading olives bending with their fruit,
No vineyards on the Hills t'adorn my suit;
No flocks nor herds my plenteous pastures feed,
Nor fields of full-ear'd corn had I to plead:
No golden roof, nor lordly seat I own,
Nor birth, nor title boast; your name alone
These wants supplies; *Serena* best can find
The poor man's friends, and bid the rich be kind.
A Goddess recommends, and is obey'd;
Wealth, title, lands, your letter all convey'd.

These are all the circumstances of Claudian's life

life that I have been able to gather from his Works, which we will next consider; and begin with the character he bears as a Poet among the Critics.

They are, as usual, divided in their opinions of him: some think his stile too florid, and are offended with the flowing ease and harmoniousness of his numbers. But this is what Claudian seems to have aimed at as a beauty, and in which he has succeeded beyond all the *Latin* Poets. But as true harmony of numbers does not barely consist in tunable and pleasing sounds, but requires a due mixture of gravity and elevation as well as smoothness and fluency to compleat it, and all of them justly adapted to the character of the subject to be described, whereby the numbers become in some sort significant as well as the expression; therefore that equability and constant fluency of Claudian's numbers has been justly objected against, as wanting both variety and strength in many places to support the dignity of the expression.

There are others, who admiring the charming ease and fluency of his numbers, with the spirit and vivacity of his style, wish he had been happier or rather more judicious in the choice of his subjects. It may be alledged in his defence, that the subjects he has chosen, though inferior to the true Epic Poems, were not only such as were likely to make his fortune at court, but were capable of the finest embellishments, and such as would admit of all those beauties of fiction and figures, which make the soul of Poetry. Besides, the rape of *Proserpine* had most of those circumstances to recommend it, which the Critics require in the fable of an Epic Poem; and it was on this Poem that Claudian proposed to build his fame: And accordingly, in his Preface to that Poem, which is addressed to his friend *Florentinus*, a person of great learning and quality, he insinuates, that this Poem was a work of much labour and difficulty, and which he had not ventured upon till he had first tried the strength of his genius by lesser Compositions.

Inventa

Inventa secuit qui primus nave profundum,
  Et rudibus remis sollicitavit aquas.
Qui, dubijs ausus committere flatibus alnum,
  Quas natura negat, præbuit arte vias.
Tranquillis primum trepidus se credidit undis,
  Littora secura tramite summa legens.
Mox longos tentare sinus, & linquere terras,
  Et leni cœpit pandere vela Noto.
Ast ubi paulatim præceps audacia crevit,
  Cordaque languentem dedidicere metum;
Jam vagus exultat pelago, cœlumque secutus
  Ægeas hyemes Ioniasque domat.

The man who first presum'd to try the deep,
And with unskilful oars the billows sweep;
Who to the dubious winds unfurl'd the sail,
And dar'd by Art o'er Nature's bounds prevail;
With caution first the sea becalm'd essay'd,
And near the shore his bark securely play'd:
Embolden'd now, he tempts the winding bay,
Forsakes the land, and gently sails away
With a fair gale; at length more hardy grown,
Disdains all fear, and rides the main unknown;
By stars directed, ploughs the swelling tide,
Victorious o'er the stormy ocean's pride.

In complaisance to CLAUDIAN's good opinion of the Rape of *Proserpine*, we will examine it first. Whether he finished it, and so the injuries of time have robbed us of what is now wanting of it, or that the Poet left it imperfect, I do not pretend to determine; though I must confess, I think the last book of those now extant, much more incorrect than the former. But leaving this nice and knotty point to the disquisition of the Critics, let us consider the plan of this Poem. It does not seem very well laid for an Epic Poem, the Poet having begun too high, and thereby prolonged the duration of the action too much: The action of the Rape is finished entirely in those books we have, so that what followed, however consequent of it, could not more properly be said to belong to it,

than

than the *Æneis* does to the *Ilias*. However, the subject, as being a most celebrated story in the Heathen Mythology, could not but be entertaining to the reader at that time; and as the Powers of Heaven, Earth, and Hell are interested in the principal action, the Poet could not fail of a fine opportunity to display his happy talent for description. It is true that some would think, that a greater simplicity in the principal action, and more human actors if possible, would have been better, and especially the latter, as affording more natural characters. It must be granted, that the Marvellous, that favourite beauty among the ancient Epic Writers, appears most in such extraordinary characters as are employed in carrying on the action of this Poem; for I cannot help thinking, that the generality of Epic Writers among the Ancients lay under a mistake, when they imagined, that as often as they introduced a wonderful incident, they added a new beauty to their work; and I almost suspect that *Virgil* himself has been misled by this affectation of the Marvellous.

CLAUDIAN is accused of sometimes falling into common-place reflections and philosophical enquiries, which lead him from the purpose of his story, and that he affects to introduce too many circumstances in his description.

He is so fine a writer, taken altogether, that I think it just to shew his faults, lest the less judicious reader might sometimes be misled by the charms of his imagery to admire what is faulty in its place, however beautiful; if considered singly and without regard to that relation it bears in proportion as a part to the whole. *Ovid* was sometimes guilty of this magnificent but unseasonable luxuriancy of fancy, which like that in leaves in fruit-trees always bespeaks them distempered, and is generally attended with, or the consequence of a small blow, and little or bad fruit. We have a lively instance of this redundancy of imagination in the beginning of the 3d book: *Jupiter* is there described as calling a council of the Gods.

Jupiter

*Jupiter interea cinctam Thaumantida nimbis
Ire jubet, totoque Deos arcessere mundo.
Illa colorato Zephyros prælapsa volatu
Numina conclamat pelagi, Nymphasque morantes
Increpat, & fluvios humentibus evocat antris.
Ancipites trepidique ruunt, quæ causa quietos
Excierit, tanto quæ res agitanda tumultu.
Ut patuit stellata domus, considere jussi:
Nec confusus honos: cœlestibus ordine sedes
Prima datur: tractum proceres tenuere secundum
Æquorei, placidus Nereus, & lucida Phorci
Canities; Glaucum series extrema biformem
Accipit, & certo mansurum Protea vultu.
Nec non & senibus fluviis concessa sedendi
Gloria; plebeio stat cætera more juventus,
Mille amnes: liquidis incumbunt patribus udæ
Naiades, & taciti mirantur sidera Fauni.
Tum gravis ex alto Jupiter sic orsus Olympo.*

Mean time Imperial *Jove* sent *Iris* down
To call the Gods to council at his throne.
Wrapt in her flushing robes she swiftly flies
On gentle Zephyrs thro' the yielding skies:
She cites the Deities, beneath the sea
And watry Nymphs, and chides their long delay.
Then calls the Rivers from their oozy caves:
At once they start and rise above the Waves,
In open air, th' important cause to know
Of the loud summons, which they heard below.
The shining Palace opes, the Powers appear,
And all in just degrees are seated there.
First the Celestials sit; the second place
Falls to the honours of the Watry race,
Nereus and foaming *Phorcus: Glaucus* last
Of double form, th' inferior rank possess'd
With varying *Proteus* in one shape restrain'd:
The better Rivers then their session gain'd:
The youthful train stand humbly by their side,
A thousand streams, which roll a modest tide.

Each *Nais* leans upon her liquid fire,
The staring Fauns the radiant stars admire.
Jabez Hughes.

Virgil says more to the purpose of his subject in five lines, than CLAUDIAN has here in eighteen.

Panditur interea domus omnipotentis Olympi,
Consiliumque vocat divûm pater atque hominum rex
Sideream in sedem: terras unde arduus omnes,
Castraque Dardanidum aspectat, populosque Latinos;
Considunt tectis bipatentibus, incipit ipse.
Lib. 10. Ver. 1.

The gates of heav'n unfold; Jove summons all
The Gods to council, in the common hall.
Sublimely seated he surveys from far
The fields, the camp, the fortune of the war;
And all th'inferior world: from first to last
The sov'reign Senate in degrees are plac'd.
Then thus th'almighty Sire began.

A description of the same kind out of the *Metamorphoses* will shew that CLAUDIAN's genius very much resembled *Ovid's*.

Quæ pater ut summa vidit Saturnius arce,
Ingemit, & facto nondum vulgata recenti,
Fœda Lycaoniæ referens convivia mensæ
Ingentes animo & dignas Jove concipit iras;
Conciliumque vocat; tenuit mora nulla vocatos.
Est via sublimis, cœlo manifesta sereno,
Lactea nomen habet; candore notabilis ipso.
Hac iter est superis ad magni tecta Tonantis,
Regalemque domum: dextra levaque Deorum
Atria nobilium valvis celebrantur apertis.
Plebs habitat diversa locis: a fronte potentes
Cælicolæ, clarique suos posuere Penates.
Hic locus est, quem, si verbis audacia detur,
Haud timeam magni dixisse Palatia cæli.
Ergo ubi marmoreo superi sedere recessu
Celsior ipse loco, sceptroque innixus eburno
Terrificam capitis concussit terque quaterque
Cæsariem,

Cæsariem, cum qua terram, mare, sidera movit,
Talibus inde modis ora indignantia solvit.
                                Lib. 1. Fab. 2.

Which when the King of Gods beheld from high,
(Withal revolving in his memory
What he him self had found on earth of late
Lycaon's guilt, and his inhuman treat)
He sigh'd; nor longer with his pity strove;
But kindled to a wrath becoming Jove:
Then call'd a General Council of the Gods;
Who summon'd issue from their blest abodes,
And fill th'assembly with a shining train.
A way there is in heav'n's expanded plain,
Which when the skies are clear, is seen below,
And mortals by the name of Milky know.
The ground-work is of stars; thro' which the road
Lies open to the Thunderer's abode:
The Gods of greater Nations dwell around,
And, on the right and left the palace bound;
The commons where they can: the nobler sort
With winding doors wide open front the Court.
This place as far as earth with heav'n may vie,
I dare to call the Louvre of the sky.
When all were plac'd, in seats distinctly known
And he, their Father, had assum'd the throne,
Upon his iv'ry sceptre first he leant,
Then shook his head, that shook the firmament:
Air, earth, and seas, obey'd th' almighty nod,
And with a gen'ral fear confess'd the God;
At length with indignation thus he broke
His awful silence and the pow'rs bespoke.

In some places I think CLAUDIAN rather more luxuriant than *Ovid:* Such is his description of the general joy of all the infernal world at the Nuptials of *Pluto* and *Proserpine*, where he seems fond of inserting every circumstance that occurred to his imagination. But as it is beautiful in itself, though disproportionate, I shall transcribe it, and add this remark,

That

That I would not be understood to condemn that for bad Poetry, which is luxuriant, nor to admire every thing that is correct. A dull Poet at the expence of much labour and pains may possibly come near to *Virgil*'s correctness, but without his spirit and thought; as an extravagant and sickly fancy may sometimes resemble the rich abundance of *Ovid* and CLAUDIAN; but examination will shew the former to be an indigested heap of Bombast, and the latter a magnificent profusion of fine images. But as true beauty consists in a just symmetry of parts concurring to make up the whole in a graceful and uniform proportion, it is the business of judgment to correct the too vigorous sallies of the imagination; as on the other hand, the fancy is requisite to adorn and enliven the regularity and exactness of the judgment.

―――――――――――*Alterius sic*
Altera poscit opem res & conspirat amicè.

But to return to CLAUDIAN's description:

Pallida lætatur legio, gentesque sepultæ
Luxuriant, epulisque vacant genialibus umbræ:
Grata coronati peragunt convivia manes:
Rumpunt insoliti tenebrosa silentia cantus.
Sedantur gemitus Erebi, se sponte relaxat
Squalor, & æternam patitur rarescere noctem:
Urna nec incertos versat Minoia sortes;
Verbera nulla sonant, nulloque trementia luctu
Impia dilatis respirant Tartara pœnis.
Non rota suspensum præceps Ixiona torquet:
Non aqua Tantaleis subducitur invida labris:
Solvitur Ixion, invenit Tantalus undas,
Et Tityos tandem spatiosos erigit artus:
Squalentisque novem detexit jugera campi,
Tantus erat; laterisque piger sulcator opaci,
Invitus trahitur lasso de pectore vultur,
Abreptasque dolet jam non sibi crescere fibras.
Oblitæ scelerum, formidatique furoris
Eumenides, Cratera parant, & vina feroci

Crine

Crine bibunt ; flexisque minis jam lene canentes,
Extendunt socios ad pocula plena cerastas.
Tunc & pestiferi pacatum flumen Averni
Innocuæ transistis aves, flatumque repressit
Amsanctus : tacuit fixo torrente vorago,
Tunc Acheronteos mutato gurgite fontes
Lacte novo tumuisse ferunt, ederisque virentem
Cocyton dulci perhibent undasse Lyæo :
Stamina nec rupit Lachesis, nec turbida sacris
Obstrepitant lamenta choris ; mors nulla vagatur
In terris, nullæque regum planxere parentes.
Navita non moritur fluctu, non cuspide miles,
Oppida funerei pollent immunia leti,
Impexamque senex velavit arundine frontem
Portitor, & vacuos egit cum carmine remos.

Lib. 2. Ver. 326.

All Hell rejoices, and the buried dead
In wanton gambols jocundly are led :
And the crown'd *Manes* with the shades combine
In genial feasts, and in the revels join.
Now chearful songs th' eternal silence break ;
No groans of ghosts the hollow caverns shake :
The gloom disperses, and continued night
Admits an infant gloom and purges into light.
Minos forgets his fatal urn to roll
No lashes sound, no punish'd spirits howl ;
Ixion turns not on his hurrying wheel,
Nor swift from *Tantalus* the waters steal :
Ixion rests, and *Tantalus* relieves
His thirst impatient, and the draught receives.
And *Tytius* stretch'd, erected on the ground
His spacious limbs, which spread nine acres round.
Such was the giant's bulk ; nor in his side
Her sharpen'd beak the rav'nous vulture try'd :
Held from the morsel she beholds in vain
The wounded liver heal and grow again.
The guilty croud th' avenging furies spare ;
They loose their fetters, and the scourge forbear ;
And for the draught the brimming bowl prepare:

Singing they quaff, and to the goblet hold
Their silent snakes, which curl'd in many a fold.
With holy fire a joyful torch they light,
And flames unwonted flash'd upon the Night.
Then first the birds across the poison'd lake
Securely could their airy journey take.
Amsanctus his impetuous roar suppreſt,
And his unruffled eddies smoothly rest;
And troubled *Acheron*, they say, with pride
Chang'd his sad wave and pour'd a milky tide:
Cocytus too, whom branching Ivies hem,
With gen'rous wine inrich'd his silent stream.
The Fates lay down their shears; no mournful cries
Nor frightful clamours, nor laments arise.
Death paus'd above; no hapless sons expire,
Nor weeping parents watch the fun'ral fire:
Nor ships at sea, nor soldiers in the fight,
Nor towns by storm are lost, for Death suspends
   his right.
Old *Charon* Reeds around his temples wears,
And sings as he his empty ferry steers.   *Hughes.*

Pluto's speech to *Proserpine* to comfort her as he is conveying her to Hell, is full of very pleasing images, very proper to pacify her sorrow and indignation, and to persuade the Goddess to entertain a better opinion of her future abode among the Shades. I shall subjoin Mr. *Eusden*'s translation, which tho' in some parts a little paraphrastical, has more of CLAUDIAN's spirit in it than Mr. *Hughes*'s, and therefore will be more acceptable to the *English* Reader.

Desine funestis animum, Proserpina, curis
Et vano vexare metu: majora dabuntur
Sceptra, nec indigni tedas patiere mariti.
Ille ego Saturni proles, cui machina rerum
Servit, & immensum tendit per inane potestas.
Amissum ne crede diem: sunt altera nobis
Sidera; sunt orbes alij, lumenque videbis
                                          Cultoresque

Cultoresque pios: illic prætiosior ætas
Aurea progenies habitant, semperque tenemus
Quod superi meruere semel: nec mollia desunt
Prata tibi: Zephyris illic melioribus halant
Perpetui flores, quos nec tua protulit Henna.
Est etiam lucis arbor prædives opacis,
Fulgentes viridi ramos curvata metallo.
Hæc tibi sacra datur, fortunatumque tenebis
Autumnum, & fulvis semper ditabere pomis.
Parva loquor: quicquid liquidus complectitur Aër,
Quicquid alit tellus, quicquid salis æquora verrunt,
Quod fluvii volvunt, quod nutrivere paludes
Cuncta tuis pariter cedent mortalia regnis,
Lunari subjecta Globo, qui septimus auras
Ambit, & externis mortalia separat astris.
Sub tua purpurei venient vestigia reges
Deposito luxu turba cum paupere misti.
Omnia mors æquat: tu damnatura nocentes:
Tu requiem latura piis: te judice sontes
Improba cogentur vitæ commissa fateri.
Accipe Lethæo famulas cum gurgite Parcas.
Sit fatum quodcunque voles: hæc fatus ovantes,
Exhortatur equos, & Tænara mitior intrat.

Lib. 2. Ver. 277.

Cease, cease fair Nymph to lavish precious tears,
And discompose your soul with airy fears;
Look on *Sicilia*'s glitt'ring courts with scorn,
A nobler sceptre shall that hand adorn.
Imperial pomp shall sooth a gen'rous pride,
The Bridegroom never will disgrace the Bride.
If you above terrestrial thrones aspire,
From heav'n I spring, and *Saturn* was my sire.
The pow'r of *Pluto* stretches all around,
Uncircumscrib'd by Nature's utmost bound:
Where matter mould'ring dies, where forms decay,
Thro' the vast trackless void extends my sway.
Mark not with mournful eyes the fainting light,
Nor tremble at this interval of night;

A fairer scene shall open to your view,
An earth more verdant, and a heav'n more blue.
Another *Phœbus* gilds those happy skies,
And other Stars with purer flames arise.
There chaste adorers shall their praises join,
And with the choicest gifts enrich your shrine.
No change of ages knows the blissful clime,
The Golden first began, t'endure with latest time.
Your world a while that Golden Age could boast,
But here it flourish'd and shall ne'er be lost.
Perpetual Zephyrs breath thro' fragrant bow'rs,
And painted meads smile with unbidden flow'rs;
Flow'rs of immortal bloom and various hue
No rival sweets in your own *Enna* grew.
In the recess of a cool sylvan glade
A monarch tree projects no vulgar shade:
Encumber'd with their wealth, the branches bend,
And golden apples to your reach descend.
Spare not the fruit, but pluck the blooming ore,
The yellow harvest will increase the more.
But I too long on trifling themes explain,
Nor speak th' unbounded glory of your reign:
Whole Nature owns your pow'r whate'er his birth,
And lives and moves o'er all the face of earth,
Or in old Ocean's mighty caverns sleep,
Or sportive roll along the foamy deep;
Or on stiff pinions airy journeys take,
Or cut the floating stream or stagnant lake;
In vain they labour to preserve their breath,
And soon fall victims to your subject Death.
Unnumber'd triumphs swift to you he brings;
Hail Goddess of all sublunary things!
Empires that sink above, here rise again,
And worlds unpeopled crowd th' *Elysian* plain.
The rich, the poor, the monarch, and the slave
Know no superior honours in the grave.
Proud tyrants once, and lawrel'd chiefs shall come
And kneel, and trembling wait from you their doom.
The impious forc'd shall then their crimes disclose,
And see past pleasures teem with future woes;

Deplore

To toss the billows of the mounting main,
And beat his ratling hailstones on the plain;
If then his God the brazen gates oppose,
And in his hold the blust'ring tempest close,
His swelling wrath in empty threats expires,
And silent to his cave the huffing blast retires.
                                                    Hughes.

AND as most of the Poets have described mount *Ætna*, as abounding with extraordinary images, the reader may be pleased to see CLAUDIAN's manner of treating it: that of *Sicily* is immediately preceding, and they are both so beautiful, that I chuse to present them in one view. He concludes the description of *Ætna* with a short philosophical enquiry into the causes of those strange eruptions. *Lucan* often expatiates much more on the like occasions, tho' I cannot altogether justify those learned digressions, yet they are entertaining if not tedious nor too intricate.

————*Trinacria quondam*
Italiæ pars una fuit; sed pontus & æstas
Mutavêre situm: rupit confinia Nereus
Victor, & abscissos interluit æquore montes:
Parvaque cognatas prohibent discrimina terras.
Nunc illam socia raptam tellure trisulcam
Opponit natura mari: caput inde Pachyni
Respuit Ionias prætentis rupibus iras:
Hinc latrat Gætula Thetis, Lilybæaque pulsat
Brachia consurgens; hinc dedignata teneri
Concutit objectum rabies Tyrrhena Pelorum.
In medio scopulis se porrigit Ætna perustis;
Ætna Giganteos nunquam tacitura triumphos,
Enceladi Bustum, qui saucia terga revinctus
Spirat inexhaustum flagranti pectore sulphur.
Et quoties detrectat onus cervice rebelli
In dextram lævumque latus: tunc insula funda
Vellitur, & dubiæ nutant cum mœnibus urbes.
Ætnæis apices solo cognoscere visu,
Non aditu tentare licet; pars cætera frondet
Arboribus, teritur nullo cultore cacumen.

                                                    Nunc

Nunc vomit indigenas nimbos, piceaque gravatum
Fœdat nube diem: nunc molibus astra lacessit
Terrificis, damnisque suis incendia nutrit.
Sed quamvis nimio fervens exuberet æstu,
Scit nivibus servare fidem, pariterque favillis
Durescit glacies tanti secura vaporis,
Arcano defensa gelu, fumoque fideli.
Lambit contiguas innoxia flamma pruinas.
Quæ scopulos tormenta rotant? quæ tanta cavernas
Vis glomerat, quo fonte ruit Vulcanius amnis?
Sive quod objicibus discurrens ventus opertis,
Offenso per saxa furit rimosa meatu,
Dum scrutatur iter, libertatemque reposcens
Putria multivagis populatur flatibus antra.
Seu mare sulfurei ductum per viscera montis
Oppressis ignescit aquis, & pondera librat.
                                       Lib. 1. Ver. 140.

Trinacria join'd with *Italy* before
Th'impetuous ocean sunder'd either shore,
With the swol'n surge, the rooted hills are rent,
And the land rested from the continent.
In neighb'ring ken the several coasts are seen,
And the victorious seas triumphant pour between.
The new made Island with three angles clos'd
Is to the rage of warring waves oppos'd:
For here *Pachinus* with his ridgy sides
Rolls off the fury of th'*Ionian* tides;
And there the billows from *Getulia*'s shore,
Lash *Lilybeum* and indignant roar;
And brookless of restraint, the *Tyrrhene* main
On firm *Pelorus* tries its force in vain.
Fix'd in the midst is fiery *Ætna* found,
Ætna for vanquish'd Giants still renown'd:
Enceladus's load who crush'd beneath
From his large breast does burning tempests breathe:
Still as the monster, weary of the weight,
Exchanges sides, he shakes the mountains height:
Sicilia heaves, and ev'ry tott'ring wall
Leans to the ground, and meditates a fall:

Her pointed summits from afar are shown,
And are accessible to sight alone:
While on her other parts fresh greens appear,
And groves of trees their leafy branches rear:
No hardy hind dares turn the sultry soil
On the high crown, and cultivate with toil;
For now black clouds and tempests force their way,
And with their loathsome pitch pollute the day.
Now massy fragments of the shiver'd stone,
Torn from her root, against the stars are thrown.
But tho' the burnings rage with such excess,
Yet faithful to the snows, they keep perpetual peace;
And hoary winter does her seat maintain,
Secure of thaws and unmolested reign;
Coldly she hovers on the freezing coast,
And the swift flames sweep harmless o'er the frost.
What forceful engines whirl aloft in air,
The craggy quarries, and the mountain tear?
From what strange source proceeds the burning stream,
Which on the wasted vallies spouts the flame?
Or in confinement choak'd th'imprison'd wind
Pushes around an open vent to find,
And in its course resisted by the rock,
Bursts the blind dens, subverted with the shock;
Or the sea, ent'ring thro' the sulph'rous veins,
Boils with the fires, and on the blasted plains
Displodes the mingled ruin; wildly thrown,
The stones and liquid flames fall with destruction down. *Hughes.*

Ceres's anxiety and concern for fear of some mischance that might have befallen her daughter, and her amazement upon the discovery of her loss, is very aptly compared to the shepherd amazed at his return to find his flocks taken out of his fold; and to the tender care of the mother bird, who has left her young in quest of food. The whole passage is full of the tenderest sentiments.

—— *Digreditur*

——— *Digreditur templis: sed nulla ruenti*
Mobilitas: tardos queritur non ire jugales.
Immeritasque movens alterno verbere pennas
Sicaniam quærit, cum nec dum absconderit Iden:
Cuncta pavet, speratque nihil: sic æstuat ales
Quæ teneros humili fœtus commiserit orno
Allatura cibos, & plurima cogitat absens:
Ne fragilem ventus discusserit arbore nidum;
Ne furtum pateant homini, neu præda colubris.
Ut domus excubijs incustodita remotis,
Et resupinati neglecto cardine postes,
Flebilis & tacitæ species apparuit aulæ;
Non expectato respectu cladis, amictus
Conscidit, & fractas cum crine avellit aristas.
Hæserunt lachrymæ; non vox, non spiritus oris
Redditur, atque imis vibrat tremor ossa medullis.
Succidui titubant gressus foribusque reclusis,
Dum vacuas sedes, & desolata pererrat
Atrio, semirutas confuso stamine telas,
Atque interceptas agnoscit pectinis artes,
Divinus perit ille labor, spatiumque relictum
Audax sacrilego supplebat Aranea textu.
Nec deflet, plangitve malum: tamen oscula telæ
Figit, & abrumpit mutas in fila querelas.
Attritosque manu radios projectaque pensa
Cunctaque virgineo sparsa oblectamina ludo
Ceu natam, pressat gremio: castumque cubile
Desertosque toros, & sicubi sederit olim
Perlegit: attonitus stabulo ceu pastor inani,
Cui pecus aut rabies Pænorum inopina leonum,
Aut populatrices infestavére catervæ:
Serus at ille redit, vestataque pascua lustrans
Non responsuros ciet, imploratque juvencos.
Lib. 3. Ver. 137.

Then issuing from the fane, she took her way,
And thinks her Dragons linger with delay:
Impatiently she lashes on their flight,
And seeks *Sicilia* ere she lost the sight
Of *Ida*'s hill; obnoxious to her tears,
Nothing she hopes, and ev'ry thing she fears.

So fears the mother-bird whose callow young
On a low ashe's trembling boughs are hung:
And while she fetches food, her little breast
With anxious doubts is carefully possest,
Lest the rude wind should shake them from the tree,
Or busy boys the humble palace see,
Or cruel serpents seize the tender prey,
And bear the helpless children far away.
  Expos'd when *Ceres* saw th'unguarded dome,
Their gate wide open, and an empty room,
All hush'd within; she yielded to her fears,
Her flowing garments mournfully she tears,
  The chaplet on her head, and rends her yellow
    hairs:
Her tears congeal, her voice is now no more,
And a deep trembling seizes her all o'er.
She ventures in, and through the quiet house
And silent courts with stagg'ring paces goes;
And, as she rolls around her heavy eyes,
Th'unfinish'd purple in the woof she spies.
In vain the maid her heav'nly art had try'd,
Arachne boldly had the rest supply'd,
And stretch'd her filmy threads from side to side.
She weeps not, nor with cries her loss deplores,
But kiss'd the vest, and dumb complainings pours:
The rock, the wheel, and ev'ry little toy
Which did the Virgin's sportful hours employ,
As her lost *Proserpine* she fondly prest
Close in her lap, and hugg'd them on her breast;
Flies to her empty bed, and ev'ry place
Where her child us'd, does the sad mother trace.
  So looks the herdsman, when he finds the stall
Silent of lowings and the bleating call,
Which wolves or nightly lions have betray'd,
Or plund'ring soldiers to the camp convey'd:
Too late the groom returns, and o'er the plain
And neighb'ring pastures seeks the ravish'd train,
And makes his mimic cries and wonted sounds
    in vain.
Hughes.

I shall

I shall give no more quotations of this Poem: But as CLAUDIAN is a Poet, whose writings next to *Ovid*'s are admirably adapted to improve the fancy of a young Poet, and abound with a variety of subjects and kinds of Poetry, I thought after having cautioned the reader of his foible, that I could not do better than to dwell somewhat largely upon him.

I shall close what I have said of the Rape of *Proserpine* with a general reflection on EPIC POETRY.

OF all the works of genius over which the Muses preside, there is nothing so difficult as to write a perfect Epic Poem. Even *Homer* and *Virgil* are found not exempt from faults when examined by the severe rules of exact Criticism; and yet, tho' some persons of good taste have reproved me as partial to *Virgil*, whose conduct I have elsewhere magnified beyond measure, I think upon good consideration, and after comparing his judgment with that of all the writers before and after him in the Epic Way, I find no cause to retract my former opinion of him, but on the contrary, it seems that many of his errors, as the *Critics* call them, are owing to his singular modesty, and the great veneration he had for *Homer* the great Father of all sublime Poetry, whose vast and unbounded genius seemed above that exact attention necessary to preserve that just distribution of parts, and fine proportion they must bear to the whole. But as all I can say would fall short of their excellency, let us return to CLAUDIAN, whom we must allow his due praise even in the Epic Way, when we recollect what a great Interval of time passed between him and *Virgil*, during which the *Roman* Empire was continually declining both in arts and arms; this consideration will incline us to treat his faults more favourably, at the same time that we may endeavour to avoid them: since it is next to a prodigy to see him breaking thro' so many impediments, and rise to a perfection that sets him above most of the Poets that preceded him, as he is infinitely beyond all that succeeded him for many ages.

THE

THE rest of his Poems are either Panegyrics or Invectives, with some Epistles and Epigrams. Several Critics are of opinion, that his Invectives are the most perfect of all his Writings, and that he has discovered in them all a superior talent for Satire. Those against *Eutropius* and *Rufinus* have so many admirers that it is hard to say which of the two deserves the preference: Not to be too prolix, I shall content my self with presenting the reader a sketch of the latter, in order to give some idea of CLAUDIAN's invention in this species of Poetry, which being a mixture of satire and praise require an artist's hand.

THE Poet introduces his subject with this reflection, that tho' he had hitherto doubted whether the world was governed by Providence, seeing the prosperity of wicked men, yet the downfall of that wicked minister *Rufinus* now fully convinced him of his errour and justified the Gods. After an invocation of the Muse, he proceeds to relate how the Fury *Alecto* being enraged at the universal tranquillity of the *Roman* Empire under *Theodosius* I. assembles in council all the furies and plagues of Hell, and proposes to make war on the Gods. *Megæra* rising up, declares against this design, but tells them, if they were content to plague the lower world, she had her self trained up *Rufinus*, who would be a fit Instrument for their purpose. After having given his character, she proposes to prefer him in the Imperial Court. The whole assembly applaud this proposal, and *Megæra* breaking it up, dips her torch in the flames of the River *Phlegethon*, and rises up from Hell near the confines of *Italy* and *Gaul*. The Sun darkens at her appearance, dismal cries fill the air, and the adjacent countries are shocked with an earthquake. The Fury disguised like an old woman hastens to the city where *Rufinus* dwelt, and at first sight of him seems amazed to find in him a being more mischievously inclined than her self. After having reproved *Rufinus* for wasting his youth at home in obscurity, when the highest honours wait him abroad, she tells him of the

power

the eastern army to return to *Constantinople*, without attacking the *Huns*. *Stilico* obeys; the eastern legions regret his departure, and enter into a conspiracy against *Rufinus*; who triumphing at his having thus supplanted *Stilico*, and full of the expectation of being declared *Cæsar*, advances with the Emperor *Arcadius* to meet the army; who, after having paid their duty to their prince, close in upon *Rufinus* and massacre him. The general joy of the people on this occasion is described by the Poet, who represents Hell itself as receiving *Rufinus* with horror. CLAUDIAN proceeds to describe the tribunal of *Minos* and *Rhadamanthus*, and the several punishments of the wicked, and relates how *Rufinus* is condemned to suffer all the united tortures of the damned, and to be thrust down into the bottom of *Tantarus*.

NEXT to his Invectives, we are to consider several panegyrical Poems of CLAUDIAN. Of this sort are those on the 3d, 4th, and 6th Consulship of *Honorius*, and that in honour of *Mallius Theodorus* on the same occasion: The praises of *Stilico*, in three books; and two Poems, one of the *Getic*, and the other of the *Gildonic* war. The Poet has stretched his fancy to the utmost in these Poems, to sound *Stilico*'s praise. It is admirable to see in how many places he has drawn his character to advantage, without repeating the same thoughts or images. He makes him shine in the several relations of parent, general, husband, patron, friend and statesman; and add a lustre to every office, by his manner of discharging it. But as true praise is founded on truth, the Poet does not borrow many ornaments from fiction, but aims at a noble unadorned manner of describing the great actions of his Hero. I should be too long, were I to dwell on the particular beauties to be met with in all these Poems: I shall only take notice of a few.

IN the Poem of the third consulship of *Honorius*, after having described the dawn of that prince's courage in his infancy, when he comes to speak of it as he approached to manhood, he makes the following noble comparison.

Ut

Ut leo quem fulvae matris spelunca tegebat
Uberibus solitum pasci, cum crescere sentit
Ungue pedes, & terga jubis, & dentibus ora;
Jam negat imbelles epulas, & rupe relicta
Gætulo comes ire Patri, stabulisque minari
Æstuat, & celsi tabo sordere juvenci. Ver. 27.

So the young lion, whom with care at home
The tender dam had suckled, longs to roam:
Now with grown claws his nervous foot distends,
And down his neck the brindled mane descends;
The cave forsakes, disdains ignoble food,
Seeks out his fire, and roars about the wood:
Now meditates t'invade the trembling stall,
And triumphs in the strongest heifer's fall.

Theodosius the Great, the father of *Honorius*, had gained a signal Victory over the *Barbarians* that had over-run all *Spain*; in which he seemed as it were favoured by Providence, that raised a strong wind, which blew with so much violence, that it turned back the enemy's arrows and javelins on themselves. This circumstance is taken notice of by the Poet in a very sublime manner.

Te propter gelidis Aquilo de montibus procellis
Obruit adversas acies, revolutaque tela
Vertit in auctores, & turbine reppulit hastas.
O nimium dilecte Deo! cui fundit ab antris
Æolus armatas hyemes; cui militat æther,
Et conjurati veniunt ad classica venti. Ver. 93.

For thee the North pours forth his freezing blast,
And furious lays the adverse armies waste:
Met by the whirlwind, back the spear recoils,
Attacks his master, and his purpose foils.
Hail, favourite of Heav'n! for whom the winds
Arm'd with their fiercest rage, the God unbinds;
The dreadful host embattled fill the sky,
And at thy signal swift with ruin fly.

The Apotheosis of *Theodosius* and taking his place among the Constellations is thus described, when he
had

had spoke his last words to *Stilico*, to whom he recommended his children.

>———*Nec plura locutus,*
> *Sicut erat liquido signavit tramite nubes:*
> *Ingrediturque globum Lunæ, limenque reliquit*
> *Arcados, & Veneris clementes advolat auras.*
> *Hinc Phœbi permensus iter, flammamque nocentem*
> *Gradivi, placidumque Jovem, stetit arce suprema*
> *Algenti qua Zonæ riget Saturnia tractu.*
> *Machina laxatur cæli, rutilæque patescunt*
> *Sponte fores; Arctoa parat convexa Bootes,*
> *Australes reserat portas succinctus Orion,*
> *Invitantque novum sidus, pendentque vicissim*
> *Quas partes velit ille sequi, quibus esse sodalis*
> *Dignetur stellis, aut qua regione morari.*
> *O decus ætherium, terrarum gloria quondam,*
> *Te tuus Oceanus, natali gurgite lassum*
> *Excipit & notis Hispania proluit undis.*
> *Fortunate parens, primos cum detegis ortus*
> *Adspicis Arcadium, cum te proclivior urges*
> *Occiduum visus remoratur Honorius ignem;*
> *Et quocunque vagos flectas sub cardine cursus*
> *Natorum per Regna vinis, qui mente serena*
> *Maturoque regunt victas moderamine gentes,*
> *Sæcula qui rursus formant meliore metallo.*
>
> Ver. 162.

This said, the Hero with a train of light
Up to the Moon describ'd his radiant flight;
Then takes his course, fair *Venus*' star to find;
His next essay leaves *Mercury* behind;
Thence to bright *Phœbus*' paths he wings his way,
Advancing meets hot *Mars*' destructive ray;
Jove's milder sphere, still soaring upwards, past,
And in cold *Saturn's* orbit rests at last.
Mean while, the heav'nly portals spreading wide,
Admit him with glad welcome on each side;
Bootes with his Wane the North unfolds;
The Southern gate *Orion* waiting holds;

Each Constellation him invites to share
Their glories, and æthereal honours wear:
Each clime each region courts the Heroe's stay,
Each star officious strives to clear the way.
O thou, bright ornament to Heav'n assign'd,
As once on Earth the pride of human-kind,
With native streams th' *Atlantic* meets thy beams,
And *Spanish* waters lave thy wearied limbs:
Thrice happy parent, whose first course displays }
Thy beams on thy *Arcadius*, and surveys
Thy lov'd *Honorius* with slow setting rays: }
Still as through various climes thy orbit roves,
Yer distant regions coresponding moves,
Through their wide realms thou go'st, whose upright sway
Has taught a world submissive to obey.
By them ev'n vanquish'd nations hope to find
Peace, and a Golden Age restore mankind.

In the fourth consulship, *Honorius* and *Arcadius*, in associated by their Father to the Empire, are pared to *Castor* and *Pollux*: *Theodosius* is described returning in Triumph with his two sons in the riot with him.

*Lætior augurio genitor, natisque superbus
Jam paribus duplici fultus consorte redibat,
Splendebatque pio complexus pignora curru.
Haud aliter summo gemini cum patre Lacones
Progenies Ledæa sident; in utroque relucent
Frater, utroque soror; simili Chlamys effluit auro;
Stellati pariter crines: juvat ipse Tonantem
Error, & ambiguæ placet ignorantia matri.
Eurotas proprios discernere nescit alumnos.*

Ver. 203.

At this fair omen their exulting sire
Feels a new spring of joy his breast inspire,
With secret pride their growing virtue views,
In each so equal, he can neither chuse.
Grac'd with these partners of his crown and fame,
Triumphant in his car the Heroe came.

Such

Such *Jove* himself appear'd, when by his side
Castor and *Pollux* stood, fair *Leda*'s pride.
In each the brother and the sister shine,
Their golden robes alike and hair divine:
Ambiguous error from their likeness flows,
Ev'n old *Eurotas* no distinction knows:
Their dubious mother views the pleasing cheat,
And *Jove* himself smiles at the fair deceit.

Theodosius's advice to *Honorius* in the same Poem is full of the noblest sentiments, and the best instructions how a Prince should govern his People, and shew the great liberty of the Poet and docility of the Prince to whom they are addressed.

But instead of singling out any more passages from these Poems, I shall conclude this Poet's life with part of his Epithalamium on *Honorius* and *Maria*, which is perhaps the compleatest Poem that was ever written on this subject: and I chuse to do so, because it has been very happily translated by Mr. *Eusden*; so that both the art and genius of the Poet may appear with advantage even to the English reader.

Mons latus Ionium Cypri præruptus obumbrat
Invius humano gressu, Phariumque cubile
Proteus & septem despectat cornua Nili:
Hunc neque candentes audent vestire pruinæ,
Hunc venti pulsare timent, hunc lædere nimbi:
Luxuriæ Venerique vacat: pars acrior anni
Exulat, æterni patet indulgentia veris.
In campum se fundit apex: hunc aurea sepes
Circuit, & fulvo defendit præta Metallo.
Mulciber, ut perhibent, his oscula conjugis emit
Mœnibus, & tales uxoribus obtulit arces.
Intus rura micant, mænius quæ subdita nullis
Perpetuum florent, Zephyro contenta colono:
Umbrosumque nemus, quo non admittitur ales,
Ni probet ante suos Diva sub judice cantus.
Quæ placuit, fruitur ramis; quæ victa recedit.
Vivunt in Venerem frondes, omnisque vicissim

Felix

Fælix arbor amat; nutant ad mutua palmæ
Fœdera; populeo suspirat populus ictu;
Et platani platanis, alnoque assibilat alnus.
Labuntur gemini fontes: hic dulcis, amarus
Alter, & infusis corrumpunt mella venenis.
Unde Cupidineas armavit fama sagittas.
Mille pharetrati ludunt in margine fratres,
Ore pares, habitu similes, gens mollis amorum:
Hos Nymphæ pariunt: illum Venus aurea solum
Edidit: ille Deos, cœlumque & sidera cornu
Temperat, & summos dignatur figere reges.
Hi plebem feriunt: nec cætera Numina desunt.
Hic habitat nullo constricta licentia nodo,
Et flecti faciles iræ, vinoque madentes
Excubiæ, lachrymæque rudes, & gratus amantum
Pallor, & in primis titubans audacia furtis,
Jucundique metus, & non secura voluptas;
Et lasciva volant levibus perjuria pennis:
Hos inter petulans alta cervice juventas
Excludit senium luco: procul atria Divæ
Permutant radios, sylvaque obstante virescunt.
Lemnius hæc etiam gemmis exstruxit & auro,
Admiscens artem pretio, trabibusque Smaragdis
Supposuit cæsas hyacinthi rupe columnas:
Beryllo paries, & Iaspide lubrica surgunt
Limina, despectusque solo calcatur Achates.
In medio glebis redolentibus area dives
Præbet odoratas messes: hic mitis amomi,
Hic casæ matura seges, Panchaia surgunt
Cinnama, nec sicca frondescunt vimina costo,
Tardaque sudanti prorepunt balsama ligno.
Quo postquam delapsus amor, longasque peregit
Penna vias; alacer passuque superbior intrat.
Cæsariem tunc forté Venus subnixa corusco
Fingebat solio, dextra lævaque sorores
Stabant Idaliæ: largos hæc nectaris imbres
Irrigat; hæc morsu numerosi dentis eburno
Multifidum discrimen arat: sed tertia retro
Dat varios nexus, & justo dividit orbes
Ordine, neglectam partem studiosa relinquens:

Plus

Plus error docuit: speculi nec vultus egebat
Judicio: similis tecto monstratur in omni,
Et rapitur quocunque videt; dum singula cernit,
Seque probat, nati venientis conspicit umbram,
Ambrosioque sinu puerum complexa ferocem.

In the fam'd *Cyprian* isle a mountain stands,
That casts a Shadow into distant lands:
Access in vain by human feet is try'd,
Its lofty brow looks down with noble pride
On bounteous *Nile* thro' seven wide channels spread,
And sees old *Proteus* in his oozy bed.
Along its sides no hoary frosts presume
To blast the myrtle shrubs, or nip the bloom.
The winds with caution sweep the rising flow'rs,
While balmy dews descend and vernal show'rs.
The rolling Orbs no wintry horrors bring,
Fix'd in th'indulgence of eternal spring.
Unfading sweets in purple scenes appear,
And genial breezes soften all the year.
The nice luxurious soul uncloy'd may rove
From pleasures still to circling pleasures move,
For endless beauty kindles endless love.
The mountain, when the summit once you gain,
Falls by degrees, and sinks into a plain,
Where the pleas'd eye may flow'ry meads behold
Enclos'd with branching oar, and hedg'd with Gold:
Or where large crops the gen'rous glebe supplies,
And yellow harvests, unprovok'd, arise:
For by mild Zephyrs fan'd, the teeming soil
Yields ev'ry grain, nor asks the peasant's toil.
These were the bribes, the price of heav'nly charms,
These *Cytherea* won to *Vulcan*'s arms:
For such a bliss he such a gift bestow'd,
The rich, th'immortal labours of a God.

 A sylvan scene, in solemn state display'd,
Flatters each feather'd warbler with a shade;
But here no bird its painted wings can move,
Unless elected by the Queen of Love;
E'er made a member of this tuneful throng,
She hears the songster, and approves the song.

           The

The joyous victors hop from spray to spray,
The vanquish'd fly with mournful notes away.
  Branches in branches twin'd compose the grove,
And shoot, and spread, and blossom into love.
The trembling palms their mutual vows repeat,
And bending poplars, bending poplars meet.
The distant plantanes seem to press more nigh,
And to the sighing Alders, Alders sigh.
Blue heav'ns above them smile, and all below
Two murm'ring streams in wild meanders flow;
This mix'd with gall, and that like honey sweet,
But ah! too soon th' unfriendly waters meet.
Steep'd in these springs (if verse belief can gain)
The darts of Love their double power attain;
Hence all mankind a bitter sweet have found,
A painful pleasure, and a grateful wound.
  Along the grassy banks in bright array
Ten thousand little loves their wings display.
Quivers and bows their usual sport proclaim,
Their dress, their stature, and their looks the same;
Smiling in innocence, and ever young.
And tender as the Nymphs from whom they sprung;
For *Venus* did but boast one only son,
And rosy *Cupid* was that boasted one;
He uncontroul'd thro' heav'n extends his sway,
And Gods and Goddesses by turns obey.
Or if he stoops on earth great princes burn,
Sicken on thrones, and wreath'd with lawrel mourn,
Th' inferior pow'rs o'er hearts inferior reign,
And pierce the rural fair or homely swain.
Here Love's imperial pomp is spread around,
Voluptuous liberty that knows no bound,
And sudden storms of wrath, which soon decline,
And midnight watchings o'er the fumes of wine;
Unartful tears and hectic looks, that show
With silent eloquence the lover's woe;
Boldness unfledg'd, and to stol'n raptures new,
Half trembling stands, and scarcely dares pursue;
Fears that delight, and anxious doubts of joy,
Which check our swelling hopes, but not destroy;

And short-breath'd vows, forgot as soon as made,
On airy pinions flutter thro' the glade.
Youth with a haughty look and gay attire,
And rolling eyes that glow with soft desire,
Shines forth, exalted on a pompous seat,
While sullen cares, and wither'd age retreat.

Now from afar the palace seems to blaze,
And hither would extend its golden rays;
But by reflexion of the Grove is seen
The Gold still varied by a waving green;
For *Mulciber* with secret pride beheld
How far his skill all human art excell'd;
And grown uxorious, did the work design
To speak the Artist and the Art divine.
Proud columns tow'ring high, support the frame,
That hewn from *Hyacinthian* quarries came;
The beams are em'ralds, and yet scarce adorn
The ruby walls on which themselves are born.
The pavement, rich with veins of agate, lies,
And steps, with shining jaspers, slipp'ry rise.

Here spices in parterres promiscuous blow,
Not from *Arabia*'s fields more odours flow.
The wanton winds through groves of Cassia play,
And steal the ripen'd fragrancies away.
Here with its load the mild Amomum bends,
There Cinnamon in rival sweets contends.
A rich perfume the ravish'd senses fills,
While from the weeping tree the Balm distills.

At these delightful bow'rs arrives at last
The God of Love, a tedious journey past;
Then shapes his way to reach the fronting gate,
Doubles his majesty, and walks in state.
It chanc'd, upon a radiant throne reclin'd,
Venus her golden tresses did unbind;
Proud to be thus employ'd, on either hand
Th'*Idalian* sisters, rang'd in order, stand.
Ambrosial essence one bestows in show'rs,
And lavishly whole streams of *Nectar* pours.
With Iv'ry combs another's dextrous care,
Or curls, or opens the dishevel'd hair;

A third.

A third, industrious, with a nicer eye
Instructs the ringlets in what form to lie;
Yet leaves some few, that not so closely prest,
Sport in the wind, and wanton from the rest.
Sweet negligence, by artful study wrought,
A graceful error, and a lovely fault.
The judgment of the glass is here unknown,
Here mirrors are supply'd by ev'ry stone.
Where'er the Goddess turns, her image falls,
And a new *Venus* dances on the walls.
Now while she did her spotless form survey,
Pleas'd with love's empire and almighty sway,
She spy'd her son, and fir'd with eager joy,
Sprung forwards and embrac'd the fav'rite boy.

Eusden.

A Critical and Historical

DISSERTATION

BY WAY OF

INTRODUCTION

TO THE

LIVES

OF THE

Roman Dramatic Poets.

SECT. I.
Of the Rise and Progress of the GREEK DRAMA.

THE politest nations of antiquisy have always considered Dramatic Poetry as a very elegant and instructive branch of their public diversions. In order therefore to trace it from its original, let us begin by a short enquiry into the nature of those public entertainments among them.

THE wisest nations have always thought it expedient, to preserve the memory of signal Victories, or other remarkable instances, as they imagined, of the divine favour, by solemn festivals appointed at certain seasons, in honour of the Deity, whose benefits at

that

that time they were defirous to commemorate. Thefe religious Rites were the objects of the magiftrate's peculiar care, and were generally accompanied by fuch fports and entertainments as were fuitable to the tafte and inclination of the people. The greateft lawgivers truly judged, that the conveniences of fociety were leaft on the common people's fide, who were tied down to hard labour at home, and moft expofed to the chance of war abroad. In order to alleviate thefe hardfhips, thofe excellent men appointed them ftated days of reft and exemption from their ufual labours: and by confecrating thefe days fo fet apart, firft to divine fervice; and then allowing the ufe of proper exercifes and diverfions, they gave their people frefh fpirit and courage to return with cheerfulnefs to their work, and filled their minds with the juft fentiments of gratitude and reverence to thofe fuperior powers, to whom, as they had been erroneoufly taught, they conceived themfelves indebted for the various bleffings of life.

These diverfions, that at firft were rude and ridiculous, nay fometimes indecent, time infenfibly improved into very ufeful and pleafing entertainments; efpecially when men of thought and leifure were openly encouraged, by the liberality of the ftate, and care of proper magiftrates, to exert their talent in regulating and polifhing thefe public fchools of inftruction. As honourable as this appellation may feem, the *Greek* ftage will deferve it, though in its beft ftate it might labour under fome irregularities and defects: Yet there it was, that the generous principle of liberty and juftice, of piety and compaffion, and indeed of every focial virtue were recommended in the moft authorized and agreeable manner. The fate of tyranny and the punifhment of vice, was fet forth in terrible examples drawn chiefly from the hiftory of their anceftors, or of the neighbouring ftates. This was the bufinefs of Tragedy, while Comedy ridiculed and ftrongly expofed the abfurdities and follies of private life. Comedy indeed

indeed was for a long time too bitter, and levelled at particular persons, and therefore was in time restrained: Yet it well deserves our notice, that it was not thoroughly reformed, till about the time of *Alexander* the Great, when the states of *Greece* had retained nothing but the shadow of their former liberty, having lost all their glory in a poor subjection to the arbitrary will of the *Macedonian* Princes.

This is a general account of the state of the *Greek* Stage. The particular ceremony to which Dramatic Poetry owes its rise, was the feast of *Bacchus*. The occasion of sacrificing a he-goat to this God, is thus related. When *Bacchus* had found out the method of planting and cultivating vines, and making wine, he communicated the secret to *Icarius*, who was then sovereign of a small territory in *Attica*. One day *Icarius* having taken a goat, that was gnawing his vines, and devouring his grapes, he justly looked upon this creature as a professed enemy to *Bacchus*; and accordingly slew the goat as an agreeable victim to that God, or rather sacrificed the mischievous animal to his own resentment. The neighbours were invited to partake of his joy; who growing merry with wine, began to dance round the altar, singing the praises of the Deity who had given them so pleasant a Liquor. The whole company were so well pleased with the ceremony, which at the same time they looked upon as a solemn act of Religion, that it was resolved by common consent to celebrate it annually with songs and dances in honour of *Bacchus*. The time pitched upon was their vintage, whence it was called * Trygody, *the Song of the Vintage*; and from the Goat that was sacrificed, Tragedy, *or the Song of the Goat*.

When *Theseus* had brought the dispersed inhabitants of *Attica* to live together in *Athens*, the people

---

* Τρυγωδία, sic dicta, ἀπὸ τῆς τρύγης, *vindemia*; vel παρὰ τὴν τρύγα, quod fœcibus ora oblinerent. *Athen.* Lib. 2. Hinc. Τρυγωδίω, *nvicior*, *scurriliter illudo*.

carried

carried this ceremony thither with them, and began to celebrate it in the city, near the temple of *Bacchus*. In time their best Poets became concerned on this occasion, and by their compositions in honour of *Bacchus*, disputed the prize of Poetry. Afterwards it was celebrated by a large chorus of musicians with songs and dances, and the execution of the solemnity was removed from the Temple of *Bacchus* to the *Forum*, but the God had the Goat still sacrificed to him; and now the hymn began to be more particularly distinguished at *Athens* by the name of *Tragedy*. The like ceremony, but more grosly executed, continued to be observed in the country villages, whence it derived the name of *Comedy*, which signifies a village song. Thus began the distinction of the two Poems, that at first were one and the same thing, from the different places where they were executed. This Account is agreeable to what *Plutarch*, *Athenæus*, *Donatus*, and others give of this matter.

We have seen how the *Greek* Drama is founded on the feast of *Bacchus*. Before we proceed to enquire into the several steps of its improvement, the following plain and elegant account of that rural solemnity from *Tibullus*, will agreeably confirm what has been said above of its rude beginning.

Agricola assiduo primum lassatus aratro
  Cantavit certo rustica verba pede,
Et satur arenti primum est modulatus avena
  Carmen, ut ornatos duceret ante Deos.
Agricola & minio suffusus, Bacche, rubenti
  Primus inexperta duxit ab arte choros.

Lib. 1. El. 4.

The chearful clowns from labour free rehearse
Their aukward songs in rude unpolish'd verse;
In honour of their Gods with chaplets crown'd,
From ill-tun'd pipes the hollow notes resound.
With belly full, and face besmear'd with red,
These artless husbandmen their chorus led.

It is natural to suppose that the genius of some of these country fellows, thus merrily assembled, might prompt them to give a little turn and harmony to their extempore song; which being relished by the company, others might thereby be induced to attempt the same at the next festival. Thus they began to study the graces of language on these occasions, which must insensibly acquire some ornaments that distinguished it from the common manner. He that accompanied the song with his pipe, may be supposed to have endeavoured to excel in proportion as his diligence was applauded. The merriment concluded with dancing, and jesting on each other. When this practice of the country had been carried, as has been said, to *Athens*, there arose some persons, though as yet hardly known by the name of Poets, who undertook to compose proper hymns for the solemnity. After this they added some satirical stories, which they rehearsed themselves to divert the people. This might give rise to what was afterwards called the *Satirica Poesis* of the *Greeks*.

The *Dionysia* or feasts of *Bacchus* were celebrated at *Athens* three times a year, which answer to our *March*, *April*, and *January*; and the *Panathenaics* in *August*. It was at these seasons that Plays were acted.

Thespis, who flourished in the 61st Olympiad, about 530 years before Christ, was the first that attempted a farther improvement: He made up a kind of company, whom he chose out of the chorus, and taught them to act on a stage; though his was nothing but a cart, with which he and his company went about from one village to another. The entertainment was partly the rehearsal of some remarkable adventure of one of their heroes, to which was added a pleasant ridicule on some of the company. The whole at first seemed only designed to relieve the chorus, who were tired incessantly with singing the praises of *Bacchus* and *Ceres*. *Thespis* finding his contrivance cceed beyond expectation, polished his dialogue, so

the best foundation both of Tragedy and Comedy. Æschylus laid aside the old raillery and buffoon stile, formed his subject upon a regular plan, to which he made the dances of his chorus subservient (*Athenæus*, Lib. 1. *Deipnosophist*.) which now became regular actors, and added another interlocutor to the one *Thespis* had introduced. The magistrates soon became sensible of the usefulness of these improvements, and granted him all necessary privileges and encouragement. Part of the public money that was applied for exhibiting the public games, began to be appropriated to the decorations of the Theatre: And about this time *Agatharcus*, a skilful architect, by the direction of *Æschylus* applied himself to make many theatrical improvements, in the scenes, &c. of which he afterwards published a treatise (*Vitruvius*, L. 7. Præf.) *Æschylus* was the first who found out the true stile of Tragedy, which according to *Quintilian*, *Inst*. Lib. 10. Cap. 1. he sometimes affected to a fault; and so much did the *Athenians* honour his memory and esteem his writings, that afterwards they by a public decree gave the poets leave to revise his pieces, which often wanted polishing and a greater correctness of stile, and then to bring them on the stage; so that he gained the prize of Poetry again many years after his death: And it was customary for boys to come with branches of myrtle in their hands, and repeat his verses at their most elegant entertainments: and *Ptolomy Euergies* gave the *Athenians* fifteen talents for the original copy of his works, for which we have no less authority than *Galen*'s. *Æschylus* is said to have been so very pathetic and successful in painting distress, that he never failed making his audience share the grief he represented. But his machinery was sometimes rather too violent; as when in his *Eumenides*, to the great terror of the

---

* *Tragœdias primum in lucem Æschylus protulit, sublimis & gravis, & grandiloquus sæpe ad vitium, propter quod correctas ejus fabulas in certamen deferre posterioribus Poetis Athenienses permisere, suntque eo modo multi coronati.*

female

female part of his audience, he filled the stage with a chorus of fifty furies: this was found so dreadful, that from that time forward the number of the chorus was not allowed to exceed fifteen. He also masked his actors, dressed them in a long flowing garment, and taught them to walk in the buskin, that they might personate the characters of heroes with more decency. *Horace* takes notice of most of these circumstances.

Post hanc personæ pallæque repertor honestæ
Æschylus, & modicis instravit pulpita tignis,
Et docuit magnumque loqui, nitique Cothurno.

De Arte Poet.

ACCORDING to *Plutarch*, *Æschylus* used to animate his vein with wine, before he sate down to compose. He died in the 60th year of his age, the 4th year of the 78th Olympiad, from the building of *Rome* 281, before *Christ* 463.

Sophocles was born the second year of the 71st Olympiad, 492 before Christ. He, in conjunction with *Euripides*, brought Tragedy to its perfection in *Greece*: added a third, and sometimes a fourth interlocutor, in the dialogue, and left nothing to be desired either in the stile, the sentiments, character, or disposition of the subject. He likewise introduced the custom of opposing one Tragedy to another, in the contention for the prize, whereas before there were either three called *Trilogia*, or four *Tetralogia*, the 4th being a satirical piece. When he was 65 years of age, he commanded some forces jointly with *Pericles*. The Poets used themselves to teach their actors to declaim their parts, but his voice was so weak, he was forced to get others to instruct them. He lived to 90 years of age.

Euripides was born the first year of the 75th Olympiad. * *Quintilian* seems to refer him to *Sophocles*,

and

---

* *Is, in sermone (quod ipsum reprehendunt, quibus gravitas & cothurnus & sonus Sophoclis videtur esse sublimior) magis accedit oratorio generi; & sententijs densus, & in iis quæ a sapientibus tradita*

and particularly obferves, that *Menander* ftudied and imitated him. He was called the Philofopher of the Poets; and his intimacy with *Socrates* was fo great, that it was commonly reported, that Philofopher affifted him in writing his Tragedies. *Euripides* died the fame year with *Sophocles*, being 75 years old. But I need not dwell on the merit of thefe two celebrated Poets, whofe works were the models of all the Tragic writers after them, both *Greeks* and *Romans*.

Let us now take a fhort view of the degrees by which Comedy was improved. It lay for fome time confounded with the old chorus and village medley, 'till, when *Æfchylus* had made fuch great improvements in Tragedy, fome Poets began to conceive, that, by imitating his conduct, they might make Comedy a regular work diftinct from the Chorus of *Bacchus*; which they afterwards laid afide, not adapting it to their Poem, as had been done in Tragedy. But we find fome very whimfical chorus's in *Ariftophanes*'s Comedies, as of clouds, frogs, &c. In *Ariftotle*'s time, Comedy was not yet perfect: *Menander* introduced the new Comedy fome years after his death

After *Lyfander* had taken *Athens*, he fet up the government of the thirty Tyrants there; and 'till then the old Comedy had continued. The fubjects of thefe Comedies were often not feigned but real, at leaft the principal circumftances were fo: the whole being a fevere and ingenious invective, and fatyrical reprefentation of the vices of the greateft men in the ftate, whofe very names the poets had the courage to mention. That this liberty might be abufed, appears from what *Socrates* fuffered by the fcurrilous wit of *Ariftophanes*; and the noble patience of the Philofopher on this occafion, is very well known. The actors

---

tradita funt, pene ipfis par, & in dicendo ac refpondendo cuilibet eorum, qui fuerunt in foro diferti, comparandus: in affectibus vero cum omnibus mirus, tum in iis qui miferatione conftant facile præcipuus. Hunc & admiratus maxime eft, ut fæpe teftatur, & fecutus, quanquam in opere diverfo. Menander. Inft. Lib. 5. cap. 1.

mafks

masks imitated mens countenances to the life. Yet so strongly were the old *Athenians* possessed with the generous love of liberty, that nothing but tyranny attempted to restrain this extraordinary liberty of the stage: perhaps it might occasionally prove a good curb on the conduct of their great men, since it is otherwise unaccountable how so polite and wise a people should have endured it so long. But it soon displeased the thirty Tyrants, whose conduct could not bear examination, and would endure no censure. *Lamachus* one of them, made a severe Decree, that forbid the Actors naming persons on the stage. This put the Poets under a necessity of using feigned names: but still the characters of the persons pointed at were so well drawn, that it was impossible for so intelligent an audience to mistake them; and this was called the middle Comedy. It flourished 'till *Alexander* the Great; who, having overthrown the united forces of *Greece* at the battle of *Cheronea*, and by the terror of the destruction of *Thebes*, forced the *Greeks* to submit to his yoke, commanded that the liberties the Poets took, should be farther restrained. It seemed as if that proud son of *Ammon* feared the Wit of a people, whose arms he despised. Upon this order arose the new Comedy, which now became a general imitation of common life. *Menander*, *Terence*'s model, brought it to the highest perfection it was thought capable of receiving. Four of *Terence*'s Plays are confessed translations from him, and so are some of *Plautus*'s: and the greatest *Roman* in arts and arms allowed the *African* but half the genius of the *Greek*. We have only a few fragments remaining of the many excellent pieces *Menander* wrote, which are reckon'd to have amounted to 109 in all. The loss of them is one of those injuries, which time and the barbarous nations, if not rather the foolish bigottry of Monks, has done the commonwealth of learning.

We have already said something of the satyrical pieces. *Pratinas* was the first, who made any successful attempts this way: he flourish'd about the 70th Olympiad. We may here take occasion to observe, that during

ring the feast of *Bacchus*, the Poets used to exhibit four dramatic pieces the same day, and on the same subject; as the adventures of *Ulysses*, the anger of *Achilles*, &c. The last of the four was a satyrical piece. This custom, as we have observed, continued 'till *Sophocles* got it altered.

Thus have we taken a summary view of the rise and progress of the *Greek* Stage. The *Roman*, which is more immediately the subject of our present enquiry, comes next to be considered.

SECT. II.
Of the ROMAN DRAMA.

THE occasion that introduced scenic games among that grave people, *Livy* has related to the following purpose.

The city being sorely afflicted with the plague, after having consulted the sacred books, the senate decreed, that * Players should be sent for out of *Tuscany*; and upon this account Scenic Games were first exhibited at *Rome*, after several other vain attempts to appease the anger of the Gods, and lessen the violence of the sickness. This happened in the year of *Rome* 392, above a hundred years before *Livius Andronicus* brought a regular Play on the stage, in imitation of the *Greeks*, whose Theatre had already attained its greatest perfection. † *Livy* goes on to observe, that 'till this time, 392, the *Romans* had no other diversions, but the shews and exercises of the *Circus*. That warlike People had as yet found no leisure to think of the more refined diversions of the mind. These

Tuscan

---

* They were only Dancers on a Stage.

† *T. Sulpicio Petico, C. Licinio Stolone Consulibus, pestilentia fuit: eo nihil dignum memoria actum, nisi quod pacis Deûm exposcendæ causa tertio tum post conditam urbem Lectisternium fuit: & cum vis morbi nec humanis consiliis, nec ope divinâ levaretur, victis superstitione animis, Ludi quoque scenici nova res bellicoso populo, nam circi modo spectaculum fuerat; inter alia cœlestis iræ placamina instituti dicuntur. Cæterum parua quoque, ut principia ferme omnia, & ea ipsa peregrina res fuit; Sine carmine ullo, sine imitandorum*

Tuscan actors (continues the Historian) at first only danced to the flute, after their own country manner. Afterwards the *Roman* youth began to imitate them, making extempore verses at the same time, in which they attempted, though grosly enough at first, to rally each other. In time too, they tried to adapt their motions to the cadence of their words. The thing took presently, and by frequent practice received some farther improvement. Then there arose actors of their own, who composed a sort of medley (*Satyras*) which was set to music, and acted in a proper manner with suitable motions, that kept time with the flutes, a rude kind of Recitativo. Some years afterwards, *L. Andronicus* ventured to represent a regular play after this medley, himself acting the Play, as all the Poets in those early times did. Being often called upon by the audience to act some passages over a-

---

imitandorum carminum actu Ludiones ex Hetruriâ acciti, ad Tibicinis modos saltantes, haud indecoros motus, more Thusco dabant. Imitari deinde eos juventus, simul inconditis inter se jocularia fundentes, versibus cœpere: nec absoni à voce motus erant. Accepta itaque res, sæpiùs usurpando excitata, vernaculis Artificibus, quia hister Thusco verbo Ludio vocabatur, nomen histrionibus inditum: qui non sicut ante Fescennino versu similem incompositum temerè ac rudem alternis jaciebant; sed impletas modis Satiras, descripto jam ad Tibicinem cantu, motuque congruenti peragebant. LIVIUS *post aliquot annos, qui ab Satiris ausus est primus argumento fabulam serere, idem scilicet, id quod omnes tum erant, suorum carminum actor, dicitur, cùm sæpius revocatus vocem obtudisset, venâ petitâ puerum ad canendum ante Tibicinem cùm statuisset, canticum egisse aliquanto magis vigente motu, quia nihil vocis usus impediebat. Inde ad manum cantari Histrionibus cœptum, diverbiaque tantum ipsorum voci relicta. Postquam lege hâc fabularum ab risu ac soluto joco res avocabatur, & ludus in artem paulatim verterat, juventus, histrionibus fabellarum actu relicto, ipsa inter se, more antiquo, ridicula intexta versibus jactitare cœpit, quæ inde Exodia postea appellata; consertaque fabellis potissimùm Atellanis sunt. Quod genus ludorum, ab Oscis acceptum, tenuit juventus; nec ab histrionibus pollui passa est. Eo institutum manet, ut actores Atellanarum nec tribu moveantur, & stipendia, tanquam expertes artis ludicræ faciant. Inter aliarum parva principia rerum, ludorum quoque prima origo ponenda visa est, ut appareret, quàm ab sano initio res in hanc vix opulentis regnis tolerabilem insaniam venerit.* Decad. 1. L. 7.

gain-

gain, and his voice growing hoarse by it, he begged leave of the audience to introduce a boy instructed for the purpose to rehearse or sing the words to the flute. This was a relief to *Andronicus*, who hereupon acted with more life and vigour; the actor having now only the dialogue part to declaim. We shall explain this part of the relation in the sequel of this essay.

By these and other regulations, of which we do not know the particulars, Stage-Plays became the object of a particular art; and the *Roman* youth leaving them (continues *Livy*) to the Poets and Players, continued to act the former medleys themselves, which were afterwards called *Exodia*, from their being acted at the end of the *Atellane* Plays. These Plays the *Romans* first learnt from the *Osci*, or antient *Tuscans*, and never admitted the Players to act a part in them. And from thence came this custom, which afterwards obtained the force of a Law, that the actors of those Plays called *Attellane*, were never degraded from their tribe, as other common Players, but were admitted to serve in the wars, as if they had never acted on the stage. *Livy* concludes this curious account with the following judicious reflection. " I was " willing to give the public an account of the first ori- " ginal of Scenic Games, that we may observe to " what an intolerable degree of extravagance they are " now brought, so as to become burthensome even to " the richest states; and this from so sober and religi- " ous a beginning."

The *Roman* Dramatic Poetry was at first divided into three sorts, some of which they afterwards subdivided into distinct species. The three sorts were Tragedy, Comedy, and the Atellane pieces. Their Tragedy was either *Palliata*; so called from the *Greek* habit *Pallium*, which the actors wore, the characters being *Greek*; or *Prætextata*, from the *Prætexta*, the habit of the *Roman* Noblemen, in which the characters were *Roman*. So *Horace*,

Vel qui Prætextas, vel qui docuere Togatas;

Speaking of a *Roman* Tragedy and Comedy. The *Togata*

gata was their serious and genteel Comedy, the characters being drawn from persons of good rank, whence it has been sometimes called *Prætextata* as well as their Tragedy. The *Toga* was the *Roman* Gown. Hence *Virgil*.

Romanos rerum Dominos Gentemque Togatam.

The *Tabernaria* or low Comedy, was so called from *Taberna* that properly signifies a shop, thereby implying, that the characters were drawn from low life; therefore the Poet to say he would not publish his works declares, they shall be found in no shop and on no shew-board,

Nulla taberna meos habeat neque pila libellos.

The * *Atellanæ Fabulæ*, seem to have been a mixture

---

* It is an obscure point of Criticism to determine justly, whether the *Romans* had Satirical Pieces, *Satiri*, as *Horace* calls them; or whether they altered their *Atellane* Plays, and made them in imitation of the *Greek* Satires. The latter is the opinion of *Diomedes* the Grammarian: His words follow, *Tertia est species Fabularum Latinarum, quæ à civitate Oscorum Atella, in primum cœptæ, Atellana dictæ sunt, Argumentis dictisque jocularibus similes Fabulis Græcis Satyricis.* There is a third species of *Roman* Comedy called *Atellane*, from *Atella*, a town in *Tuscany*, where they first began to be acted, and which in their subject and pleasantry of wit and humour are like the *Greek* satirical Plays. The only difference (adds the Critic) is this, that in the *Greek* Pieces were Satires or other buffoon characters, whereas in the *Atellanes* there was some lewd character, *Persona obscænæ*. *Vossius* corrects this reading, and says it should be read, *Personæ Oscæ*, *Tuscan* Characters; which I am the more inclinable to admit, because these obscene characters are said to have been more peculiar to the *Mimes*. But as one cannot imagine *Horace* would give rules for the Satires, if the *Romans* had none, we can have no other way to reconcile him with *Diomedes*, than by saying, that the *Romans* in time laid aside their *Tuscan* characters to introduce Satires in their *Atellane* Plays; which therefore must be considered as Tragi-Comedies, and not as Farces, an error *Horace* cautions against at large in his Art of Poetry. It is then to be supposed that like the *Greek* satirical Plays they were composed on the same subject with a Tragedy, after which they might be acted. And this is particularly agreeable to the precepts which *Horace* gives the writer of Satires. Some of those writers seemed to have mistaken the true character of this Poem, and to have confounded all rules of decency,

ture of Tragedy and Comedy, not unlike the *Greek* Satires: The Actors (as has been already hinted) were generally young gentlemen, who often took the liberty to retrench or add to their parts during the representation, just what they thought fit: Tho' perhaps this liberty may more properly be supposed to have been taken in the *Exodia* or Farces that were always acted after these Atellane Plays. Besides other privileges which *Livy* has mentioned, in the passage above quoted, we may add this; that the audience could not oblige them to unmask, an affront which was often put upon the other actors, though never so considerable. So we find *Laberius* a *Roman* Knight, a celebrated writer of Mimes (which were the lowest of dramatic entertainments, and wherein there seems to have been but one actor, who was generally the Author himself) was forced to unmask, and complains very handsomely of the affronts done him by *Cæsar*, who ow'd him a grudge for his bitter railleries against

decency, by a preposterous mixture of gravity and low ridicule in the characters, by making the Heroe, who in the Tragedy had appeared with all the dignity becoming his character, in the *Atellane* fall into the low humour and stile of the *Tabernariæ*; that sort of Comedy, whose characters were all low and ridiculous. By thus supposing the *Atellane* Plays and Satires in *Horace's* Art of Poetry to be the same thing, it may easily be presumed that the dignity of the Actors added to the great antiquity of this kind of Dramatic Poem, might make a man of *Horace's* fine taste, who studied so much to improve that of his Countrymen, think it worth his care to reduce this entertainment to a more elegant regularity than what had been practised before. There is a passage in *Cicero's* epistle to *Pætus*, which shews, that in his time the Poets were apt to make the *Atellanes* degenerate into *Mimes*, by introducing obscene characters in them; which is one of those faults *Horace* would have his writer of Satires avoid; *Nunc venio* (says *Cicero*) *ad jocationes tuas: quum te secundum Oenomaum Accii, non ut olim solebat, Atellanium, sed ut nunc fit, Mimum introduxisti*. I come now to your raillery, where after having cited the *Oenomaus*, "A Tragedy of the Poet *Accius*, "you have made, not a true Atellane, as was formerly the cus- "tom, but a perfect Mime, according to the common Practice "now-a-days." The *Atellanes* had a Chorus, which was what farther distinguished them from Comedies, and seems to argue their being like the *Greek* satirical pieces.

him.

him. This actor was so slightly shod as to appear almost bare-foot: hence he was called *Planipes*. The word *Mimi* comes from the *Greek* Μιμεῖσθαι, to imitate. There was another species of actors, who performed all in dumb shew: They were called *Pantomimes*. They were so excellent in their action, that they could represent entire Comedies and Tragedies, and were particularly in vogue under the twelve *Cæsars*: They studied the most lively expression of all the passions and sentiments by their gesticulation. *Bathyllus* and *Pilades* were two Pantomimes so highly considered in the time of *Augustus Cæsar*, that all *Rome* was divided into factions on their account. Upon complaint of this made to him, that Emperor sent for *Bathyllus*, and very much reproved him for being the occasion of such disturbances and divisions. The Player's answer spoke him a man of admirable sense, as well as great presence of mind: "Nothing could "happen better for *Cæsar*, than that the people "should always amuse themselves with the trifling "disputes of two Players." I leave the reader to make the application.

SECT. III.

Of some Particulars relating to the DRAMA *of the Antients.*

THERE were some circumstances peculiar to the *Greek* and *Roman* Stage, which come next to be explained, *viz.*

1. The BUSKIN, *Cothurnus*.
2. The SOCK, *Soccus*.
3. The MASK, *Persona*.
4. The CHORUS.
5. The FLUTES.

THE Buskin and Sock were such eminent marks of distinction between Tragedy and Comedy, that by a metaphor they are frequently made to express by

antient

antient Authors the sublime and low stile in all other compositions.

The Buskin, *Cothurnus*, is thought to have been a high square boot, which by raising the foot considerably, made the actors appear larger than the common size of men; such as the heroes were supposed to have been of old time: Besides their slow and solemn step, made them tread in a manner suitable to the state and solemnity of Tragedy.

The Sock was a more slight and easy covering for the foot, and rather proper to women; so that their being worn by the men is thought to have denoted the inferiority of the characters in Comedy to those in Tragedy: But I rather imagine, the lightness of these Socks might be the chief reason of their being used by the actors in Comedy.

The * Mask, *Persona*, is very pertinently derived by *A. Gellius* from *personare* to sound through, because their make was so contrived as to assist the voice, and make it sound with greater clearness and distinction. Madam *Dacier* was the first who observed in the draughts of a famous old manuscript of *Terence*, that theatrical Masks of the antients were not made like ours; for they had not only wide mouths, but came over the whole head, with a kind of peruke or hair fastened to them, proper to the age and character of the person the actor represented. But as that learned Lady might have said when she quoted the Fable, we need not recur to these draughts for a proof of this, since we have the positive authority of *Phædrus* for it. In the fable of the Fox and Masque, he makes *Renard* exclaim, speaking to the mask, *O quanta species cerebrum non habet!* What a fine head you have without brains! Which words can with no propriety be said of our common masks †.

And

---

* *Tully de Oratore* intimates, one could see the action of the very eyes distinctly through the mask.

† See *Plin. Nat. Hist.* Lib. 7. Cap. 53. where he speaks of *M. Ofilius Hillarius* a famous Comedian at an entertainment he made

And if the masks of the antients had not covered the whole head, it would have been absurd in *Phædrus* to alter *Æsop*'s manner, who relates the same of a carved head the Fox saw at a statuary's. But that ingenious freed-man of *Augustus* was too judicious not to consider what he did; and his alteration is certainly for the better, because of the mask's being hollow and having nothing within it, whereas the carved head was solid at least, tho' it had no brains: And as the theatrical masks were fitted up with great art to express the countenance and humour of the persons represented, this passage of *Phædrus* must be admitted as an unquestionable proof of that which the draughts above-mentioned very happily serve to confirm. The wide opening of the mask at the mouth, not only assisted the actor's voice, but according to the different manner of his striking the lips and breath against a thicker or thinner plate of brass, as the character to be represented required, enabled him very much to humour his voice agreeably to his subject: there being proper artists to instruct the young actor in this managment*. Such a strength and good ma-

---

made on his Birth-day, dying suddenly as he was looking at the mask he had that day worn, and which he set before him, and crowned with a garland. *Is cum populo admodum placuisset natali die suo, conviviumque haberet, edita cœna calidam in pultario poposcit; simulque personam, ejus diei acceptam intuens, coronam e capite suo in eam transtulit; tali habitu rigens, nullo sentiente donec accubantium proximus tepescere potionem admoneret.*

* *Quintilian* has observed, that the Actors had great variety of masks, which they had often changed both in Tragedy and Comedy. *Inst. L. 1. C. 1. Major in personis observatio est apud Comicos Tragicosque, multis enim utuntur & variis.* And a little lower the same great Critic goes on to observe of the Masks, *Itaque in iis, quæ ad scenam componantur fabulis, artifices pronunciandi a personis quoque affectus mutuantur, ut sit Niobe in tragœdia tristis, atrox Medea, attonitus Ajax, truculentus Hercules. In Comœdiis vero præter aliam observationem qua servi, lenones, parasiti, rustici, milites, vetulæ, meritriculæ, ancillæ, senes austeri ac mites, juvenes severi ac luxuriosi, matronæ, puellæ inter se discernuntur; patet ille, cujus præcipuæ partes sunt, quia interim concitatus, interim lenis est, altero, erecto, altero composito supercilio: Atque id ostendere maxime Latinis actoribus moris est, cum iis quas agunt partibus congruat.* Cap. 1. Lib. 7.

nagement

nagement of the voice was highly necessary on the *Greek* and *Roman* Stages. We have already said, their Plays were exhibited by the care of a proper magistrate, and their theatres were made to contain, not a small audience, but the greater Part of the inhabitants: For their Plays were acted only occasionally, at certain feasts, or at the funerals of great men; when they were represented with such circumstances of grandeur and magnificence as almost exceed the imitation of the most powerful states at present.

The Ædileship was the first office of distinction among the *Romans*. This magistrate was surveyor of the publick buildings, and had the care of exhibiting at his own charge shews and games to the people. As this office paved the way to those of the greatest power, which were only to be obtained by the favour and votes of the People, it was always exercised in a very splendid and liberal manner. *Julius Cæsar*, by his profusion and munificence when Ædile, wherein he spent almost his whole patrimony, seems to have beforehand, as it were, laid out for the Dictatorship. Under the Emperors, every thing of this kind was performed with yet more prodigality and pomp; so that the modern Stages cannot give us any tolerable idea of the antient Theatres. That of *Pompey* the Great, is said to have had places for 80,000 men besides the *Cavea*, or Pit, which was left for the vulgar to stand in, and in which at other times all kinds of Exercises were performed.

Now if we consider the extent of such a Theatre, and the distance of the greater part of the audience from the stage, and that the antients acted always by day-light, the scene being always laid in the street, or some open portico, the use and expediency of their masks will evidently appear: for the natural features of the face at such a distance, and without the help of false lights, could not appear distinguishable enough to express, in that lively manner that the antients required, their several characters on the stage. Besides, their extream nicety to adapt the masks to every

every several character, very much contributed to the entertainment of the audience; since hereby they could better imagine they saw the persons represented in the play, than we can, who are still apt to lose the character in the player. Thus we think of *Booth* and *Wilks*, when we should only consider *Shakespeare's Henry* the VIIIth and VIth: not to mention this other disadvantage of the same face appearing in the different characters of Prince and Pimp, Heroe and Villain, old and young. *Horace* makes *Æschylus* the first inventer of masks, but they received many improvements since.

THE Chorus is defined to be a company of actors, representing such an assembly of persons as might properly be supposed present, where the affair is transacted.

THE *Greek* Dramatic Poets were exact observers of the Chorus in Tragedy: but it seems the Poets soon found it needless in Comedy; the few remaining *Latin* Tragedies that go under *Seneca*'s name, are most of them faulty in this respect, and one of them has no Chorus at all. *Horace* gives the following rules for the behaviour of the Chorus. They were sometimes maids of honour, and ladies attending on princesses, courtiers, friends, Counsellors, &c. The Chorus likewise justified soliloquies, or rather made them not such: and these soliloquies and the part of the Chorus we know were the noblest parts of the Poem. The *Choragus*, or chief of the Chorus, must be a very good Actor, his part was set to the finest music, which accompanied his Declamation. But let us see *Horace*'s rules.

Actoris partes Chorus, officiumque virile
Defendat, neu quid medios intercinat Actus
Quod non proposito conducat & hæreat apte.
Ille bonis faveatque & concilietur amicis,
Et regat iratos, & amet peccare timentes.
Ille dapes laudet mensæ brevis, ille salubrem
Justitiam, legesque & apertis otia portis:

Ille

Ille tegat commiſſa: Deoſque precetur & oret,
Ut redeat miſeris, abeat Fortuna ſuperbis.
De Art. Poet.

The meaning of this will beſt be underſtood in proſe. "Let the Chorus act a part in the Play du-
"ring the acts, and be conſidered only as one *Dra-*
"*matis Perſona*; and in the interlude ſay nothing
"but what is agreeable to and connected with the
"ſubject: Let it expreſs great willingneſs to protect
"the good, to maintain and ſupport the intereſt of its
"friends, to pacify thoſe that are provoked to anger:
"It muſt be full of love: to ſuch as abhor and com-
"mit crimes, ſhould recommend ſobriety and tem-
"perance; and praiſe the excellent benefits that the
"ſtrict obſervation of juſtice beſtows on mankind.
"It muſt praiſe the happy attendants of peace and
"quiet; inviolably keep the ſecrets that it is intruſted
"with, and earneſtly pray the Gods to recall their
"bleſſings of proſperity and happineſs from the
"wicked, and mercifully to relieve the good that
"labour under affliction and diſtreſs." Thus we ſee the Chorus was to be one continued leſſon of the moſt ſublime morality.

At firſt Comedy had a Chorus as well as Tragedy, The licentiouſneſs of its ſatire, and the bitterneſs of its raillery, ſeem to have been the occaſion of its being forbid at *Athens*; I ſuppoſe about the time, when the old Comedy was laid aſide. I have *Horace* for my Author.

——————————*Choruſque*
Turpiter obticuit, ſublato jure nocendi.

The Flutes, *Tibiæ*, are generally reckoned one of the obſcureſt points of antiquity; and yet without ſome idea of their uſe, the very titles of *Terence*'s Plays are not to be underſtood. *Horace* only ſays, that during the ſimplicity of the earlieſt times, the Flutes gave a ſlender ſound, having but few holes; but that the luxury of his age had ſo increaſed the number of them, that it rival'd the trumpet's ſound;
and

and that the stringed instruments, *Fides*, had been improved much after the same manner.

> *Tibia non ut nunc orichalco vincta, tubæque*
> *Æmula, sed tenuis, simplexque foramine pauco.*
> *Aspirare & adesse choris erat utilis, atque*
> *Nondum spissa nimis complere sedilia flatu.*
> *Quo sane populus numerabilis, utpote parvus,*
> *Et frugi, castusque, verecundusque coibat.*
> *Postquam cœpit agros extendere victor, & urbem*
> *Latior amplecti murus: vinoque diurno*
> *Placari Genius festis impune diebus,*
> *Accessit numerisque modisque licentia major.*
> *Indoctus quid enim saperet, liberque laborum*
> *Rusticus, urbano confusus, turpis honesto?*
> *Sic priscæ motumque & luxuriam addidit arti*
> *Tibicen, traxitque vagus per pulpita vestem.*
> *Sic etiam fidibus voces crevere severis.*

SOME Commentators understand what is said in the last line, as meant only of the *Greek* Tragedies; but it is absurd to think *Horace* would mention it here, if he did not likewise mean it of the *Roman* Tragedies, which were accompanied sometimes by stringed as well as wind instruments. *Dio* expressly says, that *Nero* played on the harp in some Tragedies, and does not mention it as any innovation made by that prince in the music of Tragedy. It is notorious how that Emperor affected to excel in the execution of all the parts of a Musician, an Actor, and Poet.

INSTEAD of giving the Reader Madam *Dacier's* account of these flutes, which seems hardly intelligible, tho' it is counted the best we have had yet, let us try by a passage from *Donatus*, and another from *Diomedes*, if we shall be more successful in clearing this matter. *Donatus's* words follow from his fragment of Tragedy, &c. *Diverbia histriones pronunciabant, Cantica vero temperabantur modis non a poeta sed a perito artis musicæ factis. Neque enim omnia iisdem modis in uno cantico agebantur, sed sæpe mutatis, ut significant, qui tres numeros in Comediis ponunt, qui tres continent mutatos modos cantici illius. Qui hujuscemodi modos faciebant, nomen in principio fabulæ scriptoris & actoris superponebant. Hujusmodi adeo carmina ad tibias fiebant, ut his auditis, multi ex populo ante discerent quam fabulam acturi scenici essent, quàm omnino spectatoribus ipsis antecedens titulus pronunciaretur. Agebantur autem tibiis paribus aut imparibus, dextris aut sinistris. Dextræ autem & Lydiæ sua gravitate seriam Comœdiæ dictionem pronunciabant. Sinistræ & sarranæ acuminis levitate jocum in Comœdia ostendebant. Ubi autem dextrâ & sinistrâ acta fabula inscribebatur, mistim joci & gravitates denunciabantur.* Thus far the *Grammarian*. I shall have occasion afterwards to consider the former part of this passage, let us now particularly attend to what relates immediately to the Flutes. We find them here distinguished into right and left-handed. The right, which he calls *Lydian*, had few holes, and sent forth a low deep sound, and therefore accompanied the serious parts of the Play, to which their tone was suited. The left, which he calls *Sarrane*, had more holes, and yielded a clear, shrill, and louder sound, and were played upon during the more lively and pleasant scenes of comedy. When the scene was partly serious and partly merry, the Musicians plaid on both sorts occasionally, and then the play was said to be acted *tibiis imparibus*, with unequal Flutes; that is, some right, and some left handed. But if they us'd only right, or only left handed, it was then said to be perform'd *tibiis paribus dextris, aut sinistris*. Where the Numbers 1, 2, 3, are set to the titles of a Comedy, it denoted, that the Flutes were chang'd so often in the course of the play. This leads me to take notice of Madam *Dacier*'s mistake, who notwithstanding the clearness of what *Donatus* here says, thought the music was never chang'd during the course of the play's acting; and therefore being to account for the meaning of the words in the title of *Terence*'s plays,

plays, she understood them to signify, that the play was acted with flutes not suited to the subject itself, but to the occasion when the play was acted. For example, if a comedy was acted at the funeral games, then it would be accompanied with serious music; that is, right-handed Flutes, and so *vice versa*. But such a supposition is too absurd to be admitted. For how can one bear to imagine one hears an arch fellow joking upon the stage, whilst his declamation is accompanied by the heavy sound of a deep-ton'd Flute? Or at other times, to hear a grave story told, as one may say, to the tune of a *Scotch* jigg? But the Fact seems to be no more than this; that the Flutes were shifted with the scene, as in the *Heautontimorumenos*, or *Self Tormentor* of *Terence*, the melancholic scene between the two old fellows, which is the first in the play, was declaim'd, or acted with the grave, or right-handed Flutes, and other scenes that had a mixture of the serious and merry were accompanied by the right and left-handed Flutes together. This very observation will enable us to explain the title of the *Andrian*, which runs thus. *Acta Ludis Megalensibus, M. Fulvio, M. Glabrione, Ædilibus Curulibus, egerunt L. Ambivius Turpio, L. Attilius Prænestinus. Modos fecit Flaccus Claudii, tibiis paribus dextris & sinistris: & est tota Græca. Edita M. Marcello, C. Sulpicio Cass.* Here it is evident, that these words *Modos fecit Flaccus Claudii, tibiis paribus dextris & sinistris*——make one sense together, and can signify nothing else, but that *Flaccus*, the son of *Claudius*, had set the words of the *Andrian* to music, which was to be executed in some parts with right, and in others with left-handed Flutes. In the Life of *Terence* we shall take occasion to explain the rest of the title, which does not relate to the Flutes.

DIOMEDES the Grammarian mentions another distinction of Flutes, namely, that there was one sort of them to accompany the chorus, and another the soliloquies; for so we shall find *Cantica* to signify. But this must chiefly relate to Tragedy, whose music was more labour'd than that of Comedy. *Quando chorus canebat, choricis tibiis, id est choraulicis artifex concinebat: In Canticis autem Pythaules Pythicis respondebat.* This latter musician took great pains to excel in his art, striving to answer, that is, to equal the actor's voice, whom he accompanied: For so *responsabat*, a frequentative verb, must signify; and not that he answered the player, when he had done acting, by the music between the acts. I hope the attentive and learned reader will find this account of the Flutes more intelligible, when he has examin'd and compar'd it with the following account of the music of the antients, as far as it relates to the Drama.

SECT. IV.
Of the DRAMATIC MUSIC of the Antients.

WHAT is here said will be only historical, without pretending to any knowledge of this art in particular. However, something of this kind I thought might be expected, as necessary to clear up several difficulties, and seeming absurdities relating to the conduct of the Theatre of the Antients.

THEIR notion of music, as an Art, was infinitely more extensive than ours. For under this name they included the whole art of elocution and action as reducible to rules, and taught by method. Thus dancing, declaiming, and gesticulation, fell under the general head of music, as well as singing and music now properly so call'd.

THE saltation or dancing of the Antients was characterized, and not meerly composed, as ours, of motions form'd to give grace and freedom to the body. It comprehended all the art of gesture and theatrical action, which is rather executed by the face and hands, than the feet. The misunderstanding of this has occasion'd the wrong translations of many passages in antient Authors, who have taken the word

Saltatio

which, he was also further regulated by the Flutes that accompanied him. Something like this method is to this day observed by the *Jews* in the musical accents that are set over the words in the Bible, by which, the People, who from their infancy are taught the use of them, chaunt the service in the proper manner in their synagogues.

THE Antients divided their music into hypocritical and metrical. The hypocritical taught to follow the measure and time in acting; the metrical, to observe both in singing and declaiming. *Numeros musicæ duplices habet* (says *Quintilian*) *in vocibus & in corpore.* Lib. 1. C. 10. It should seem from another passage in the Rhetorician, that there was a particular person who beat time with his foot on the stage, and that the music regulated both the Actor and him that declaimed. *Atqui corporis motui sua quædam tempora, & ad signa pedum non minus saltationi quam modulationibus adhibet ratio musica numeros.* Lib. 11. C. ult. And to this purpose we find *Seneca* admiring that the actors could be so exact to adapt their motions so well to the time of the words and music. But this would not be half so extraordinary, if the same man was to execute both. *Mirari solemus Scenæ peritos, quod in omnem significationem rerum & affectuum parata illorum est manus, & verborum velocitatem gestus assequitur.* Epist. 121. But *Livy* in his account of the first institution of Scenic Games, has expresly mentioned this division of the Action and Declamation. Let us again consider that part of it, which mentions so extraordinary a particular. Speaking of *Livius Andronicus*, he says, *Idem scilicet quod omnes tunc erant, suorum carminum actor, dicitur, cum sæpius revocatus vocem obtudisset, venia petita puerum ad canendum ante Tibicinem cum statuisset, cantiam egisse aliquanto magis vigente motu, quia nihil vocis usus impediebat. Inde ad manum cantari Histrionibus cœptum, diverbiaque tantum ipsorum voci relicta.* The only difficulty of this passage consists in the meaning of the words *Canticum & diverbia*.

We

We find this removed by *Diomedes* the Grammarian, who explains them as follows. *Membra Comœdiarum tria sunt, Diverbium, Canticum, & Chorus. Diverbia sunt partes Comœdiarum, in quibus diversorum personæ versantur; in Canticis autem una tantum debet esse persona, aut si duæ fuerint, ita debent esse, ut ex occulto una audiat & eloquatur, sed secum si opus fuerit verba faciat.* Lib. 3. Cap. 4. Here it is plain, the Dialogue is called *Diverbia*, and the Monologue or Soliloquy *Canticum*; and that *Canticum* does not signify a Song, or the music between the intervals of the acts, as some commentators have absurdly imagined. *Livy*'s words, *cantare ad manum*, directly intimate, that one comedian sung to the other's hand, that is to his action. The actor, as we there find, was the principal comedian. The singer was a person instructed for the purpose, and as the Historian observes, placed in the back part of the stage just before the Musician. *Macrobius* has a passage very much to our present purpose, by which we learn, that *Roscius*, that celebrated comedian, chiefly excelled in this dumb action: for *Cicero* used to contend with this player, with whom he was very intimate, who could best express any sentiment or passion, the orator by his eloquence, or the comedian in his Action, *Et certe satis constat contendere eum cum Histrione solitum, utrum ille sæpius eandem sententiam variis gestibus efficeret* (I would read, *effingeret*) *an ipse per eloquentiæ copiam sermone diverso pronunciaret.* SATURN. Lib 2. Cap. 10.

But, as this circumstance must appear strange to us, notwithstanding *Livy*'s authority, let us see if *V. Maximus*, who gives an account of the same thing, cannot convince us beyond all possibility of doubt. Speaking of *Livius Andronicus*, he says, *Is sui operis actor, cum sæpius a populo revocatus, vocem obtudisset, adhibito pueri & tibicinis concentu gesticulationem tacitus peragit.* (Lib. 2. Cap. 4.) That is, being the Actor of his own Play, and his voice growing hoarse by the people's often recalling him to act some parts over again, he made use of a boy or servant, who sung or declaimed in concert with the flute, whilst he himself silently acted his part, that is, executed all the gesticulations. And *Donatus*, as quoted in the last section, says, the comedians themselves pronounced the dialogues, but the cantiques were set to music, modulated, not by the poet, but by some able musician. Perhaps it may be meant here that the poet, who accented his play for the direction of the actor in his declamation, left the cantiques or monologues unnoted, which were set to music by some able master in the art. But the part of the singer or declaimer became afterwards so considerable, that somewhat before *Isidore*'s time, about the 4th century, the Poets themselves affected to pronounce or sing the monologues, whilst the player acted. *Ibi Poetæ, Comœdi & Tragœdi ad certamen descendebant, iisque canentibus, alii gestus edebant.* ORIGEN. Lib. 1. Cap. 44. We may add another Passage from *Suetonius*, concerning *Caligula*, who was so passionately fond of acting and declaiming that he could not forbear at the public spectacles, pronouncing the part aloud with the declaimer, and acting along with the player, who executed the gesticulation. *Canendi ac saltandi voluptate ita efferebatur, ut ne publicis quidem spectaculis temperaret, quo minus & Tragœdo pronuntianti concineret, & gestum histrionis effingeret.* It is observable, that *Suetonius* here distinguishes the declaimer from the actor, and declaiming from acting. *Ovid* has also used the word *saltare* for acting, in answer to his friend's letter, who had sent him word that his Tragedy named *Medea*, a Play much admired by the Antients, met with great approbation during the representation: he says,

Carmina cum pleno saltari nostra Theatro
Versibus & plaudi scribis, amice, meis.
De Ponto. Lib. 5. El. 7.

And *A. Gellius*, to intimate that long before his time the

this more composite manner? From *Andronicus*'s first introducing it to the reign of *Honorius*, when it was still practised, they had had the experience of near seven hundred years, and yet found no reason to alter it. We should therefore mistrust our own judgments a little, and not hastily condemn a practice that seems strange to us. Their great progress in all arts, poetry, painting, sculpture, oratory, architecture, &c. should prevail with us to think favourably of their judgment in this particular. Persons of the highest rank appeared on the *Greek* stage; and though the *Romans* were more reserved in this respect, we know that from their first condition of slaves, good actors have been able to raise themselves immense riches, and purchase their freedom during the commonwealth, and they grew much more considerable under the Emperors, when it became the general complaint, that players, freedmen, and such upstarts ran away with all honours and places of profit, and engrossed the prince's favour. One must never have read *Tacitus* and *Juvenal*, not to mention many other authors, to doubt the truth of what is here advanced. Let this teach us to suspend our censures, and to be not so ready to condemn every thing that is out of our own way of thinking and practice.

LET us now examine the notion of the antient Plays being noted, and partly set to music. The word *Carmen* properly signifies a Song or Poem set to music. So *Ovid*, above quoted, used it to mean his *Medea* a tragedy. And *Cicero*, speaking of a tragedy, says, Præclarum Carmen, est enim rebus, verbis & modis lugubre. (*Tuscul. Quæst. L 5.*) Rebus, means the subject or composition of the fable; verbis, the expressions; modis, the music fitted to the words, or the words set to music. More could not be said of one of *Handel*'s Opera's if the poetical part of those compositions were equal to his excellent music.

WE have already seen *Livy*'s account, which is full to this purpose, and the Reader may turn to it again if he please.   LET

LET me observe in this place, that, if the critics, who condemn the Antients for the many soliloquies in their Plays, had known the reason for this practice of theirs, they would have with-held their censures. The continual presence of the Chorus, we have before alledged as a sufficient justification of soliloquies in tragedy, which thereby are rendered, indeed, not so. Another inducement to the frequent use of them, we find, must have been, to adorn the whole performance by the excellency of the Music which accompanied the more labour'd declamation of the soliloquies. *Cantica*, says *Diomedes, temperabantur modis, non a poeta, sed a perito artis musicæ factis.* The Poets did not set the *Cantics* themselves to music, but employ'd some skilful artists to compose the music. It hence seems plain, the Poets noted the dialogue part themselves, as coming within their sphere, the music being here more simple, and low, and serving only, as it were, to assist the actor's voice, in the just expression of the tones and accents, which in *Latin*, are said to have been ten, according to *Priscian*, of which he gave the marks, but that work of his is lost. *Sergius*, the Grammarian, reckons eight only. *Tenores*, says he, *sive accentus dicti sunt, qui naturalem uniuscujusque sermonis in vocem nostræ elationis tenorem servant. Dictus autem accentus est, quasi ad cantus; sunt omnes Latini accentus octo.* *Quintilian* proves, that they who compos'd the music for the plays, did not barely compose the music to distinguish acts, as has been falsly imagin'd, but to accompany the declamation. * In those plays that are compos'd for the stage, (that is, whose music is composed) the masters of the art of declaiming have a strict regard to every character. The *Latin* says, borrow'd the affections (that is, of their composition) from the masks.

---

* *In iis, quæ ad scenam componuntur fabulis, artifices pronunciandi a peritis quoque affectus mutuantur.* Inst. Orat. L. 11. C. 3.

I cannot but think it probable too, that the Poets in the order in which they placed their words, had some regard to the music that accompanied the declamation, and this more in the cantiques than the dialogues, more in tragedy than comedy. *Horace* blames this luxurious improvement of the numbers.

Accessit numerisque modisque licentia major.

The Poet would never put *numeri* and *modi* together, if they had not an immediate influence on each other. But I should never have done, if I would go on with observations of this kind, that prove the Plays being acted to music among the Antients. But to return. *Lyrick* poetry also, which was allowed the greatest variety of numbers, and the bold transpositions to be met with in the odes, both *Greek* and *Latin*, may reasonably be thought, in a great measure, owing to the poet's skill in music. And * *Cicero* says to this purpose, of *Roscius*, that this great master of action intended, as he grew in years, to make the musicians soften their notes and slacken the composition of the Cantiques for the ease of his action: For the declamatory part, we find, was executed by another. And we have already seen, that *Roscius*'s talent lay in dumb shew, and that he would often contend with *Cicero*, who could best express a circumstance, he, by the force of action, or *Cicero* by that of eloquence. † He elsewhere observes, that such as had a little skill in music knew by the beginning of the ouverture what play was a going to be acted. This we can do at our Operas too, because the music is part of the Drama. But at the play-house, no body knows by the first, second, or third music, what play is to be acted, but by the bills; because it is arbitrary, and has no relation to the play that is to

---

* *Solet idem Roscius dicere, se, quo plus sibi ætatis accederet, eo tibicinis modos, & cantus remissiores esse facturum*, De Oratore L. 1.

† *Quam multa, quæ nos fugiunt in cantu, exaudiunt in eo genere exercitati: Qui primo inflatu Tibicinis, Antiopam esse aiunt aut Andromacham, cum nos ne suspicamur quidem.* Academ. Quæst. L. 4.

follow.

follow. * In another place he remarks, That some verses, even in tragedy, had such bad numbers, that, but for their being set to music, (accompanied by the flute, in *Latin*) there would be no distinguishing them from Prose. These passages prove, that comedy and tragedy had their proper measures, tho' they were sometimes too much neglected.

This may serve to justify *Horace* in censuring the negligence of *Plautus* in the metre of his verses, but in what particulars this negligence most appear'd, and why, according to *Quintilian* trimeters were best, is hard to discover, unless we had a more particular knowledge of the manner of the Antients in noting and declaiming their comedies. But it is at the same time evident, that *Varro, Priscian, Donatus, Asper, Juba, Scaurus, Probus* and *Sulpitius*, all great grammarians, would never have applied themselves to find out the metre of *Terence* and *Plautus*'s verses, had they understood no more of it than our modern critics can. As these antient grammarians were all acquainted with music, which *Quintilian* lays down as a knowledge essentially necessary to the grammarian, they were able to find and restore the misplacing of a word in a verse much more readily by the help of the musical intonation and accents. And yet if the matter was so obscure in *Priscian*'s time, that he says, there were several, who denied that *Terence* had any metre, and others pretended they alone had the secret key of them, and that none but themselves could pretend to measure his verses, it is a little hard to conceive how our critics, let them be persons never so distinguished by their learning and great abilities, can come nearer the truth than those antient grammarians.

Some indeed have had a conceit, that they should soonest attain to the truth, by taking it for granted, that the comic Poets used those measures that were most agreeable to the subject, as we find *Virgil* has

---

* *Quae, nisi cum Tibicen accesserit, sunt orationi solutae simillima.* De Orat.

very succesfully done in many places. But it has been observ'd by succeeding criticks, that when they came to examine the Comedies of *Plautus* and *Terence* by this rule, it only served to confound, and lead them into new intricacies.

LET it suffice us from such imperfect notions as antiquity has left, to have proved the fact, both as to this and other particulars which we have had occasion to take notice of under this head of the theatrical musick of the Antients.

SUCH as are well acquainted with the state of antient *Greece* and *Rome*, do not wonder at their elaborate study of every artifice capable of adding life and ornament to their declamation: The genius of the people easily moved by every passion, supported by a great vivacity and quickness of conception, as they continue to this day, though oppressed by ignorance, slavery, and superstition: This disposition, I say, made eloquence lead the way to the highest honours; and even under the Emperors, the Sovereign studied to recommend or palliate his conduct, by a graceful and eloquent manner of speaking in publick: and it was no small reproach even to *Nero*, that he was forced to employ others to compose his harangues for him. Eloquence in pleading at the bar was so fashionable even in *Horace*'s time, that he mentions it as a becoming ornament in the character of a pretty fellow.

> *Namque & nobilis & decens,*
> *Et pro solicitis non tacitus reis,*
> *Et centum Puer artium*
> *Late signa feret militiæ tuæ.*   Lib 4. Od. 1.

SECT. V.

Of Dramatic Fiction and Imitation.

THE foundation of Dramatic Poetry is not barely imitation, which it has in common with all other kinds, but probable fiction, or a well-invented fable.

fable. I need not say much in justification of fiction: the best writers have often employed it to make the strongest impressions, and to convey the most important truths. The *Greeks* always began the education of their children by it; their first theology and philosophy was concealed under it. *Strabo* in his first book has a fine passage that makes to this purpose. " In the first place (says that judicious wri-
" ter) Poets are not alone in the use of fables:
" Critics and Lawgivers have done so long before
" them, both for their usefulness and in conformity
" to the natural inclination of a rational creature.
" Man is willing to learn, and fable opens him the
" way. By this our children begin to hearken to
" what we say; the reason of which is, that fable is
" a kind of a new story, not of what really is, but
" of something very different. Now nothing de-
" lights the understanding more, than what is new
" and strange, and it is this makes us love the
" sciences. Therefore if you add the wonderful
" and marvellous to fable, that infinitely increases
" our delight, which is the first inducement to learn.
" It is therefore highly proper to make use of fable,
" to draw the tender minds of children to the love
" of knowledge; and when they are more advanced
" in years, and their understanding has gathered
" strength, so that there is no longer occasion to
" caress and indulge them, then let them be intro-
" duced into the real sciences, and taught to know
" things by what they are." Thus far *Strabo*.

It is certainly true, that the strong propensity to imitation, which nature has implanted in us, is the source of all study and application. This disposition gives fiction, which is only a happy imitation of what might probably happen, a great advantage over truth itself, which being artless, and of ordinary occurrence, has less power to excite and keep up our attention. Besides, in a just imitation one discovers that subtilty and address in the contrivance, which by setting the mind upon making proper reflections,

puts

puts it in the way to discover something new: And according to *Aristotle* (Rhet. Lib. 1. Cap. 11.) the pleasure we take in seeing a just imitation, does not arise from the beauty of the original imitated, but from the mind's thereby finding the means to reason and instruct itself agreeably. Hence some philosophers very justly argued against the Epicureans, when they maintained, that the pleasure people take at shews can arise neither from the sense of hearing nor seeing, but from the mind only, which understands and judges. An instance from painting will illustrate *Aristotle*'s position. Most grotesque figures, that please by their ridiculous deformity in a picture, would give disgust in the originals. So monsters, and other hideous shapes, that we can consider without emotion, upon the canvas, and in colours, would, if they were really present, fill us with horror and aversion. But to return to fiction.

As it is the soul of all Poetry, but particularly the dramatic and epic, so it is that which makes the most essential difference between the historian and the poet. *Aristotle* (Poet. Cap. 9.) seems to have established this truth. Should any one, says the Philosopher, put *Herodotus*'s history into verse, it would be but a history still. Here then is the difference. The historian describes what has happen'd, and the poet, what might, or ought to come to pass. So that poetry is more grave and moral than history, because the former says general things, and the latter only particulars. A general thing is what every man, of such a certain character, should probably say or do, &c. This is the very method which poetry follows, when it gives proper names to its characters. A particular thing is what *Alcibiades*, for instance, has actually said, or done, &c. This most evidently appears in comedy; (meaning the middle *Greek* comedy) for the comic poets having formed the plan of their subject agreeable to probability, impose what names they please afterwards upon their characters, not imitating the satirists, who apply them to particulars.

of the real adventures of those persons to their fiction, and extract such ingenious episodes from them, as very much heighten the probability of the whole, and make it sometimes pass with the audience for a true history.

SECT. VI.

Of Tragedy, according to Aristotle.

HIS *Art of Poetry* is so celebrated a piece of criticism, that I thought to speak of tragedy and comedy without taking notice of his account of them, would be looked upon as presumption, though I doubt his concise and metaphysical manner of treating the subject may not be agreeable to the generality of readers; they may pass this Section over.

The Philosopher (*Cap. 6. Poet.*) defines Tragedy to be, The imitation of an important and compleat action, of a just extent with a suitable stile, properly varied in the several parts, which, without the help of narration (whereby it is chiefly distinguished from an Epic Poem) by the means of terror and compassion, purges those and all other the like passions in us.

By a suitable stile he understands verse, number, and harmony, and properly varied, refers to verse being the principal in one part, and number and harmony in the other.

This imitation (says the Philosopher) being made by such as carry on an action, it necessarily follows, that the decorations of the scene are in some sort a part of Tragedy, as well as the melody and discourse with which the imitation is made. Discourse is the composition of the verses, and melody the music.

Tragedy therefore has these six parts; the Fable, the Manners, the Sentiments, the Language, the Music, and Decoration.

Tragedy is the imitation of some action, and they who do any action are necessarily what they are by their manners and sentiments, which are the causes of men's happiness or misery. The

THE imitation of an action is properly the Fable; by Fable is meant the composition of matters.

THE Manners are that which points out the qualities of those who do an action, and the sentiments are the discourse, by which those persons make any action known or whereby they discover their thoughts. After having proved that the good constitution of the Fable is principally to be considered in Tragedy, our great critic proceeds thus.

THE Manners come next, with which it is, as in painting; for should a painter lay confusedly the finest colours upon the canvas, it would not please so much as the out-lines or sketch of a picture. So as Tragedy is the imitation of some action, it must principally be the imitation of those who do the action.

Aristotle's meaning is, That if the characters are not well marked, so that all that the persons of the Drama say or do be consistent with the characters given them, the rest is only confusion, as not relating to or being contrary to the subject; For the manners (continues the Philosopher) are that which discovers the inclinations of him that speaks, and what measures he intends to take on any occasion, where it would else be difficult to know them. So that all such discourse as does not immediately tend to unfold the designs of him who speaks, are without the manners.

THE sentiments explain what is, or what is not; that is, discover to us the thoughts of him who speaks.

THE fourth thing, which only regards the discourse, is the Diction, which is the explanation of things by words, and has the same power in prose and verse.

THE fifth is the Music, which is the greatest and most agreeable ornament Tragedy can employ.

THE Decoration is the last, but does not properly regard the Poet, nor make a part of Dramatic Poetry, but concerns other artists.

I shall not trouble the reader with a larger extract from *Aristotle*'s Poetics; this may suffice to give an idea of his method.

SECT.

SECT VII.

Of the Measures of DRAMATIC POETRY.

AS the mind of man is formed for imitation, it is also pleased with numbers and harmony. This taste for harmony taught the *Greeks* to distinguish different measures for different kinds of Poetry. The Hexameter was found fit for Epic or Heroic Poetry; the Sapphic, Alcaic, Phaleucian, &c. for Lyric Poetry; and the Iambic for Tragedy. And though *Strabo* says, verse was more ancient than prose, among the *Greek* Writers, yet the appropriating certain measures to certain kinds of Poetry, was of a much later date. *Homer* seems to have been the first, who fixed the hexameter verse for epic Poetry. *Aristotle* has observed, that his *Margites*, a comic Satire, which *Homer* composed before the *Iliad*, was an irregular mixture of several measures, possibly not unlike the old Saturnian verses in use among the old *Roman* Poets before *Ennius*.

Thespis among the other improvements he made in the infancy of the *Athenian* stage, chose the Iambic measure as fittest for dialogue. The Tetrameter had been used in the old satirical pieces before. Comedy used the Iambic trimeter as well as tragedy, but not so strictly, as running nearer to prose: Nay trimeter itself was chosen for the same reason, as of all regular and measured verse coming nearest to the language of conversation. *Archilochus* a satiric Poet was the first inventer of the Iambic measure. *Horace* speaks of it as follows.

Archilochum proprio rabies armavit Iambo.
Hunc Socci cepere pedem grandesque Cothurni;
Alternis aptum sermonibus, & populares
Vincentem strepitus & natum rebus agendis.
                    De Arte Poet. ver. 79:

Archilochus first us'd Iambics keen,
As a fit measure to convey his spleen,

Both

Both Sock and Buskin since adopt this foot,
As sounding clearly through the people's shout,
And form'd dramatic Action well to execute.

Aristotle having observed how fit this measure is for the stage, by its coming so near to prose, adds, That the Hexameter verse was very seldom to be found in *Greek* prose, as the Iambic was; so that dramatic writers had good reason to prefer the Iambic to all other measures, as fittest for the stage.

SECT. VIII.
Of COMEDY.

ARISTOTLE (*Cap.* 5.) has said but little of Comedy; I shall therefore join some of my own observations with his concerning this branch of dramatic Poetry.

THE Philosopher's definition of Comedy is very short and obscure: he calls it, An imitation of bad men; but he explains himself, saying, That by bad men he means not persons guilty of all or the greatest vices, but such vices as are capable of ridicule. " Ridicule (says he) is properly a defect or defor- " mity without pain, which does not tend to the " destruction of the subject in which it exists: for in- " stance, we call that a ridiculous countenance which " is disagreeable and mishapen, without being pain- " ful to the person that is made ridiculous by it." Thus far *Aristotle*.

THE changes the *Greek* Comedy underwent in its infancy, have not been discovered to us so well as those of Tragedy; for it was late before the magistrate began to defray the charge of exhibiting Comedies. Those who acted them before were free and voluntary actors, who had no dependance upon, nor encouragement from the state.

THE contrary seems to have happened among the *Romans*, who I believe had their Atellane plays and
Exodia

Exodia or Farces acted almost to perfection, before Tragedy was much cultivated among them.

The first improvers of the *Greek* Comedy had nothing to do, but to borrow from Tragedy such theatrical ornaments as were proper to their subject and design; and this may be a reason why what was done by them in this part, has been so little taken notice of, whilst we have several particulars of such improvements of Tragedy.

Epicharmus and *Phormis* are said to be the first that laid aside the old satiric dialogue, to form a subject, and lay the plan of the old Comedy, which, though not properly of the Poet's invention, as exposing real characters and persons, was, however, fashioned and cast into what form the Poet judged fittest to cast a ridicule on his characters. Thus the *Athenians* were beholden to the *Sicilians* for the first plan of Comedy. *Crates*, an *Athenian*, took the hint, and composed several pieces with success. He flourished about the 82d *Olympiad*, near 45 years before *Aristophanes* published his first Comedy; and some of his last pieces come very near the regularity of the new Comedy. Thus we find Comedy attained not its perfection in so few years as Tragedy. *Aristophanes* began to flourish the 4th year of the 94th *Olympiad*: And *Menander* flourished the beginning of the 123d *Olympiad*, which is an interval of 72 years. *Epicharmus* was not many years after *Thespis*, though at first he applied himself to philosophy, and was an old man before he wrote any Comedies. He was born at *Coos*, but was brought into *Sicily* at three months old, which is the reason so many authors have thought him a *Sicilian*. *Hiero*, tyrant of *Sicily*, having forced him to quit the publick teaching of the *Pythagorean* philosophy, he first rehearsed on the stage some of the doctrines of his philosophy, which he couched in verse, and afterwards set himself to write Comedies, which he did to the number of 52, according to *Suidas*. *Meursius* has collected the titles of 40 of them; and there are some sentences out

of

of them extant among the fragments of the old comic writers. *Phormis* was cotemporary with *Epicharmus*, and had the instructing of *Gelo* the tyrant's sons. He was a native of *Syracuse*. These old comedies of *Phormis* were written in so grave a stile, that some critics, by their fragments, have mistaken him for a tragic writer, contrary to the testimony of *Aristotle*, and all antiquity. C. 5. Poet.

Eupolis flourished about the 92d *Olympiad*, being an imitator of *Cratinus*, who was cotemporary with *Crates*. It is reported by some writers, that *Alcibiades*, during his great power at *Athens*, ordered the Poet to be cast into the sea, for having expos'd him in one of his comedies. And *Ælian* says, That *Ephialtes*, a slave of *Eupolis*, running away from his master with some plays which he had stolen, was seized and killed by *Eupolis*'s dog. *Suidas* says, that *Euetes* and *Euxenides* published some comedies at *Athens*, at the same time that *Epicharmus* published his at *Syracuse*. But if this were a fact well proved, *Aristotle*, where he enquires into the antiquity of comedy, would not have allowed the *Syracusans* the honour of its invention.

Menander and *Philemon* were cotemporaries. *Philemon* is said to have lived to upwards of an hundred years, and died of an immoderate fit of laughter. Both *Quintilian* and *Gellius* are surprized the *Athenians* should so often prefer *Philemon*'s Plays to *Menander*'s, who meeting *Philemon*, after the judges had decreed him the prize, said; *Tell me truly, Philemon, did not you blush yourself to bear the Prize from me?* *Menander* was the scholar of *Theophrastus*, and born the third year of the 109 *Olympiad*, and died the 4th year of the 131. *Menander* made no scruple to imitate the best comic writers that had preceded him. He wrote 108 comedies: or, according to *Apollodorus*, 105; yet gained the prize but eight times.

O saeclum insipiens & infacetum.

SECT. IX.

Of the Efficacy of DRAMATIC POETRY, *in purging the Passions:* PLATO's *Objections against it answer'd, and the Usefulness of a well regulated Stage asserted.*

THE great End of Tragedy, according to *Aristotle*, is to purge the Passions, as he calls it. This contradicts *Plato*'s opinion, who condemns Tragedy for exciting the Passions. Let us see how these two great men may be reconciled, and Tragedy justified. Had we *Aristotle*'s second Book of Poetry, wherein he has fully cleared this matter, as he declares in his politics, we should not be under any difficulties. The immediate words of the definition are; "Which, "by the means of terror and compassion, purges "these passions, and all others of the like nature "in us."

First, Let us explain the term, *To purge the Passions.* The academic, and after them the stoick Philosophers have used this expression, to signify a driving out and extirpating of the Passions. But Tragedy cannot be said to purge them in a sense which exceeds its power. The peripatetics, or followers of *Aristotle*, being persuaded, that it is the excess of the Passions which renders them vicious, and that when regulated they become useful and necessary, mean, by purging the Passions, to remove that excess by which they are bad, and to reduce them to a just moderation. This is the end which Tragedy proposes, and the only one in which it can succeed. It is easy to shew how it excites terror and compassion in our breasts, in order to purge these Passions. It is done, by setting before us the misfortunes which men have been plunged into by involuntary faults, and by making them familiar to us, teaches us not to apprehend such misfortunes too much when they befall us,

and

and how they may, in some measure, be avoided. The Emperor *Antoninus* has a fine reflection to this purpose, in the 6th Article of the 11th Book. "Tragedies, (says that excellent moralist) were first introduced to put men in mind of the many accidents that happen in life, and to give them notice, that such accidents must of necessity happen; and to teach them, that those calamities which entertain them on the stage, ought not to be thought insupportable in the great theatre of the world." But secondly, by purging these passions, it also purges such other passions in us, as might lead us into the like misfortunes. For instance, who could see the Tragedy of *Oedipus*, *Sophocles*'s I mean, and not learn to correct in himself all rashness and blind curiosity, which are the immediate causes of the dreadful calamities that Prince suffered, and not any deliberate crimes? This seems to be *Aristotle*'s meaning in his definition, and this should be the design of Tragedy, as a fable or fiction: since all fables were intended to form the manners by proper instructions, concealed under the allegory of some action.

It is now time to consider *Plato*'s objections. The power of theatrical representations seemed so great to him, that he excluded them and their composers from his ideal commonwealth. Epic poetry was involved in the same censure. "Epic and dramatic writers, says he, give us no description of a wise man's character; do not set forth that inward tranquillity of mind, which enables him to maintain an even temper, undisturbed by pleasure or pain." So far *Plato* is right. A philosopher, stripped of his Passions, would make but a dull figure on the stage. He goes on to observe, that the poets exhibit to us men given up to strong desires, and commonly made a prey to the violent agitations of some darling Passion; or, at best, struggling with it. It is confessed that Poets are so well convinced of the necessity and influence of this practice here condemned, that as soon as the agitation and anxiety is over,

over, and it is clearly determined whether the person's conduct has render'd him happy or miserable, he disappears. The cause of that affecting pleasure the audience felt, to hear and see a great man struggling with his Passions, and to mark all the fatal consequences attending their too prevailing power over him, no longer subsisting when his fate is once fully decided.

The best way to take off the force of this objection of *Plato*'s, I conceive, may be to shew a little more fully the several degrees by which Dramatic Poetry recommends itself to us as useful in the regulating our Passions.

We can generally make but imperfect guesses at the true motive of men's actions, and very rarely penetrate to the bottom of their designs. That which breaks out, and appears as a spark, is often produced by a fire that burns furiously within. So that, on the one hand, we too often deceive ourselves, when we imagine we have discovered men's real intent, and men as often deceive us on the other, when they pretend to inform us of the true situation of their minds.

But theatrical persons pull off their mask to the spectators, making them the confidents of their most secret views and intentions. If they leave any thing for conjecture, it is what the judicious part of the audience cannot possibly fail to discover. And this is true both of Tragedy and Comedy. But further.

The Poet's design engages him to describe the Passions, and their Effects, just as they really are, without exaggeration. His method of instruction is the clearest and surest, that of example, and what may fully convince us, that the picture is truly drawn, many cannot help discovering their own character, every man finds his neighbours in some character or other of the stage.

A faithful picture of the Passions is of itself sufficient to make us fear them, and take a full resolution to avoid them. I chuse to instance from some of our own Tragedies, as most generally known. Who that has seen or read the *Orphan*, but dreads the sad effects of an indiscreet reserve, occasioned by love and jealousy. *Castalio*'s and *Polydor*'s ruin are the fatal consequences of this error in the former; whilst *Polydor*'s blind passion thinking to enjoy *Monimia* in *Castalio*'s place, makes him defile his brother's marriage-bed, and be unawares guilty of adultery and incest. When we are present at such representations, do we not promise ourselves not to give way to the like Passions; and wish *Castalio* had been more sincere, *Polydor* more cautious, and *OEdipus* more discreet? Do not the characters of *Pyrrhus* and *Orestes*, in the *Distressed Mother*, shew all the force of a violent and blind love. The former forgets his interest and dignity, and most solemn engagements, injures a fair Princess, to whom he was betrothed, to marry the widow of his most deadly enemy; *Orestes* forgets the ties of honour, justice and hospitality, and, hoodwinked by his Passion, assassinates a Prince, to whom he was sent ambassador, in the temple, and at the very altar of the Gods. *Hermione* employs a man she despises, tempting him with hopes of marriage, to murther the man she loves, prompted at once by pride and jealousy to be revenged on him who could neglect her for another. In short, every well written Play is pregnant with such instances, which the reasonable part of the audience will apply to their own hearts, and there form such resolutions, as may be of use to them in the conduct of their lives.

There is another thing we may learn from the stage, that all the Passions burn faintly at first, and would soon be extinguished, if by a just diffidence of ourselves, we were determined to fly from such objects as we know to be apt to inflame them.

Tragedy proposes, that all the passions it describes in the characters of the stage should move and affect, but does not mean that this emotion of the audience should be the same with that of the person on the stage, who is tormented by some Passion;

nor does Tragedy design they should espouse his sentiments. Most commonly its aim is to excite sentiments altogether opposite to those that are exhibited in the play.

When *Medea*, to be revenged on *Jason* for leaving her, murders her own children by him in a fury of revenge, the picture is so drawn as to give the audience a just horror for the passion of revenge, which is capable of carrying a mother to such unnatural extremities.

The Poet would raise the affection of his audience only to virtuous characters, and there only what is praise-worthy is to be commended. We pity their errors whilst we resolve to avoid them.

Comedy has its efficacy in the same manner. Avarice, knavery, debauchery, coquetry, vanity, rusticity, &c. are ridiculed in Comedy, to make men hate those vices and imperfections, and thus it becomes useful in a lower degree to restrain the follies and vices of common life, which are often not taken notice of, and sometimes not understood by the speculative philosopher: yet, when become habitual to a people, they prove destructive of the peace and happiness of society, and tend to the subversion of the state. Every one's reflection may furnish him with instances of this kind both antient and modern, when certain vices and follies that escaped the censure of the magistrate, whose power is limited within the compass of the laws, have been successfully ridiculed and laughed out of countenance on the stage. But the Poet who makes his Hero in Comedy a successful rake, a triumphant debauchee, openly affronts the sense as well as manners of his audience. For the lewd villain that invades the bed of his friend, or debauches his daughter, will be as jealous as any man to guard his own honour, and preserve his family from shame and disgrace.

In great and flourishing states, Comedy under proper regulations may do good service. Many villanies as well as follies may be exposed in a manner so as to meet with general approbation. As pride is the darling passion of the heart of man, there is nothing he can bear less than to be made ridiculous: Some have gone so far as to think that there have died more martyrs to pride than to the truth. Honour in its common acceptation among well-bred people, say they, is but a genteel name for it: how much evil goes uncommitted, because honour forbids it! But as it is beneath the dignity and sanctity of religion to play one Passion against another, the stage is the only place where this is allowable, and which, by shewing certain vices to be ridiculous, renders them odious. If licentious poets have abused this liberty, by affixing the marks of ridicule to subjects that deserve a much better treatment, we are not to argue against any thing from the abuse of it. It is well known the pulpit itself has been abused to the worst purposes; yet no sober man would from thence argue against the present use of it.

AGAIN, many virtuous characters in life may be rendered so amiable on the stage by the Poets address, as may tempt some men to be at the pains to attain them. Next to pride, sloth is most predominant in men; so that motives and incitements of all sorts had need be set before them to stir them up to action, and form virtuous habits in them: For if it is sure on the one hand, that much more evil would be committed were men less indolent, so on the other it is as certain, that much more good might be done in the world, if men would be prevailed upon to put their good designs in practice, and follow their good inclinations: And as evils are often greater in imagination than reality, so most duties in life seem much more difficult in practice, than they are found to be upon trial. If then a just representation of the ease that attends the discharge of many virtues, and the attainment of good accomplishments be made, by an able hand, I doubt not but many may, by such representations on the stage, be drawn to try what seems so practicable, so becoming, and so advantageous in it consequences. BUT

THE LIFE OF SENECA.

LUCIUS ANNÆUS SENECA the Philosopher was not author of all the ten Tragedies, that are commonly published under the name of ANNÆUS SENECA. *Lipsius* attributes only the *Medea* to him; the *Thebaid* he thinks should be ascribed to some writer of the *Augustan* age; and the last, called *Octavia*, he, with most other critics, supposes the work of some bad Poet of the *Augustan* age. The rest in his opinion were written by a nephew of the Philosopher, whom some critics rather believe to have been his son; which I cannot assent to for this reason, because history mentions but one son of his by his first wife, who died a boy some time before his father's banishment. See *Consol. ad Helviam*: and *Tacitus* no where says he had any children by his second wife *Paulina*. *Maurus Terentianus* speaks of ANNÆUS SENECA a tragic Poet, who flourished after *Pomponius Secundus*; and *Pomponius* was cotemporary with SENECA the Philosopher.

In tragicis junxere choris hunc sæpe diserti
Annæus Seneca & Pomponius ante secundus.

Sidonius Apollinaris actually distinguishes between SENECA the Philosopher and *Seneca* the Tragedian.

Quorum unus colit Hispidum Platona,
Orchestram quatit alter Euripidis.

But

But whether the tragic Poet was so nearly related to the Philosopher as to be his Nephew, may be questioned 'till we find some authority for this conjecture. But let him be who he will, as we have no account of his life, nor of the author of the *Thebaid*, nor yet of the writer of the *Octavia*, we must pass them by to say something of the Philosopher, who is on all hands presumed to have composed the *Medea*, and by some good critics is reckoned author of the *Troades* and *Hyppolitus*.

Lucius Annæus Seneca was born at *Corduba* in *Spain*, about the beginning of the vulgar *Æra*: for we find he died the 12th year of *Nero*, of *Christ* 65, being upwards of threescore. His Father *Marcus*, who was of the order of Knights, distinguished himself by his eloquence at *Rome*, and some of his works that are now extant, shew him to have been a man of an exquisite taste, a bright genius, and a good critic; At his death, he left our Author possessed of an ample fortune, which he afterwards immensely increased: for notwithstanding his application to philosophy, he applied himself to public affairs, and was both Quæstor and Prætor; but it does not appear whether he obtained these honours before his banishment, which happened on this occasion.

Julia the daughter of *Germanicus* having been long notorious for her incontinency, the Emperor *Claudian* thought it expedient to banish such Persons as were said to have had any intrigues with that Princess; and the Empress *Messalina*, having conceived some disgust to Seneca, involved him, whose continency was as universally acknowledged as it was admired, in the number of those criminal lovers, and banished him into the island *Corsica*; where he lived eight years, which he spent in the amusements of study, and is thought to have often comforted himself with writing Poetry during his exile.

Messalina being dead, *Agrippina*, whom *Claudius* married, and who was convinced of the innocence of Seneca, prevailed with the Emperor to recall him:

After which, as a proof of her good opinion of him, she made him Præceptor to her young son *Nero*, for whose succession to the empire she was then making way. SENECA so carefully and successfully discharged this important trust, that had the young Prince continued to hearken to his wise counsels, as he did during the first five years of his government, he would have been the delight, as he afterwards made himself the abomination of all his subjects. SENECA's riches are said to have increased so much under the favour of the Prince, that his estate in *Britain* was computed at two millions sterling.

BUT insensibly, as *Nero* gave ear to flattery, and his depraved appetites, SENECA's interest began to decline at court; from whence he at length held it prudent to retire, when he found it in vain to oppose *Nero*'s humour, who now only wished for some pretence to get rid of this troublesome monitor.

SENECA had spent some time in a peaceful retirement, when *Piso* and some other *Romans* of note, growing impatient of *Nero*'s tyranny, and entering into a conspiracy against him, were discovered and put to death. *Tacitus* leaves it undecided, whether SENECA had entered into this conspiracy: however, *Nero* is supposed to have privately instructed *Natalis* (one of the conspirators, who impeached the rest) to accuse SENECA of being in the plot. The historian observes, that *Nero* had not long before endeavoured, by corrupting some of the family, to poison SENECA; which, either through the philosopher's great abstinence or his precaution, had no effect. When an officer came to him from *Nero* to examine him, as to what knowledge he had of *Piso*'s measures, he answered to the several charges laid against him with such an air of innocence and indifference, as provoked the tyrant, when he heard it, to send him an order to die. His wife *Paulina*, a lady of great beauty and virtue, so earnestly intreated her husband to let her die with him, that after having used all his art and eloquence to dissuade her from it, he was at length forced to consent to her importunity. THE

THEIR veins were opened at one time, but SENECA, who was in years, and dried up by a long course of abstinence, bled very slowly. Fearing therefore that the sight of his ling'ring death might increase *Paulina*'s pains, and that the sight of her in the same condition should break through his best resolutions, and make him act at his death in a manner unbecoming the constancy of his life, he intreated her to be conveyed into another apartment. Having thus avoided that dangerous trial of his constancy, with a chearful countenance and perfect composure of mind he addressed himself to his weeping friends, and gently reminded them of the just reproach they made themselves liable to, by yielding so much to their grief: then as it were collecting all his sinking spirits, he employed all the charms of his eloquence in discoursing to them of the excellency of virtue, and in explaining to them the most sublime moral truths. These his dying words were carefully taken down in writing by some of the assistants, and were afterwards communicated to the public, "For which reason (says *Tacitus*) I have forborn inserting them in my history." The dying words of great men are always valuable, so that the loss of this curious Piece is much to be lamented.

AT length, SENECA perceiving his death too tedious and lingering, swallowed a strong poison, which his friend *Statius Annæus*, an able physician, administered to him; but his body was already so exhausted, and decayed, as to be proof against it. Then SENECA ordered his attendants to lead him into a hot bath, and as soon as he came in, took some of the water and sprinkled it upon them, saying, He made that libation to *Jupiter* the deliverer: He was soon after suffocated by the vapours of the bath, and so expired.

NERO, who had no particular reason to be offended with *Paulina*, had dispatched some officers to prevent her death: they found her so faint, that it was generally believed, she was altogether insensible of what was done, when they bound up her arms. Though she was snatched from death by the tyrant's mercy, and the care of her friends, and survived her husband a few years, yet the paleness of her countenance, which shewed the great quantity of blood she had lost, gloriously witnessed to the world that generous affection which she bore her husband.

It is not my province here to say any thing in particular of SENECA, either as a polite writer in prose, or as an excellent moral and natural philosopher; though his character, in these respects, is much more considerable than as a writer of Tragedies. He shewed himself likewise a very witty writer in that excellent satyrical piece, which is called, *The Apotheosis of the Emperor* Claudian.

But before we enter into his character as a dramatic Poet, I shall make a previous reflection or two on the conduct of the Antients in dramatic poetry, as far as it seems to deviate from the received rules of our modern critics, who, in many respects, have taught us, in theory at least, to improve on the Antients.

The parts of a Play, in which its morals should appear, are the fable, and the characters: In their characters they have been tolerably exact; and their chorus took care to rectify or palliate whatever might seem contrary to the strict rules of virtue, or was dubious and admitted of a double sense. The Reader will observe, that I speak only of Tragedy. The fable, which *Aristotle* calls the soul of Tragedy, if well constituted, should be moral. I cannot say, that I find many of the Antients attended to this rule. This neglect might sometimes proceed from their adhering too closely to the historical accounts of their heroic ancestors, whose adventures were the subjects of most of their Tragedies. And they might imagine a strict observation of what we call poetical justice, neither so agreeable, nor so conducive to the great end of their Tragedy, which was to fill the minds of the audience with terror and compassion.

ANOTHER

ANOTHER great fault in their Drama seems to have been, their making the Gods interpose so often without any visible necessity, and sometimes act very unjustly. Both these faults are also chargeable on their Epic Poetry, only, as this species of Poetry aims at the sublime and the marvellous in the œconomy of its fable, which this machinery of Gods intervening promotes, it is hereby rendered more probable, or at least more excusable in Epic than Dramatic Poetry. So that the defect of their fable, in point of morality, must be given up to the severity of the modern critics, some of whom, and particularly *Dacier*, have in vain attempted, out of their great zeal for the antients, to find a moral, where they never thought of any themselves. Yet, in justice to some of them, we must grant, that the absurd doctrines of their theology should, in some sort, excuse their conduct with respect to the characters of their Gods. Thus, whenever, according to the received doctrine of their priests, and even of the stoic philosophers, *Jupiter* is confounded with Fate and blind Destiny, no justice can be expected from his Dispensations. And so long as the whole tribe of inferior Gods is supposed subject to all the extravagancies of human passions and infirmities, it cannot be presumed, that they should either dispence their favours, or wreck their vengeance according to the real merits or demerits of mankind.

THERE are two Tragedies out of the ten extant under SENECA's name, which I propose to examine. The first is *Medea*, which, as being on all hands attributed to the philosopher, will shew his character as a tragic Poet.

THE second is *OEdipus*, the most celebrated subject in all antiquity, which, I think, is to be ascribed to the other SENECA, who, in the dramatic part, has not only out-done the philosopher, but even rivals *Sophocles*, his great original, though this Play is esteemed the *Greek* Poet's master-piece.

To begin with the Tragedy of *Medea*. It has but five persons or characters. *Medea*, her confidant, *Jason*,

son, *Creon*, and a messenger. The scene is at *Corinth*, before *Creon*'s palace. The chorus may be supposed a company of *Corinthians* waiting there. The first act consists of but one scene, and the song of the chorus. *Medea* having heard of *Jason*'s nuptials with *Creüsa*, *Creon*'s daughter, declares her resolution of being revenged on her husband for his infidelity. Then she goes out, and the chorus sing the hymeneal song in praise of *Jason* and *Creüsa*.

In the first scene of the 2d act, *Medea* enters with her confidant, who endeavours to calm her passion. *Creon* comes in the second scene, and finding *Medea* there, orders the guards to bid her instantly depart out of his dominions. She advances to speak to the King, but all that she obtains by her expostulations and entreaties, is one day's time to see and bid her children farewell. Then both leave the stage, and the chorus concludes the act, by declaiming against the criminal boldness of those men who first ventured to sea, * yet foretells, the time shall come when all nations shall, as it were, be joined and united by universal trade and commerce. *Medea* and her confidant begin the third act. She grows more enraged, and the other uses more arguments in vain, to dissuade her from giving way to her passion and revenge. In the second scene, *Jason*

---

* It was 1500 years, before what the Poet there speaks of came to be verified by our navigation to the *East* and *West-Indies*, and above 700 between *Jason* and SENECA. The poet having described the trade of the *Greeks*, *Ægyptians* and *Phœnicians* of those times, or rather of the *Romans* of his own time, goes on thus;

——————*venient annis*
Sæcula seris, quibus oceanus
Vincula rerum laxet, & ingens
Pateat Tellus, Tiphysque novos
Detegat orbes; nec sit terris
Ultima Thule.

Ortelius, the geographer, remarks with pleasure, That the poet, who was a *Spaniard*, has here prophetically described the discovery of the new world by his countrymen the *Spaniards*. This passage, however extraordinary, was absurd in the mouth of the *Corinthian* chorus.

comes

comes to *Medea*, solemnly protesting his great trouble and concern, that he is forced to divorce her, which he had not consented to so much for the preservation of his own life, as out of a fatherly tenderness for their two children, who would else inevitably be involved in the same ruin with their parents. Their case was this. *Medea*, to be revenged on *Pelias*, King of *Thessaly*, for his cruelty to *Jason*, had pretended, by virtue of her enchantments to restore the old King to youth and vigour. But having persuaded his daughters to consent, she treacherously killed him in the operation. This so exasperated the neighbouring *Greeks* against her and *Jason*, that he fled the country, and came with his family for refuge and protection to *Corinth*. *Creon* offers him both, on condition he would divorce *Medea*, and marry his daughter *Creüsa*. *Jason* comes in this scene, to justify his conduct to *Medea*; he assures her, it was owing to his most earnest request, that *Creon* had been prevailed with to change the sentence of her death into banishment. *Medea*, far from being satisfied with his apology, reproaches him with great bitterness for his ingratitude and reminds him, that all the crimes she is accused of, were committed for his sake and advantage. Then she tries to persuade him to fly with her from *Corinth*; or, at least, desires he would let her have the comfort to take her children along with her, to be the companions of her exile. Here *Jason* betrays a father's fondness for his two sons; which *Medea* immediately lays hold of as a fit occasion of revenge, and obtains his consent to take her last leave of them. The chorus conclude the act, by commemorating the terrible manner in which *Neptune*, according to the *Greek* fables, is said to have punished the presumption of the *Argonauts*, who were the first considerable sailors among them; and then follows a prayer to that God, to spare *Jason*, who was innocent, since it was by the direction of the Gods that he undertook the *Colchian* expedition.

Medea's confidant opens the 4th act, and describes with horror the deadly preparations which her mistress

stress was making to execute some dreadful design. The second scene discovers *Medea* in the midst of her magical ceremonies, and invoking all the infernal powers to prepare the rich, but fatal garment she intends as a present for *Creüsa*, and which was to be so impregnated with fire, that, as soon as the princess put it on, it should consume her, and all the Palace of *Creon*. When this is done, she sends for her children to carry the fatal gift to the bride. The chorus close the act, expressing their apprehensions of *Medea*'s ill designs in general, which they pray the Gods to avert.

The fifth act begins with a person who brings a dreadful account how *Creüsa*, with her Father *Creon*, were consumed by a terrible fire that broke out in the palace, as soon as *Creüsa* had put on the robe which *Medea* had sent her. The sorceress now triumphing in the general distress, and this immediate success of her revenge, prepares to compleat it by the murder of her children: Nature and rage for a time strive in her heart. In the interim, *Jason* comes out with some persons to seize her, which she apprehending, at first sight of them retires to the top of the house with the children. There she cruelly insults him a while, and then kills one of her sons in his sight. The afflicted Father uses all his intreaties to save the other's life, but in vain: then in his distraction he calls upon her to kill him too; but *Medea*, satisfied with this full vengeance, rides away in triumph thro' the air in a chariot drawn by flying dragons. *Jason* in despair cannot forbear accusing providence, and concludes the Play with this miserable reflection, That where-ever she goes, she must be a witness to the world that there are no Gods.

As this subject has been so highly celebrated by all the antients, I was the more willing to give this sketch of it; but cannot discover what there is in it, that deserved their admiration. It has absolutely no moral: for though it may be granted, that *Jason* could have no excuse to leave *Medea*, who had made her

Roman Poet: But the *Greek* has no more regard to poetical justice in the catastrophe, than the other: Indeed *Medea* does not kill her children on the stage, they are heard by the Chorus crying out for mercy to their mother behind the scenes.

It is observable, that *Aristotle* prefers what he calls the Pathetic to the Moral Tragedies; but whether he does this as a Philosopher, or as a Critic, who forms his rules from the practice of the most celebrated Poets, I cannot pretend to determine.

Seneca's stile is magnificent, the sentiments are sublime, and the images very lively and poetical; but he wants that noble simplicity and pathetic manner which recommends *Euripides*, and in the whole it seems to have been written for the closet rather than the stage.

But let us see whether the younger *Seneca*, author of *OEdipus*, had not a better genius for dramatic poetry: The historical fable of the play is as follows.

Laius King of *Thebes* and Father of *OEdipus*, was informed by an Oracle, that his wife *Jocasta* would bear a son, that should kill him. To elude the danger threatened by the Oracle, *Laius*, as soon as the child was born, gives him to one of his servants to be killed. The man being touched with compassion, instead of taking away the innocent infant's life, having bored his feet, and passed an ozier twig through them, hung him by the heels in a wood, and there left him to the farther disposal of Providence. It was the child's good fortune to be found thus hanging by a domestic of *Polybus* King of *Corinth*, who took little *OEdipus* down (who was so named from his swelled feet) and carried him to his master. The King being childless, adopted *OEdipus*, and brought him up at *Corinth* as his Son.

About the time *OEdipus* was grown to man's estate he happened to have some words with a *Corinthian*, who in the heat of dispute let fall some words reflecting on the uncertainty of his parentage, which had hitherto, by the express order of *Polybus*, been

concealed

concealed from him. *OEdipus*, who grew very uneasy at this reproach, went to consult the Oracle at *Delphi*, there to learn a more certain account of his parentage; but is forbid by the Oracle to make any farther enquiry about it, for it was his destiny to kill his Father, and beget Children on his Mother. Alarm'd and perplexed at this terrible answer, he resolves to abandon *Corinth*, which he still believed to be his native country: on the road to *Thebes* he meets *Laius*, and, a quarrel arising between them about the way, kills his Father in the fray, and soon after proceeds on his journey to *Thebes*, which at his arrival he finds in confusion, both on the account of their King's unfortunate death (the news of which was just arrived) and because of the ravages committed by the cruel monster *Sphinx*. The only means of deliverance from this last calamity, was for some body to expound the riddle she proposed, but as many as failed in the attempt forfeited their lives; which having been the fate of several already, deterred others from so dangerous an undertaking. As an encouragement, the *Thebans* now publickly offered the Crown and Queen *Jocasta* in marriage to him that should succeed. This tempted *OEdipus* to undertake to expound the riddle, which he did, upon which the monster through grief and indignation cast itself headlong from a rock, and so perished. Thus was *Thebes* delivered, and the generous deliverer receiving the promised reward, ignorantly mounted his Father's throne and bed.

Thus far the history of *OEdipus* precedes the action of the Play we are about to examine; and as the whole action of it naturally arises from the foregoing account, *Sophocles* artfully introduces a narration of the whole story at the unravelling of the plot, which is esteemed as beautiful as any of the ancients or moderns.

Thus far *OEdipus* is to be supposed to have maintained the character of a just and wise man: invincible ignorance excuses the secret guilt or rather calamity of his actions; and accordingly in the first
scene

scene of the *Greek* Poet, the Priest of *Jupiter* addresses him as a good and innocent Prince. But to come to SENECA's Play.

HE omits that circumstance, and introduces *OEdipus* and *Jocasta* in the first scene of the first act, lamenting their people's distress, and a Chorus of *Thebans* imploring the mercy of the Gods, and describing the dreadful havock which the plague makes among them, concludes the act. As they go off the stage, they see *Creon*, *Jocasta*'s brother, who was just returned from *Delphi*, where *OEdipus* had sent him to enquire what was to be done to stop the plague. *OEdipus* opens the second act with *Creon*, whom he presses to acquaint him with the answer of *Apollo*. At length *Creon* informs him, that the Oracle order'd that the murderer of *Laius* should be driven out of the city, and then the plague would cease. *OEdipus*, having made heavy imprecations against the murderer, desires *Creon* to inform him of the particular manner of *Laius*'s death: *Creon* tells him, that the King being on the road with but a few attendants, as in time of peace, was attack'd by some robbers and kill'd: Then observing the blind prophet *Tiresias* and his daughter *Manto* advancing, *OEdipus* orders a sacrifice to be prepared, that the prophet may by that means consult the Gods and discover the murderer. The whole process of the sacrifice, which is performed on the stage, is full of the most ominous indications: but the prophet not being yet able to find out the criminal, resolves to have recourse to necromancy, and calls up the ghost of *Laius*; but before he goes off the stage for this purpose, he orders the Chorus to sing an hymn in praise of *Bacchus*, which closes the second act.

IN the third, *Creon* comes with *OEdipus*, and tells him, that *Tiresias* having enquired of the ghost of *Laius*, who had killed him, was told that *OEdipus* was the man. He being still, in a great measure, persuaded that *Polybus* was his Father, denies his having killed his Father, or committed incest with his
Mother,

Mother, and so being enrag'd with *Creon*, who seem'd to charge him with those crimes, sends him to prison, suspecting it was a plot laid between *Creon* and *Tiresias*, to procure the former the crown. The Chorus ends the act by excusing OEdipus's conduct, and accusing the hard fate of *Thebes*, which, from its first foundation, had been doomed to undergo a series of calamities.

OEDIPUS opens the fourth act, being conscious to himself of his own innocence, yet seemed confounded at the contrary declaration of the Gods, and by degrees begins to mistrust, that the person whom he had killed in the fray on his way to *Thebes* might be *Laius*, and asking *Jocasta*, who was now come on the stage, about the time and place of the King's death, her account confirms his suspicion. In the next scene comes a messenger from *Corinth*, to acquaint him with his Father *Polybus*'s death, and that the Queen his Mother sent to invite him to come and take the government upon him. OEdipus is overjoy'd to hear that his Father had died a natural death, but being still mindful of the first Oracle, fears to go to *Corinth*, because of his Mother. The zealous messenger, who, according to SENECA, is supposed to be the very man that had received OEdipus from the shepherd, that *Laius* had sent to kill him, assures OEdipus, he need not fear the Oracles, for that he was not the son of *Merope*, Queen of *Corinth*, and then proceeds to give him an account of the whole adventure. For SENECA differs a little from the received story, and supposes that *Phorbas*, the shepherd of King *Laius*, meeting with this servant of *Polybus*, whilst he was going to hang up the child by the feet, which he had already bored, instead of doing so, gave him to the *Corinthian*; who brought him to *Polybus*. *Phorbas* being now sent for by OEdipus, and threatned with the rack, is forced to discover all, which plunges the wretched OEdipus into distraction and despair: the song of the Chorus shuts up the act, preferring the security of private life in a middle station,

tion, to the dangerous changes to which the throne is exposed. A *Theban* enters in the first scene of the fifth act, giving an account of the consequence of *OEdipus*'s despair, and his putting out his eyes. The Chorus excuse this action, only blaming him for striving to avoid the decrees of Fate, which we shall find was intended by SENECA for the moral of the Play. But to proceed; in the second scene, *OEdipus* being blind, comes forward, and meeting *Jocasta*, after some melancholic expostulations, suitable to their present horrors of mind, she snatches the sword from his side, and kills herself. *OEdipus* goes off, and banishes himself from *Thebes*, as the Oracle had directed, which ends the Play.

I think most of the alterations which SENECA has made from *Sophocles*, are for the better, and particularly the last, of making *Jocasta* kill herself with *OEdipus*'s sword. In *Sophocles* she hangs herself behind the scenes. The *Greek* has more decorum, the *Roman* is more natural in this point.

I come now to the passage from the Chorus in the 5th act, in which I think SENECA has given the moral of the Play.

Fatis agimur; cedite Fatis;
Non sollicitæ possunt curæ
Mutare fati stamina sui.
Quicquid patimur mortale genus
Quicquid facimus, venit ex alto
Servatque suæ decreta colus
Lachesis. Dura revoluta manu
Omnia certo tramite vadunt;
Primusque dies dedit extremum.
Non illa Deo vertisse licet,
Quæ nexa suis currunt Causis.
It cuique ratus, prece non ulla
Mobilis, ordo: multis ipsum
Timuisse nocet; multi ad Fatum
Venere suum dum Fata timent.

The conclusion of this passage very strongly and particularly intimates, that *OEdipus*, by seeking to decline,

THE LIFE OF PLAUTUS.

PLAUTUS was born at *Sarsina*, now *Sezza*, a small town in *Umbria*, a Province of *Italy*, now called *Æmilia:* His proper name was *Marcius Accius*, and from his splay feet is supposed to have got the sirname of PLAUTUS. His Parentage seems to have been mean; some think him the son of a slave, *Libertus*.

As if the memory of writers were sufficiently preserved in their works, we meet with very slender accounts of their lives among the ancients, and of none less than of PLAUTUS. Nor can we fix the time of the first acting of any of his Plays, and hardly ascertain his age by any circumstances of his life. *Cicero* has in general told us, that our Poet was some years younger than *Nævius* or *Ennius*, and that he died the first year of the elder *Cato*'s Censorship, when *Claudius Pulcher* and *Lucius Portius Licinius* were Consuls, about the year of *Rome* 569, 184 years before the birth of CHRIST. *A. Gellius* (Lib. 3. Cap. 3.) says, that PLAUTUS flourished at the same time that *Cato* the Censor was distinguished at *Rome* for his eloquence: He adds out of *Varro*, that PLAUTUS's Plays were so well received by the *Romans*, that the Poet having been handsomely paid for them, thought of doubling his stock by trading; in which he was so unfortunate, that he lost all he had got by the Muses, and for

have made the number of his Plays exceed an hundred, as *Gellius* affures us some had done, and mentions the names of several of them.

PLAUTUS is said by *Varro* to have composed the following Epitaph for himself, which, as favouring of vanity, has been rejected by some Critics as not of his making: but as *Gellius* (Lib. 1. Cap. 24.) expreffly cites *Varro* for it, I shall give it the Reader with the translation, leaving it to him to censure, or acquit the Poet for speaking so advantageously in his own praise.

Postquam est mortem aptus Plautus; Comœdia luget,
Scena est deserta; hinc risus, ludusque, jocusque,
Et numeri innumeri simul omnes collachrymarunt.

Wit, laughter, jests, and all the train that use
T'adorn the Scene, and grace the Comic Muse,
Forsook the Stage, at *Plautus*' death to mourn,
And Harmony undone sat weeping o'er his urn.

BEFORE we enter into a particular examination of PLAUTUS's works, it may not be disagreeable to take a short view of the state of the *Roman* Comedy, when he began to appear as a writer for the stage; a cursory review both of the *Greek* and *Roman* stage will most naturally lead us to our purpose.

THE old *Greek* Comedy did not begin 'till some time after *Æschylus*; its subjects were not feigned, but real; they spared not the persons of the chief magistrates, whose dignity could not protect them from the insolent invectives of the Poets. They were all introduced on the stage with their true countenances, and as it were *in propriâ personâ*. In time toleration rendered this liberty excessive, and the Poets were forbid naming the persons whose actions they would expose: Yet under borrowed names they drew mens characters so justly, that with the help of the mask, none could mistake the person intended. As this proceeding was a medium between the old and the new, it was named the Middle Comedy. Some of *Aristophanes*'s last pieces are of this nature.

he wrote the twelfth book of his annals. *Terence* was about nine years old when Plautus died, in the year of *Rome* 569, and his *Andrian* was acted in the twenty-eighth year of his age; though I think it very probable, that was not *Terence's* first Play: so that here was not an interval of above eighteen years between Plautus's last and *Terence's* first Play. *Cæcilius Accius*, and *Pacuvius*, were contemporaries with our author, and *Licinius* was not much elder. There were many other Poets sprung up during this time, but these are the most considerable. Thus in less than eighty years, comedy was begun and perfected among the *Romans*.

After this general view of the *Greek* and *Roman* stage, let us carry on our enquiry into what more particularly relates to Plautus. He has been particularly esteemed by the best judges, both antient and modern on these two accounts: 1. The exact propriety of his expression, which has been made by many the standard of the purest *Latin*. 2. That which set him above all the *Roman* Comic writers, is the true ridicule and humour of his characters. This is the constant opinion of *Varro, Macrobius, Gellius,* and *Cicero*; and the most eminent modern Critics, as *Lipsius*, the *Scaligers, Muretus,* and *Turnebus,* not to name a long catalogue of others, who have not disputed Plautus's excellency in these two respects. *Quintilian* indeed speaks little to the advantage of the *Roman* Comedy in general, in which he thinks his countrymen very deficient. It were to be wished he had explained himself more largely on this head. *Horace* has dealt more ingenuously with his Readers, in express terms condemning his Countrymen of the preceding age for commending and admiring Plautus's wit and numbers, and charges them with folly for so doing.

At nostri proavi Plautinos & numeros &
Laudavêre sales; nimium patienter utrumque
Ne dicam stultè mirati; si modo ego & vos

Scimus inurbanum lepido seponere dicto,
Legitimumque sonum digitis callemus & aure.
De Arte Poetica.

HORACE, as appears by many passages in his Epistles and Satires, was very zealous to abolish a false taste, which prevailed even in the *Augustan* age, of preferring the old Poets to all that succeeded them, without examining into their respective merit. In order to this, he thought it necessary to shew the *Romans* they were mistaken. Thus he has condemned *Lucilius*, which censure however *Quintilian* disapproves, saying, that Poet's Satires were as much above his reproaches, as they fell short of the immoderate praises bestowed on them by the admirers of *Lucilius*. I think we may apply this to PLAUTUS, whose wit was sometimes low in compliance with the taste of the age, and his numbers generally irregular thro' the imperfect state of music, and the want of a good ear in the age he wrote for: yet the generality in succeeding times excused his numbers, and liked his wit, perhaps too much, as thinking it without alloy.

As to his numbers, PLAUTUS himself seems to have made no great account of them, according to the last line of his Epitaph, *Et numeri innumeri*, &c. that is, irregular numbers. It has been observed in the Introduction to the Dramatic Poets, that the chief merit of these numbers seems to have consisted in their fitness to the music that accompanied them in the actor's Declamation. Now the recitative music, to which PLAUTUS's Plays were set, was probably much more simple and unharmonious, than that composed in the *Augustan* age, when all the arts that serve to enliven and adorn life, were carried to their height: And this reflection will partly justify his low wit, which is generally suited to his characters, and possibly was well adapted to the taste of his audience.

Horace was certainly to be commended, for endeavouring to introduce a better taste, than that which had so prejudiced them in favour of antiquity, that they were blind to the grossest faults of those writers, and were incapable of doing justice to the best modern performances. But he might, one should think, have avoided so general a censure, which he passed in contradiction to the opinion of many of the best judges: and granting PLAUTUS should abound in false wit, if it is introduced in the character of a slave or parasite, I do not see how the poet is affected by the censure, whilst he makes them speak in character. It was the audience, who should be blamed for applauding what the poet might mean to ridicule.

The generality of writers I believe find it hard to resist the temptation of being witty when they can; and yet it is judged to be so nice a point, that not one in a hundred is truly so, where he pretends to it most.

There hardly ever appear'd a brighter genius than that of *Ovid*; yet by too great a complacency in indulging it, he fell short of that perfection for which nature seemed to have designed him.

Virgil's flegmatic temper corrected the heat of his fancy, yet I doubt his more juvenile works were not quite exempt from false wit; which indeed is manifestly true, if we allow some of these little Poems to be of his composing, which are vulgarly called his *Juvenilia*.

Lucan and *Seneca* were both of a noble spirit and unbounded fancy, that led them too far in pursuit of wit; but their eagerness has often made them with *Ixion* embrace a cloud instead of the real beauty they thought to enjoy.

Even our grave Censurer has sometimes given into this false wit, where he pretends to be most witty, as in some of his Epodes, and the Satire on *Persius* and *Rupilius*.

Terence I believe was aware of *Plautus*'s foible, and has cautiously avoided it, but has not escaped the other extreme of coldness, in the general opinion, as well as of *Julius Cæsar*, to whom the following Verses giving the character of *Terence* are ascribed.

"are deficient still in the stile of our Comedies;" though *Varro* has said, the Muses would speak in PLAUTUS's manner, had they spoke *Latin*. It is plain *Quintilian* thinks they had between them both what was united in *Menander*'s stile, who was the perfection of the Attic wit and elegance. This great Critic adds something about the numbers of *Terence*, which is well worth our notice. "*Terence*'s Poetry (says "he) would have been much more agreeable, had "he kept to the Senarian or Trimeter Iambic mea- "sure." I do not pretend to explain this particular beauty, which *Terence* wanted: The curious Reader may consult a *Hare* or a *Bentley* in this nice particular. But I cannot but observe from hence, that this is a corroborating proof of what has been laid down as a certainty in the introduction, that the antients were very careful to acquire an exact taste and a nice ear to judge of harmony and numbers. If we suppose that by neglecting the Trimeter measure, *Terence*'s verses were too prosaic, it will justify *Horace*'s condemning PLAUTUS's measures, which were yet more neglected, and so more grating to the delicate ear of the *Augustan* age.

WE have now gone through with our examination and censure of the stile and measure of PLAUTUS; let us see if we can fare better with respect to the Dramatic part of his character. That he is lively and entertaining, and hastening with his characters to the winding up of the Play, is what *Horace* has allowed him to be, after the manner of *Epicharmus*:

Plautus ad Exemplar Siculi properare Epicharmi,
Epist. 1. Lib. 2.

THIS *Epicharmus* was scholar of *Pythagoras*, and flourished in *Sicily* in the time of *Servius Tullius*. *Plato* is said to have made great improvements by the reading his Comedies. This Poet was banished by *Hiero* King of *Sicily* for having spoken too freely of the Queen his wife. *Aristotle* in his poesies mentions the claim the *Sicilians* made to precedency in
point

the sequel, such as that of *Simo* in the *Andrian* of *Terence*: The story is admirably well told I confess, but that is due to *Terence*'s diligence and fine genius, and does not take off the general force of the objection. So confidants are necessary characters in Tragedy, to enable the Poets handsomly to acquaint the audience with what is in agitation, more than to carry on the action of the Drama. This is not offered with a design to approve PLAUTUS's method, which he has himself oftentimes found unnecessary, but to hint rather at some of the motives which might have probably induced the Poet to this practice: To which we may add this other consideration, That as the arts were but then in their infancy at *Rome*, the people's fancy was yet heavy and slow in apprehending, and consequently insensible of the many refinements in theatrical Entertaiments, which the ensuing conquest of *Greece* and *Asia* soon after introduced among them. In twenty years time, the smallest interval that can be allowed between the last of PLAUTUS's and the first of *Terence*'s Plays, many alterations might be and were made for the better, in a people so well disposed as the *Romans* then appeared to be for improvements of all kinds. Then flourished *Paulus Æmilius*, whose noble example in the compleat education he gave his children, had a general influence among the Patricians. *Cato*'s was but a single voice for banishing the eloquent ambassadors of *Greece*, whose discourses were listened to by the generous *Roman* youth, like that of a voice from Heaven, bidding them cultivate Philosophy and all the pleasing arts of peace. It was not any aversion to the Muses that animated the Censor's zeal on this occasion; he himself had too much learning and eloquence to be an enemy to either, and was cotemporary with our Author, and is said to have studied the *Greek* tongue in his old age: but as he supposed it to be a just observation, that luxury and dissolution of manners too often attend a learned people, as the *Roman* Satirist observes of the *Greeks*,

Grammaticus,

Grammaticus, Rhetor, Geometres, Pictor, Aliptes, Græculus esuriens in cœlum jusseris ibit.

This made *Cato* unwilling to countenance these refinements. But to return to Plautus and *Terence*. The latter had an undoubted advantage, when he composed his pieces at a Villa of *Scipio* or *Lælius*; whereas poor Plautus was forced to make some at the Mill. But though his necessitous circumstances might hasten the birth of some of his productions, the vivacity of the offspring argues the strength of that wit that could form them so well notwithstanding their hasty birth. If *Terence*'s were more mature and timely, he may thank the happiness of the times at least as much as his own genius for it. So *Virgil* has surpassed *Homer* in some respects, which must be thought owing to the same advantages. Yet *Homer* will ever maintain the precedency as to natural accomplishments. The Critics observe, that *Terence* has imitated Plautus as closely as ever *Virgil* did *Homer*, and it must be owned with the same good judgment and success.

Since we are entered upon it, let us carry on the parallel between our two Dramatic Poets a little farther. *Plautus*'s sentences have a peculiar smartness in them, that conveys the thought with clearness, and strikes the imagination strongly; so that the mind listens with attention and retains it with pleasure. This makes his Dialogue more interesting, though less laboured than that of *Terence*. In short, *Plautus* is more gay, *Terence* more chaste. The first has more genius and fire, the latter more manners and solidity. *Plautus* excells in low Comedy and Ridicule, *Terence* in drawing just characters and maintaining them to the last. Their plots are both artful, but *Terence*'s is more apt to languish, whilst *Plautus*'s spirit maintains the action with vigour. His invention was greatest, *Terence*'s art and management. *Plautus* gives the stronger, *Terence* a more elegant delight: *Plautus* appears the better Comedian of the two, as *Terence* the finer Poet. The former has more compass and variety, the latter more regularity and truth in his characters. *Plautus* shone most on the Stage, *Terence* pleases best in the closet. Men of a refined taste would prefer *Terence*. *Plautus* diverted both *Patrician* and *Plebeian*.

AFTER this comparison, let the reader bestow the Lawrel where he thinks it best deserved.

I should now proceed to give an account of his several Plays, of the time of their being acted, how far he was a translator of the *Greek* Poets, and what improvements he made from his own genius. But there are no titles at the head of his Comedies to give us any light into this matter, as we find to *Terence*'s; nor have we those books of *Varro*, which being written upon *Plautus*'s works only, very probably would have satisfied our curiosity in these matters. However we may take a cursory view of his Comedies in the order they are now printed, contenting ourselves with such little hints as the Poet has himself afforded us in the Prologues; and taking in such other helps as may be had from *Cicero* or *Gellius*.

THE 1st is *Amphitryo*; which *Moliere*'s and *Dryden*'s imitations have made pretty well known. The *Frenchman* has done *Plautus* most justice. We do not find whether this Comedy is of *Plautus*'s invention or a translation. He calls it a Tragi-Comedy, not that there is any thing tragical in the subject, but because the principal characters are Gods and Princes. *Euripedes* wrote an *Amphitryo* and *Archippus*, two Plays of this name. How far *Plautus* was beholden to them for his incidents, is uncertain.

THE 2d is *Asinaria*, the Ass-Driver, translated from the *Greek* of *Demophilus*, a writer of the Middle Comedy. *Plautus* assures his audience it is elegant and does not want for wit and humour.

THE 3d is *Aulularia*, the Casket: *Moliere*'s Avare, and *Wicherly*'s Miser, are copies of this Play. Whence *Plautus* has taken it, it is no where said; though it is pretty certain he had it, as indeed almost all his Plays, from the *Greek* Poets.

THE 4th is *Captivi*, the Captives. The Poet pretends to have taken particular care in writing it, both as to stile and sentiments, and that the characters are uncommon.

THE 5th is the Discovery, or *Curculio*, from the name of the parasite. This Play having no Prologue, we must pass on to the next.

THE 6th *Casina*, the name of a female slave; in *Greek* it was called Κληρούμενοι, *Sortientes*, casting Lots. The Prologue to this Comedy seems not to be of *Plautus*'s making, but of the principal actor, who revived it after the Poet's death. This Prologue farther observes, that when it was first brought on the stage it met with great applause. " * This (adds he) " and the favour you have shewn to all *Plautus*'s Co- " medies, encouraged me to revive the *Casina*." It is a great pity we cannot ascertain the time of this revival of the *Casina*; the soonest we can suppose it, must be in *Terence*'s time, because *Plautus* died

---

* *Qui utuntur vino vetere sapientes puto,*
Et qui libenter veteres spectant Fabulas;
Antiqua opera & verba quum vobis placent
Æquum placere est ante veteres fabulas.
Nam nunc novæ quæ prodeunt Comœdiæ
Multo sunt nequiores quam nummi novi.
Nos postquam populi rumorem intelleximus
Studiose expetere vos Plautinas fabulas,
Antiquam illius edimus Comœdiam,
Quam vos probastis, qui estis in senioribus.
Nam juniorum qui sunt non norunt scio,
Verum ut cognoscant dabimus operam sedulo.
Hæc quum primum acta est vicit omnes fabulas,
Ea tempestate flos Poetarum fuit
Qui nunc abierunt hinc in communem locum.

Quam vos probastis qui estis in senioribus. This Verse shews that it could not be above thirty years after the first acting of the Play in *Plautus*'s life time, because the old men, who sate now spectators (says the Prologue) were judges of its goodness when they saw it acted before. Here we find *Plautus* declared by the Player to the whole audience the best Poet of his time. *Ea tempestate flos Poetarum fuit, qui nunc abierunt hinc in communem locum.* And the very first lines put an equal value on their judgment, who chuse old wine and prefer old Plays. And another verse observes, That their new Plays were worse than their new Money.

young,

young, and was survived by most of the Poets of his time, who are said in this Prologue to have been all dead some time before the revival of the *Casina*.

THE 7th, *Cistellaria*, the Basket: The Prologue of this Play comes in at the end of the first Act, and is the God *Auxilium*, Help. Having given an account of the subject as usual, he concludes, bidding the *Romans* to overcome the *Carthaginians*, and punish them as they deserved. This seems to prove the Play to have been acted before the end of the second *Punic* War, which was in the Year of *Rome* 552. This must therefore have been the first of *Plautus*'s Plays; for he died A. U. 570. (*Cicero in Bruto*.) so that he lived not above eighteen years after his writing the *Cistellaria*, supposing it to have been acted the eighteenth year of the *Punic* war, that is, within one year of the end of it: and as the *Romans* hardly began to have a taste for learning 'till after this war was ended, the general ignorance of the audience when this Play was acted must be some apology for the absurdity of this God's speaking a Prologue, at a time when the Poet had no real occasion for him; and if the audience wanted to be let into the subject, the common Prologue might have done as well. True, but then *Plautus* could not have made so handsome a compliment to his countrymen on their valour, their justice, &c. as he does in the character of the God, and at the same time encourage them to pursue their victories over the *Carthaginians*. This reflection turns the seeming absurdity to the Poet's Honour; and as to his coming in at the close of the 1st act, it is consistent with the liberties of the Middle Comedy, which *Plautus* in his first pieces chiefly imitated.

THE 8th, *Epidicus*, the Litigious: This was one of our Poet's favourite Comedies, as he says himself in the character of *Chrysalus*, Act. 2. Scene 2. of the *Bacchides*; and by its having no introductory Prologue may be thought to have been one of the last.

THE 9th, *Bacchides*, so called from two sisters that

that are the chief characters in it. The Comedy is not inferior to any of *Plautus*'s but has no Prologue.

THE 10th, *Mostellaria*, the Ghost, has been imitated by the *French* and us. *Johnson*'s Alchymist is partly copied from it. This has no Prologue.

THE 11th, *Menæchmi*, the Twins, has also been copied by writers of both nations. *Shakespeare*'s Comedy of Errors is in imitation of it. In the Prologue *Plautus* observes, that the Poets, to make their Plays seem to be taken from the *Greek*, chose to lay the scene at *Athens*. " His subject is *Greek* too " (adds the Poet) but the subject is from *Sicily* at " *Syracuse*, though the scene is at *Epidamnus*." From whence we may observe, that *Greek* Comedies translated were most acceptable to the *Romans* in *Plautus*'s time, and they seem to have been so in *Terence*'s, or he would not have been at the pains to translate them.

THE 12th, *Miles Gloriosus*, the Bragging Captain: *Terence* has copied the character of his *Thraso* in the Eunuch from hence. This Play is without a Prologue, and is reckoned an excellent Comedy. The character of *Periplectomenes*, an old Batchelor that helps to bubble the foolish Captain, is very humorous and original.

THE 13th, *Mercator*, the Merchant; translated from the *Greek* of *Philemon*. The Prologue is spoken by *Charinus*, who is the merchant, and the principal character of the Play. The reflections, which *Charinus* intermixes with the account of the subject, shew the sense the Antients had of the disadvantage of their loose morals, which we are but too apt to imitate and encourage on our Stage, under the notion of modern gallantry. One may wonder to meet with so much morality in *Plautus*'s Plays, considering the great immorality of their principles as well as practice, and the infant state of learning and philosophy at *Rome*.

The 14th, *Pseudolus*, the Cheat. This was a favourite Piece of *Plautus*'s, according to * *Cicero*, and

---

* Cato Major; sive de Senectute.

has been variously imitated by the modern Poets. I shall here take occasion to observe from the Prologue, that the *Roman* taste was then something like ours under King *James* I. Many of *Plautus*'s Prologues have a spice of false wit, as well as many of the characters of his slaves and parasites. But the Prologue to this Comedy, gives no account of the subject, and is only addressed to the audience to recommend the Play to their favour. In order to succeed, the Poet runs on for a dozen lines together in a strain of quibbling upon the words *bonus* and *malus*; After this follow some six or seven lines extreamly witty upon full bellies and empty stomachs. I think it must be granted our Poet had sense enough not to trifle so strangely, without knowing it was suitable to the general taste of the People; though *Plautus* certainly wrote too fast to write always correctly, or think of mending the publick taste: And his avarice might be the great inducement of his writing perhaps more than fame. This is the opinion of *Horace*:

————— *Aspice Plautus*
Quo pacto partes tutetur amantis Ephebi,
Ut patris attenti lenonis ut insidiosi,
Quantus sit Dorsennus edacibus in parasitis;
Quam non astricto percurrat pulpita socco.
Gestit enim nummum in loculos demittere, post hoc
Securus cadat an recto stet fabula talo.
Epist. 1. Lib. 2. Ver. 170.

Therefore our Poet seems to have had his present interest more than his future reputation in view; he little regarded what after ages might think fit to censure, when the general taste should be altered. That we find *Terence* so free with this low humour, so far beyond his cotemporaries, and indeed most that came after him, I think we may very justly attribute to the excellent education his noble Patron gave him, and the happy familiarity he contracted with those great men who were suspected to have so much assisted him in his writings. On the other hand, *Plautus*'s birth and

The LIFE of Plautus.

and education were, it is likely, very mean; and nothing but great strength of natural genius could have attained the elegance he was master of. Add to this, that we cannot say whether this same vein of low wit did not prevail in those *Greek* Poets, whom he translated. *Terence* had this farther advantage, that he formed himself upon *Menander*, whereas *Plautus* chiefly followed the Poets of the Middle Comedy, whose manner was reckoned much inferior to *Menander's*, whom even *Terence* is said to have but imitated by halves.

The 15th is *Pœnulus*, the *Carthaginian*: In his Prologue *Plautus* calls it *the Uncle*. The *Greek* name was Καρχηδόνιος; the Poet from whom it was translated is not named. The remains of the *Punic* language, that have been corruptly preserved in the copies of this Play, have found good work for the Critics to restore them to the true reading, and are esteemed a very curious Piece of Antiquity. From the Plot of this Play we have this farther hint, that the Children of the *Carthaginians* were often stolen from their Parents, and carried away and sold for slaves in other Countries. History speaks of the *Numidians*, as a people who lived by continual depredations of this kind; and in this manner we may probably suppose *Terence* to have been stolen when a child from *Carthage*, and sold to *Terentius* the *Roman* Senator.

The 16th is *Persa*, the name of a slave in the Play; here is no Prologue to shew from whence this Comedy was translated.

The 17th is *Rudens*, the *Cable*, but might more properly be called the *Happy Shipwreck*. This Comedy is translated from the *Greek* of *Diphilus*, as the Prologue informs us, which is spoken by the God or Constellation *Arcturus*; whose heliacal rising and setting the Antients reckoned stormy.

The 18th *Stichus*, a slave's name in the Play. Or from the subject, this Comedy may be called the *Triumphs of Conjugal Love*. Here is no Prologue.

The 19th *Trinummus*, the *Hidden Treasure*; the
Prologue

Prologue is spoken in the characters of Luxury and Penury, who come to take possession of the extravagant young man's house, who prodigally squanders away all his father had left him during his absence. This Comedy is translated from *Philemon* the *Greek* comic an elegiac Poet.

The 20th and last is *Truculentus*, the *Churl*. This is one of those Plays for which, according to *Cicero*, *Plautus* expressed the most value. The short Prologue to it, gives no account from whence *Plautus* took it, though it is clear enough, that as they are all *Greek* subjects, he translated this as well as the rest, from the *Greek* comic Poets.

Having thus taken a brief and general view of *Plautus*'s Plays, as far as his own Works could direct us, we should now enter into Particulars, and examine the Plot and conduct of his Drama in some one of his Comedies; and then set it as it were in parallel with one of *Terence*'s, thereby to enable the Reader to form a judgment of their Abilities in this most essential part of Dramatic Poetry. Though we are not so well able to judge of *Plautus*'s or *Terence*'s diligence or neglect in this respect, since we have not the *Greek* Plays extant that they translated, and so not knowing what they took from, or what they altered in them, we can but imperfectly determine whether they altered with more or less judgment in this respect. Yet, notwithstanding this impediment, it is hoped the following Examination may be of some Use and Entertainment.

Examination of the Asinaria *of* Plautus.

MY reason for choosing this Comedy, is not because I think it one of the best, since it is rather the contrary: But if the Drama is regularly executed, and the Incidents well prepared, the Reader that is not at leisure to examine the rest, may fairly presume they do not fall short of it, particularly such, as by the foregoing enquiry appear to have been much esteemed by the Antients, and most of
them

them imitated by the Moderns. Such are *Amphitryo, Aulularia, Captivi, Casina, Epidicus, Bacchides, Mostellaria, Menæchmi, Miles Gloriosus,* and *Rudens.*

The Critics generally agree, that a Dramatic Poem, in order to succeed, must have one simple continued Action, the Time not to exceed twelve hours; that the Incidents be well prepared and spring from the subject. That the Dramatis Personæ should always have a necessary or probable pretence for being on the Stage; and the same for going off: That the Intervals between the Acts be filled, as serving to carry on the Action, and continue it, as much as what is done on the Stage. That the Catastrophe arise from all the Incidents together, and entirely satisfy the curiosity of the spectators. Lastly, The Poet must observe unity of Place, that is, that the Scene must not be shifted nor changed throughout the Play.

It is allowed, *Plautus* has not been so scrupulously exact as never to transgress any of these Rules. But Madam *Dacier* has proved, that the Poet has observed them all in *Amphitryo, Epidicus,* and *Rudens.* It would be no hard matter to shew the same of some of the rest. But to begin with the Examination of the *Asinaria.* The subject is the trick put upon a man that dealt in Apes, to get the money he brought in payment for some he had bought, to employ it in supplying the pleasures of a wild young fellow. The Incidents are the exclusion of this young fellow from his mistress's house, for want of money; his father's loving the same woman: the troublesome and imperious temper of his mother, who on account of the great fortune she brought, governs the whole house: the absence of her principal slave to whom the money was due, which the dealer in Asses brought; and lastly, the mortification of a rival, who at last discovers the cheat.

The Time does not exceed eight hours; beginning but a little before noon, to give the dealer time to come from the Country; and it ends before night, for it is said, (Sc. 2. Act 4.) that the Entertainment, in which the Catastrophe happens, is to be given by day-light. The Place must be supposed an open Place near the old man's and the curtezan's houses, with this difference, that the latter should be fronting, and at the lower end of the stage. I must begin by observing, that the moral of this and some other of *Plautus*'s Comedies is abominable, though the subject of many of our *English* Comedies that are much esteem'd, resemble it too much. Perhaps the ignorance of the Antients may deserve our pity, but what excuse can we plead for the Immorality of our Stage?

Act 1. *Sc.* 1. opens with *Demenetus*, the old Gentleman and his servant *Libanus*. They may be supposed to have been talking together before they came on the Stage. The man is uneasy, and fears his master is going to send him to work in the mill, perhaps for some fault he had done, which makes him very earnest to find out what the old Gentleman would be at; at last *Demenetus* rids *Libanus* of his fears, by telling him he knows his son's Intrigues, and instead of blaming him, is willing to promote them. To hide his own scandalous design, he pretends the fondness of a father, is the reason of this complaisance. Having thus secured *Libanus*, and given him leave to get the money his son wanted, where he could, they separate.

Sc. 2. *Argyrippus*, the old man's son, who was forbid the Curtezan's house for want of money, comes on the Stage lamenting his misfortune. He complains bitterly of the old Baud her mother, and of the Curtezan, and resolves to be revenged. But love soon helps him to excuses for the daughter, so that he is determined to wreck his whole vengeance on the Mother. As he is in this resolution, he sees the Baud coming out of her house, and resolves to speak to her.

Sc. 3. Their Conversation shews the pernicious maxims of those creatures. It ends by making up the quarrel, upon condition, that for a sum of money *Argyrippus* shall have the Curtezan to himself for a year. Upon this, *Argyrippus* goes to get the money on any terms; and this makes the Interval between the first and second Act. Besides, *Libanus*, instead of seeking for the money, as he was ordered, had fallen asleep; and the dealer in Asses comes and enquires for *Demenetus*, but not finding him, goes to the public Baths, waiting for his return.

Act 2. *Sc.* 1. *Libanus* opens the scene; waking in a surprize, he recollects what he had to do: Whilst he is preparing to undertake it, he sees *Leonida*, another servant of the family coming in a hurry, and almost out of breath: he steps a little aside, not to be discoverd by the other who advances.

Sc. 2. After having told the reason of his coming, *Libanus* appears. *Leonida* informs him, that the dealer was arrived, who brought the money in payment for the Asses. How the man asked him which was the master's house; that he had made the dealer believe he was the Baily, to whom he was to pay the money, but that the other would not give into the bite: Whilst these two servants are consulting how to trick him, they see the man coming. *Leonida*, to make sure work, runs to give his master *Demenetus* notice of it, and *Libanus* comes forward to give the man no room to mistrust any thing.

Sc. 3. The dealer opens the Scene, and knocks at *Demenetus*'s door. *Libanus* comes and amuses him till *Leonida* appears, who counterfeiting *Saurea*, the principal slave, who had authority over the other slaves, and this begins the 4th Scene.

Sc. 4. *Leonida* coming up to *Libanus*, begins to reprimand him for having neglected to obey some orders he pretends to have given him, without seeming to take any notice of the dealer. After having made sport in this manner a while, he makes as if he just perceived the dealer in Asses, and asks his business. Being informed, it was to pay the price of some Asses that had been sold him, *Leonida* tells the man he may pay him. The other refuses it, saying, he does not know him, and that he will not pay him without *Demenetus*'s order. Thus ends the second Act. During

ring the Interval they find *Demenetus*, by whose direction the man pays *Leonida* the money.

Act 3. *Sc.* 1. *Cleareta*, and *Philenium*, her daughter, begin this Act; the mother reproaches her daughter for having so little regard to her instructions. And she, who really loves *Argyrippus*, cannot resolve to refuse to see him, as her mother would have her do, because he has got no money. Their conversation makes the first scene. The second (*Sc.* 2.) is made by *Leonida* and *Libanus*, who make themselves merry with the account they give of their bubbling the dealer in Asses of his money. Whilst they are in the height of their joy, they perceive *Argyrippus* just coming out of his mistress's house with her, and both in tears. They listen some time to learn the cause of their sorrow, and after having been witnesses to their mutual tenderness at parting, they come up to them (*Sc.* 3.) to give *Argyrippus* the good news of their having got him the money he wanted. But the rogues fool with him for a while before they give him the money. At length they give it him, upon condition that his father shall be in company with *Philenium* that night. And thus ends the 3d Scene and 3d Act. The Interval is filled up by *Leonida*, who is sent by *Argyrippus* to invite his father to sup with him and his mistress.

Act 4. *Scene* 1. The 4th Act opens with *Diabolus Argyrippus*'s rival, and a Parasite with him. *Diabolus*, to improve the opportunity of his rival's disgrace, had agreed with *Cleareta* for a certain sum, to have her daughter a year, on certain conditions drawn up in writing. He had given the Parasite this commission, who is now come, and reads him the Articles, which *Diabolus* approves, and they go out together to make the mother sign them. Here seems to be a Scene wanting, for *Diabolus* returns (*Scene* 2.) immediately with the Parasite, in a great fury against *Demenetus* and his son, though he does not seem to have had time to be informed how *Argyrippus* had made up his affairs with his mistress. However, he threatens to go and give *Demenetus*'s wife notice of his scandalous conduct, but the Parasite persuades him to let him go on that errand. Thus ends the 4th Act.

The Interval is filled up by the Parasite's giving *Artemona* notice of her husband's management, and her getting ready to go and surprize *Demenetus* with her son *Argyrippus* and *Philenium*.

Act 5. *Scene* 1. The Scene opens and represents the three last named persons at the bottom of the Stage, just going to supper, and in the height of joy. But, unluckily for them, the Parasite brings in *Artemona*, who stands a little aside to observe her husband. *Sc.* 2. At last, she comes in transported with anger, and having called him all to naught, soon obliges him to quit the company, and go off the Stage. Then the Actors, when the Play is ended, come forward together and laugh with the audience at what had passed, which they are far from disapproving. Nothing can be more immoral than this conclusion. But indeed, the heathens, in their practice especially, had little regard to chastity, where their leudness did not disturb the public peace. Fornication of all kinds, unless with citizens, was publicly tolerated, and that in the most infamous degree, as we see from the example before us. But that it would be wrong to argue from these abuses of the stage against all dramatic entertainments in general, has been already shewn.

As for *Terence*'s Plays, they are generally so well known, that a shorter examination of the *Andrian* (which I choose as most regular in the Drama) will be sufficient, without dwelling upon the minute incidents of every scene, as we did in *Plautus*'s *Asinaria*, because it is less known and read. *Donatus*, and the old critics, were content to divide the whole Play into three parts, which they called *Protasis*, *Epitasis*, and *Catastrophe*, and thus explain.

Protasis, is the first Act, the beginning or opening of the Play.

Epitasis, is the progress, and as it were the whole process of the various errors and perplexities of the subject as it is carrying on. *Catastrophe*,

Catastrophe, is the turn, the unravelling and clearing up of all difficulties, by a thorough discovery, which concludes the Play.

(*Protasis*.) *Pamphilus* was in love with *Glycerium*, who was supposed to be a stranger at *Athens* where the scene lies, and sister to *Chrysis* a Curtezan of *Andros*, but lately deceased at *Athens*. He had given *Glycerium* his word that he would marry her, and the intrigue was gone so far between them, that she was with child by him. *Simo* being informed of his son's passion for this stranger, in order to break off the engagement, pretends a design of marrying him speedily, and desires he would shew his obedience by accepting of the wife he would choose for him. *Pamphilus*, who sincerely honoured his father, and passionately loved *Glycerium*, was in the greatest distress how to behave on this occasion. His slave *Davus*, who had overheard the old gentleman's sham plot, advises his young master to promise his father an entire obedience, from whence he could apprehend no danger, since it was only a counterfeit marriage. The lover, though with some reluctance, is persuaded to do so, and promises to marry the person his father should please to choose him.

(*Epitasis*.) In the mean time this marriage of *Pamphilus* began to be talked of abroad, so that *Glycerium* came to hear of it, and through the violence of her grief at the news, being near her time, falls in labour, and is delivered of a boy. *Simo*, now he had got his Son's consent, which was above his expectation, began seriously to think of marrying him in earnest; and accordingly breaks the matter to his friend *Chremes*, who readily accepts the proposal of marrying his daughter *Philumena* to *Pamphilus*. The lovers affairs now seemed desperate; he had consented, and his father was for hastening the wedding. Upon this, *Davus*, whose indiscreet zeal had brought his master into these perplexities, endeavours to deter *Chremes* from the marriage, giving him to understand, that *Pamphilus* was in love already with another person,

person, by whom he had a son, which was true. This stratagem partly succeeds and makes *Chremes* hesitate.

(*Catastrophe*) But *Simo* so earnestly presses him to give his daughter, that at last all his scruples are removed, and *Pamphilus* finds himself as much embarrassed as before; when luckily *Crito*, a stranger of *Andros*, comes to *Athens*, as being next heir to *Chrysis* the Curtezan lately deceased, the reputed sister of *Glycerium*. *Simo* at first supposes him suborned by his son to interrupt the marriage; but at length *Crito* discovers to *Chremes* and him, that *Glycerium* was not related to *Chrysis*, but really a daughter of *Chremes*, whom he had for many years looked upon as lost. *Philumena* is married to her first lover *Charinus*, whose character is a foil to the merit of his friend *Pamphilus*, as the dulness of his man *Byrrhia* sets off *Davus*'s subtilty and contrivances.

By this sketch the reader will be inclined to judge, that the turn of PLAUTUS's Plays is more to ridicule and humour, as that of *Terence*'s is to politeness, and to move the affections: and whoever could happily unite the genius of these two, would be able to write a compleat Comedy; which, as being concerned to represent the passages of common life, has, by a wrong and hasty judgment, often been presumed to be an easy task for a Poet of common abilities. But *Horace* was long since of another opinion, for the same reason that persons of less reflection judged it so easy, namely, because it is only conversant with the occurrences of common life; for this not only makes it much easier for the generality to judge if a character is well expressed, if the dialogue is natural and well turned, and the plot well laid and happily executed; but makes every person expect to find more perfection in the whole performance than is generally in the power of most writers to give it. From this great mistake of ours, we are as liberal of our censure as sparing of applause, and condemn every error, which we think might have been mended with so little trouble to the Poet.

Creditur, ex medio quia res arcessit, habere
Sudoris minimum; sed habet Comedia tanto
Plus oneris, quanto veniæ minus———
                              Epist. ad AUGUST. ver. 168.

THE LIFE OF TERENCE.

TERENCE was born in the year of *Rome* 560, about nine years before the death of *Plautus*, eight years after the end of the second Punic war, when learning began to flourish among the *Romans*. They had now subdued though not destroyed *Carthage*, and by the overthrow of the *Macedonian* Kingdom had partly conquered *Greece*. This was the state of affairs about the time of TERENCE's captivity: so that the politer arts and sciences began to meet with encouragement, and *Paulus Æmilius*, who was a friend to them, set a noble example to the other Patricians by the liberal education he gave his children, which *Plutarch* particularly mentions in his life.

WHETHER TERENCE was of mean or noble parentage, whether an *African* in general, or a *Carthaginian*, is uncertain; though it seems more likely he he might be a *Carthaginian* of a good family, and made captive in the wars the *Carthaginians* continually had with the *Numidians* and other neighbouring nations. The *Romans* sent their deputies at three different times to compose these differences between the *Numidians* and *Carthaginians*; at one of which it is most likely some of them might purchase our Author among the other slaves that were sold. He fell into the hands of a generous master, *Terentius Lucanus*, a *Roman* Senator, who was so taken with the early marks he discovered in his young slave of a bright genius, that he gave him the advantage of a good education to improve it; and soon after, by giving him his liberty, put him in a way of raising his fortune by it.

His merit soon recommended him to the acquaintance and familiarity of the chief Nobility; and particularly to the friendship of *Scipio Æmilianus*, son of the aforesaid *P. Æmilius*, and adopted by the son of the elder *Scipio Africanus*. This nobleman was about nine years younger than our Author, but he had bravely distinguished himself in the wars at seventeen years of age, and we have already observ'd above, how well his father brought him up. He was the hero of the age, and compleated the destruction of *Carthage* some years after TERENCE's death. *Lælius*, son of the great *Lælius*, so intimate with the elder *Africanus*, was as intimate with the younger *Scipio* and our author; whose enemies were glad to give out that his Plays were composed by these noblemen, in order to lessen his growing credit. *Furius* was another of TERENCE's Patrons, but his merit is less known; though he is mentioned by TERENCE's enemies as one of the greatest men in *Rome*. In his Prologue to the *Adelphi*, TERENCE does not so much as offer to refute the calumny; but *Suetonius* observes it was done to pay his court to those great men, who perhaps might not be displeased at the report; and indeed in the Prologue to the *Heautontimorumnos*, TERENCE desired the audience not to credit the slanderous reports of his brother writers:

Ne plus iniquûm possit, quàm æquûm, oratio.

Suetonius adds a story of *Cornelius Nepos* to this purpose. "That the first of *March*, which was the feast of the *Roman* Ladies, *Lælius* being desired by his wife to sup a little sooner than ordinary, he prayed her not to disturb him; and that coming very late to supper that night, he said he had never composed any thing with more pleasure nor success; and being asked by the company what it was, he repeated some verses out of the 3d Scene of the 4th Act of *the Self-Tormentor*." All Commentators are agreed, that these verses are extremely fine. This report did not lessen after our Author's death; for *Valgius*, a Poet contemporary with *Horace*, says as much in positive terms;

Hæ, quæ vocantur Fabulæ, cujus sunt?
Non bas, qui jura populis, recensens dabat
Honore summo affectus fecit Fabulas?

The Plays however were certainly TERENCE's; not but that those gentlemen might be diverted sometimes by composing some Scenes for a Poet, whom they so familiarly conversed with.

THE *Andrian* does not seem to have been TERENCE's first piece; the very Prologue to the Play seems to intimate the contrary, and the circumstances *Suetonius* mentions about TERENCE's reading it first to the Poet *Cæcilius*, prove the *Andrian* not to be the first piece, and that *Suetonius* has mistaken the name of the Play; for *Cæcilius* died two years before the *Andrian* was brought on the Stage. *Vossius* therefore pretends to correct the words of *Suetonius*, and instead of *Cæcilius* reads *Acilius*, who was one of the Ædiles: but there is no likelihood of this, it being absurd to suppose the Ædiles would take the trouble to examine a Play privately first, since they had it always acted before them, before it was brought on the Stage. *Cæcilius* was the best Poet of the age,

and

and *Segeditus* has given him the preference to all the comic Poets. *Horace* makes him excel in the dignity of his sentiments, and *Varro* in the disposition of his subject. He was near fourscore when our Poet offered his first Play; and being unacquainted with TERENCE, it is said, that when he waited on him by the Ædiles order, who had desired to have *Cæcilius*'s judgment before he received the Play, the old gentleman being at table, bid our young author take a stool and begin to read it to him. It is observ'd by *Suetonius*, that TERENCE's dress was but mean, so that his outside did not much recommend him. But he had not gone through the first Scene, when *Cæcilius* invited him to sit at table with him, deferring the reading of the rest of the Play 'till after supper. This was a proof of TERENCE's merit, and *Cæcilius*'s good discernment and generosity. When he had heard the Play read throughout, he was charmed with the beauties of it, and commended the author as he deserved. With this advantage and approbation did TERENCE's first Play appear on the stage, when TERENCE could not be twenty-five; for the *Andrian* was acted when he was but twenty-seven years of age, 166 years before CHRIST. The *Hecyra* was acted the year following; the Self-Tormentor, *Heautontimorumenos*, two years after that: The *Eunuch*, two years after the other: The *Phormio*, the latter end of the same year; and the year afterwards the *Adelphi* or Brothers was acted, before Christ 160, when TERENCE was thirty-three years of age.

AFTER this *Terence* went into *Greece*, where he staid about a year, in order as it is thought to collect some of *Menander*'s Plays. He fell sick on his return from thence, and died at sea according to some, others say it was at *Stymphalis* a town in *Arcadia*, whither he put back from sea, before he was quite thirty-five years of age.

ACCORDING to this account, we cannot have lost above one or two of *Terence*'s Plays: for it is ridiculous to credit what *Suetonius* reports from one *Consentius*, an antient Author, of whom we find no mention

tion elsewhere, that *Terence* was returning with above an hundred of *Menander*'s Plays, which he had translated, but that he lost them by shipwreck, and that he died of grief for this loss.

Terence was of a middle size, very slender, and of a dark complection. He was married and left a daughter behind him, who was afterwards married to a *Roman* Knight. *Terence* left her a house and gardens on the *Appian* Way, near the Villa *Martis*. So that it seems very strange his enemies should give out that he died very poor. The friendship of those great men he so much conversed with, must have procured him some advantages. He received 8000 Sesterces for his *Eunuch* the first time it was acted; and was no doubt well paid for the rest: for it appears from the Prologue to the *Hecyra* or Step-mother, that the Poets used to be paid every time their Play was acted, and that the *Ædiles* employed the principal Actor or Head of the Company to agree with the author about the price. At this rate *Terence* must have made a handsome fortune before he died; for most of his Plays were acted more than once in his life time. The *Hecyra* we have been speaking of was brought twice upon the Stage and interrupted, so that not above one Act had been represented. The Poet here suffered in his reputation, but his purse was the better for it, as he says himself in the first Prologue, and in the second Prologue, spoken when it was brought the third time on the Stage; *Ambivius Turpio*, after having in a handsome manner requested the Attention of the Audience, desires for his sake they would hear the Play out; hinting as if he were ready to reimburse the Magistrate the money he had paid the Poet, in case the Piece did not take; which seems reasonable, since the Ædiles purchased it on his judgment, and at a price agreed on between the Poet and him, the chief Actor. The *Eunuch* was acted twice in one day.

We are now come to consider him more particularly with respect to his Plays that are extant, and his Character as a Dramatic Writer. It were endless to

mention

mention the Testimonies of the antients in his favour, or the many fine things said of him by modern Commentators and Critics. His chief excellency consists in these three points: The beauty of his characters, the politeness of his dialogue, and the regularity of his scene. I shall not insist on a particular comparison between him and *Plautus*, which we have done already in the Life of that Poet. The first thing wherein he surpasses all other comic Poets without exception, is the beauty of his Characters; in which *Plautus* has often grosly failed. In *Terence*, the Characters are maintained throughout the whole Play. *Varro* himself gives the palm to our Author for the manners. *In Argumentis Cæcilius poscit Palmam, in Ethesin Terentius.* A general knowledge of the world is not sufficient to attain this excellency. You must know all the secret springs that move the soul, and find out the progress of every incident in affecting the mind. It is objected, that *Terence* could not express the passions strongly: But it was not his business, and Comedy is the more difficult on that account, as requiring a greater experience of the humours and inclinations of men.

The manners, according to *Aristotle*, may be expressed these three ways; either by describing men as they are, or making them worse or better. The former, as leaving least to fancy, seems most difficult, and more suitable to good Comedy. Tragedy makes men better or worse than they commonly are, as well as Epic Poetry. Panegyrick makes them always better, and Satire worse.

Terence reigns without a rival in this particular, that his characters are all extremely natural; you hardly see a thought or humour strained through the Play; and hereby he submits himself, as it were, to the judgment of every reader in every age. Where ridicule is too much affected, you cannot follow nature so well; you will always compose an absurd character out of several real ones in life. Such a character then is a creature of the fancy, and cannot be so truly entertaining

tertaining, nor so improving, though by being more ridiculous it will be more diverting for a while, than one drawn after nature. This makes the grand difference between *Plautus* and *Terence*, and indeed between the middle and new Comedy of the *Greeks*.

As to the Disposition of a Play, in which *Terence* is thought not to excel, I know nothing more perfect in that kind than the *Andrian*. But this does not seem to be so strictly necessary in Comedy as Tragedy, and therefore more excusable. As in a picture, you will often excuse some fault in the disposition of the whole design, provided all the parts are well executed, and every particular figure well drawn.

BUT *Terence* is so far from being faulty in this respect, that I think this regularity of the characters in *Terence* gives him another advantage over writers of *Plautus*'s genius. Wit and Humour please the mind as distinct from the heart or affections; but every character in *Terence* interests the reader, and stirs his affections. *Terence* first moves, and then pleases you. You feel all *Pamphilus*'s concern in the *Andrian*, find all his reflections just, and pity his perplexity. *Simo*'s narration in the first scene of this Play is inimitable; and a careful reading of that alone will give the intelligent reader a more lasting pleasure than the merriest scene in *Plautus*; just as a fine piece of painting, after a good examination, must please more than the best grotesque piece can; though it will not so immediately strike a vulgar eye, nor tickle the fancy so much. Not but that I must do *Plautus* that justice to allow that he has often very fine Scenes of a more serious kind; but after all, his chief talent was ridicule, and *Terence*'s the propriety of the manners.

IN his Sentences again, *Plautus* is either too philosophical or proverbial. *Terence* is prodigiously cautious in this respect, and suits them so well to his subject by the politeness of his language, that they always seem to rise from the present occasion on which they are spoken, and not to have been sought for by the Poet.

The LIFE of Terence.

No Comic Writer can be more scrupulously exact than he is, in observing the proper Decorum of the stage. The characters of his Dramatis Personæ are never, as in *Plautus*, and other antients, confounded with that of the Actor. While *Plautus* introduces a tedious prologue in the character of *Mercury*, to let you into the whole secret of the play, *Terence* most artfully introduces old *Simo* in the *Andrian* deliberating with his Freed-man *Sosia* how to manage *Pamphilus*, whose Amour with *Glycerium*, the Manner of his discovering it, and the other previous Circumstances necessary to lead the reader into the design of the play, are there so delicately introduced and so clearly related, that one would never suspect *Terence* intended that first scene only to inform the Audience as far as was requisite to make them understand the sequel. That other Scene again, where *Pamphilus*, to assure *Mysis* that he will not forsake her Mistress, calls to mind the solemn Promise he made *Chrysis* on her Death-bed to be as a father, guardian, and husband to his beloved *Glycerium*; that scene, I say, is conducted with such Address, that it is not 'till after some reflection that we discover the Poet's art in taking this opportunity of giving the audience, who now began to grow uneasy, and mistrust his Fidelity, the fullest assurance to the contrary.

These are some of the masterly Strokes by which our Author exerts his Talent in the conduct of the Drama. We may find numberless Instances of this kind in every Play of his, wherein he did not content himself only to follow *Menander*, but often consulted his own genius. For he frequently made two plays of *Menander*'s into one; moulding them together into one compleat Comedy. Finding the incidents too few in *Menander*'s Plays which he imitated, he thought it necessary to fill the scene with more characters, which obliged him sometimes to make two into one. Some Writers jealous of his growing fame, highly blamed his conduct herein. *Terence*, in his prologue to the *Andrian*, pleads guilty to the charge; and justifies what he had done by the necessity of it, to give the audience a compleat entertainment; and by the example of the best Poets that had preceded him.

The best modern writers for the stage, I think are agreed in the usefulness, if not necessity of an under plot, so that I need say nothing in defence or commendation of our author's practice in this particular. So to the *Eunuch*, a plot of *Terence*'s own invention, he has boldly and judiciously added the characters of the captain and parasite from the *Colax*, a Play of *Menander*'s. Without this under-plot, which is admirably interwoven with the other, every attentive reader must perceive the play would have been barren of incidents, which is now the most admired of the six, though perhaps, each has its several excellencies. *Terence* has perfectly justified himself in the Prologue, where he owns the fact as usual. "But (says he) if an author may never borrow a "character of those who have writ before him, and "adapt it to his purpose, he may as well never write, "since it would be difficult to find out any character "that had not been brought on the stage before.

Nullum est jam dictum, quod non sit dictum prius.

I can't help taking notice of an odd circumstance, that shews the great liberty every private man took in those public entertainments. *Lavinius*, whom *Terence* has described as a dull Poet, and a servile translator of the *Greeks*, when the *Ædile* having bought the Play, had ordered it to be acted, and had admitted this Poet as a spectator, he bawled out in the height of the representation, that *Terence* was a plagiary, and had stolen from others the two characters aforesaid. What I would observe is, that this insolence, tho' the Magistrates, who had given the Play themselves, presided at the Theatre, is no farther taken notice of in *Terence*'s prologue, than as an absurd piece of ill-nature in *Lavinius*; nor does *Terence* say that the Ædiles thought fit to punish or reprimand him for it, which he would not have failed to do, if they had, in a prologue that was spoken on purpose to expose his adversary's and justify his own conduct to the Public. I shall not justify such a sufferance of so public a breach of good manners

ners, but must, at the same time, remind the reader, if he be censoriously disposed, to consider how frequently the Action has been interrupted in our Theatres by the insolence and riot of the meanest of the audience, when persons of the first distinction, or the sovereign himself have been present.

Terence continued his former method in composing the *Heautontimoreumenos*, or *Self-Tormentor*. He therein had an Eye to one of *Menander*'s of the same name, but supplied the barrenness of the plot, by doubling the characters; introducing, instead of one of each, two old fellows, two young men, two mistresses, and two slaves. *Menander*'s whole play consisted in *Menedemus*'s tormenting himself for his son's absence, whom he had forced to go into the army, by his severity in not allowing him the common freedoms of the young fellows of his age. A play with no other incidents but what related to *Menedemus* and his son, *Terence* rightly judged would be too barren of entertainment, and has accordingly given it a new life by the addition of so many characters co-incident with the main plot.

A Passage in this Prologue gives me occasion to mention another distinction the *Romans* made of their Comedies, into *Stataria*, *Motoria*, and *Mixta*. The first was like the *Self-Tormentor*, with few changes of the Scene. The second, like the *Amphytrio* of *Plautus*, had many changes, and was full of Action. The last was, like the *Eunuch*, a mixture of these two.

The *Adelphi*, or *Brothers*, *Terence* composed much after the same method as he had observed in the *Heautontimorumenos*. To enliven this Play, he translated from a Play of *Diphilus*, a *Greek* comic Poet, the Characters of a young fellow taking a Curtezan by violence from a merchant of slaves. It is easy to see how many incidents arise from this one through the Play; and what a fine opportunity the Poet has hence taken to thicken his Plot, and display the contrary Characters of the two old Men the Brothers, by their behaviour on this occasion. But I have only room to suggest this hint to the Reader's notice, to do more would be to deprive him of the pleasure of the search and the satisfaction of the discovery.

The same detracting old Poet, continued to reproach *Terence* with his being assisted by Persons of the first Quality in composing his Plays. One would have thought our Author had here a fine opportunity of retorting upon his adversary, and shewing his inconsistency, first, in saying that persons of the greatest genius had a hand in his Pieces, and then blaming them as faulty, or stolen from others. But *Terence* knew how to keep his temper, and politely appeals to the audience, whether such a reproach must not rather turn to his praise, that persons so distinguished by their birth and actions, both at home and abroad, should condescend to bear a part with him in composing, and treat a man of his low condition with that intimacy and friendship.

Terence has left us no account of his manner of composing his *Phormio* and *Hecyra*. They are both imitated from the *Greeks*, and if he had found it necessary, he would have added some new Characters, as his practice was, and he had declared in the Prologue to the *Brothers*, that he intended to do.

Why he should always choose to imitate the *Greeks*, rather than sometimes lay the Scene at *Rome*, and compose what the *Romans* called *Togatæ Fabulæ*, I shall not pretend to determine. Perhaps his genius was not so good at invention as improvement. This is known to be true not only of particular men, but whole nations, of which I dare name ours as a pregnant example. Though many other nations claim precedency for invention, none that I know of will contest our merit in improving every Art we have received from them. What *Terence* might have done, had he lived, is uncertain. It is rather to be admired, that with all the advantages he might reap by imitating the *Greeks*, he should be able to write six such finished Pieces as are yet extant of his, before thirty four years of age, and not a *Roman* by birth neither. I will here add the testimony of *Velleius Paterculus*.

Paterculus, an Author, whose good taste was never questioned. He declares, that the *Roman* Dialogue and Urbanity attained its full perfection under *Cæcilius*, *Terence*, and *Afranius*. *Varro* indeed gives the first the preference as to the Conduct of the Stage, as *Horace* does in the Sentiments; but they both allow *Terence* inimitable in the Conduct of the Stage, as *Varro* does in the Characters. *In Argumentis Cæcilius palmam poscit: In Ethesin Terentius.* But I should choose to make *Horace* my judge in this matter, whose Art must extend to the Conduct of the Stage as well as to the beauty and propriety of the Characters, *Vincere Cæcilius gravitate Terentius Arte.* And *Paterculus*,——*Dulces Latini leporis facetiæ, per Cæcilium, Terentiumque & Afranium suppari ætate nituerunt.* To conclude these observations on this part of *Terence*'s character. His Scene, as the ingenious Mr. *Congreve* very well observed, and in one Play has particularly endeavoured to imitate him, always proceeds in a regular connection, the persons going on and off for visible reasons, and to carry on the Action of the Play. He has indeed no witty meer chit-chat in these Plays of his, nor surfeits his audience with Scenes full of repartee, simile, or gross ribaldry, nor dares absurdly to shift his Scenes from one Country to another, nor has any lame Chasms in the midst of his Acts, whereby the whole Action is for a while at a stand, to be poorly botched up again in the next Scene. If these defects are to be found in modern Performances, it is evident, the censure must fall upon the Author's want of genius, and not on the nature of a double Plot. *Terence* having incontestably proved by his practice, that an Underplot, if well adjusted, is so far from destroying the principal design, that it carries it on with more spirit and vigour, and furnishes new incidents, without which the whole Action would be faint and heavy. Should an unskilful Artist attempt a History-piece, and commit gross mistakes in the grouping and attitude of his figures, so as many of them should seem to have no Part in the grand defign of the Piece, the Connoiffeurs I believe would call his abilities in queftion, without blaming the Art for his mifcarriages in the execution. From what has been obferved, I believe the Reader will be inclinable to do our Author juftice, and allow his talent for forming the Characters, and conducting the Drama. Which fecond point, I think, Madam *Dacier* was too eafy in giving up, as if fhe miftrufted *Terence* were deficient in this refpect. Though perhaps, *Varro* and fhe meant only the laying the Fable or Plan of the Play, and in which alone the learned *Roman* may have given *Cæcilius* the preference. This firft ground-work indeed is moft effential to the forming a good Tragedy. Comedy, whofe fuperftructure is more light and eafy, will bear a flighter foundation. If therefore Tragedy demands invention and elevation, Comedy requires more genius, penetration and exactnefs, and I may add compafs of underftanding. And here it is we may fay, that nature feems to have led *Terence* by the hand; who, though he was fo compleat a Mafter of polite converfation, and has filled his Comedies with fo many fine Reflections, yet he fo nicely difcerns the bounds of every Character, that all that is faid feems juft what became each perfon at that time, and in thofe circumftances. This is the genius that *Horace* approved of in a Poet to his tafte.

―――――― *Ut fibi quivis*
Speret idem, fudet multum, fruftraque laboret
Aufus idem   Art. Poet.

But our Author's moft undifputed excellency yet remains to be confidered, the Politenefs of his Dialogue the confummate Elegance and Purity of his Diction.

The firft language of Comedy was very mean and vulgar, and the Dialogue as it were ftuffed with obfcene Wit and Ribaldry. The fatirical Characters of fome Perfons obnoxious to the public diflike, thus infolently pointed out, made up the firft rude Effays of the old *Greek* Comedy at *Athens*.

THE *Romans* grew not much acquainted with the
Greek

Greek learning 'till after the reformation of the *Athenian* Stage. *Menander*, the most polite *Greek* comic Poet, whose pieces were so admired, that, according to *Paterculus*, they who followed him in the same way fell short of it; him *Terence* chose for his Model, having throughly studied and improved his Manner; as we have shewn above. If *Terence* could not attain all his Wit and Humour, as *Julius Cæsar* seems to question, he was confessedly more chaste and correct. *Plautus*, who was not inferior to *Menander* in wit or humour, we see sometimes gave too much way to his genius, and it is a question whether he has not taken some of his witticisms as well as good turns from the *Greek*, whom he almost equalled in most respects, allowing for the difference of language. The *Greek* being much more capable of turns of all kinds, and the genius of the people more gay and lively than that of the *Romans*, and at the time of *Menander's* writing much politer than the *Romans* ever were.

Terence therefore, though a foreigner by birth, was by temper and education more truly *Roman* than *Plautus*. There is a dignity and gracefulness in his sentiments, suitable to the gravity of a noble *Roman*, and it may be truly said of him with respect to his language, that like the Graces he is often seen to smile, is ever chearful, but never breaks out into a strong fit of laughter. His strokes of ridicule are so finely expressed, that a vulgar eye often cannot discern them; upon a closer view they appear so just and natural, that we wonder at our own inattention, that could let them escape our observation.

And indeed the true *Attic* Wit and *Roman* Urbanity does not seem so much to have consisted in what we now call Turns of Wit and Pleasantry, as in a polite and elegant propriety of Sentiments and Diction, that sometimes glanced upon, but seldom directly aimed at a strong Ridicule. Such *Plato's* writings are said to be: and none that ever read them, will compare that Philosopher's Stile and Manner to that of our Modern Wits.

THIS

THIS happy ſtile it was, that made *Terence*'s jealous rivals give out, That *Scipio*, *Lælius*, *Furius*, and other the greateſt Men of the Age, compoſed the greater part of thoſe Pieces, which he only father'd and uſher'd into the world as his own. Thoſe Poets could never attain the Court language, as the *French* call it. It is here worth our notice, that *Terence* has been found ſo entirely free from the *African* genius in his ſtile. The other writers of that part of the world, as many as have written in the *Roman* tongue, ſome of whom were Men of great parts and learning, have diſtinguiſhed themſelves by the viciouſneſs of their ſtile. It abounds in points, is flaſhy, ſwelling, broken and impure: witneſs *Apuleius*, *Capella*, and *Tertullian*. *Maurus Terentianus* is indeed ſomething better.

HENCE I think it evident, that *Terence* was made a ſlave very young, and his education wholly *Roman*, ſince it is otherwiſe inconceivable how he ſhould not have ſucked in the leaſt tincture of that corrupt turn of thought and expreſſion, that ſo diſtorts the ſtile of thoſe elſe eloquent writers.

IT would be too great a deviation from our ſubject to enlarge upon the difference of Genius of different Nations, which has been in ſome meaſure attempted in the Introduction to the firſt Volume: yet thus much let me add, that as the language of *Athens* was the only ſtandard of a good ſtile for many Ages among the *European Greeks*, ſo none of the *Aſiatics* (generally ſpeaking) except the *Rhodians*, could attain to a nervous and manly eloquence.

IF I might dare to offer my opinion of our own comic writers on this occaſion, I ſhould think Mr. *Congreve*'s Plays excel in wit, purity of ſtile, and polite language, unleſs the Author of the *Careleſs Huſband* ſhould diſpute the firſt place with him. *Wicherley* and *Farquhar* will come next, unleſs diſputed by Sir *John Vanbrugh* or *Shadwell*. Mr. *Addiſon*'s *Drummer* is beyond any of that kind in our language, and comes neareſt to the manner of *Plautus* without his faults.

My chief view in what has been here said of our Poets, is to give the *English* Reader some tolerable idea of *Plautus*'s and *Terence*'s stile, which I am afraid they cannot have from any translation extant. The stile of an Author, which is often what characterizes him most, is hardest to express in a translation; I had almost said impossible: For when you have done all, you can give but a faint resemblance, by making him speak, as you think he would have expressed himself had he been an *Englishman*: For to come nearer, would be to make a servile, that is, a very bad translation. The Genius of Languages are so very unlike, as well as the many customs, and even ways of thinking, that arise in different times and nations, from Religion, Learning and Government, that we ought to make an Author great allowances, who has used his best endeavours to give us a good translation of an antient writer: though I must absolutely condemn the modernizing way of the famous *Ablancourt* who has translated *Tacitus*, *Lucian*, and many other of the Antients; but was so full of his own thoughts, that you only read the *Frenchman* when you think to read the *Greek* or *Roman*. You have the polite *Ablancourt*'s manner, for the grave and sententious *Tacitus*, or the censorious and sneering *Lucian*.

Populo ut placerent quas fecisset fabulas, was the aim of our Poet in the regulation of his Drama, and it is unquestionably the true test of a good Play when it has a great run, and pleases all orders of men. It may be defective in what the Critics call the Constitution or Fable, may exceed in point of duration of time, and shift the Scene too irregularly to consist with critical probability; yet all this notwithstanding I dare pronounce that a good Play, which with any or even all these irregularities, has pleased both Court and City, Town and Country. I do not say that an attention to the rules of good Critics is amiss; but I will maintain, a Poet may fail in some or all these points, and yet if he be true in marking out his Characters, just and ingenious in his Sentiments and
Dialogue,

Dialogue, polite and elegant in his Language, he will please in spite of the Critics and their Rules. This observation will hold good in Epic as well as Dramatic Poetry. *Homer*, with *Bossu*'s leave, is not only deficient in the Fable of his Poem, which has been acknowledged by the most unprejudiced judges, but is often absurd in his Characters: whether the Age he wrote in does not carry an excuse with it for this, I shall not dispute, as being out of the present question: Yet the magnificence of his Diction, and the genuine beauty of his Sentiments, will make him the object of universal admiration, as long as a taste for the politer Arts and Languages shall last among us.

It is the same in Painting: The best judges observe great faults in *Rubens*'s Manner and his Design, besides the absurdity of his modern Dresses, and the clumsy fleshiness of his Figures; but his colouring is so admirable, which is in Painting what the stile is in Poetry, that with all his faults he stands in the foremost rank of Artists, and takes place of many who are his inferiors in Colouring only.

'Tis this excellency of Diction and Dialogue that sets *Terence* above all other Comic Writers. *Plautus* had more Wit; *Cæcilius* more skill in laying the Plot:

I own that our Taste is different from that of the *Romans* in *Terence*'s time. We should like his Elegance, but think him cold and spiritless: yet this simplicity I am persuaded best suited the prevailing taste of his time. There was a gravity in the character and conversation of the *Romans*, to which we are strangers; but when they were come to the highest pitch of grandeur and magnificence I am persuaded they quitted their antient simplicity of character, and in compliance with a luxurious court, took up an air of Wit and Gaiety, which soon degenerated into affectation: Thus we find it began to do in *Nero*'s time, as appears from the writings of the gravest Authors, *Seneca*, *Lucan*, *Tacitus*, *Quintilian* in his Declamations, and *Pliny* the younger; nay, what may seem strange, so strong was the ill habit, that whilst
some

some of these great men complained of the decay of true Eloquence, they were themselves the great examples and promoters of it.

YET there are some Points left, wherein our Author seems to have failed most; one of which is in not making his Characters *Roman*. The more immediately we are acquainted with those Characters that are made the subject of Comic Ridicule, the more readily do we enter into the humour and spirit of the Play, and consequently receive a more agreeable entertainment from thence, than foreign characters, though those of the neighbouring nations, could possibly give us. In *Terence*'s time indeed the *Romans* were no strangers to the *Greek* Manners and Customs, but they were indisputably better acquainted with their own. Therefore both *Terence* and *Plautus*'s Plays would have been better relished, had they laid the Scene at *Rome*.

ANOTHER deficiency seems to be a want of variety of Characters: a raking Son, a griping old Father, a tricking Slave, a greedy Strumpet, a pimping Parasite, a Daughter exposed or stolen, and owned in the Catastrophe: These are the constant Characters of their Comedies, tho' not without some variation. It may be said, that their Manners were not arrived to that height of luxury, nor had they yet discovered the various arts of life, which time and necessity have since taught us. Besides, that inexhaustible fund of Characters, *Love* was treated in a very different way among the *Greeks* and *Romans* from what it is among us. I think in general we do the fair sex more justice now than they did; and Religion has made s[ome a]mendment, outwardly at least, in our Morals. A[ll] considered, perhaps that sameness of Character [that] makes *Plautus*'s and *Terence*'s Plays less agree[able is] more excusable than some have imagined. [But] in respect to this variety of Chara[cters] much improved among us, and [not so] in any other Nation. The i[nfluence of Go]vernment, and the humour pe[culiar] to be two sources of it. Besides, our Comic Writers have taught persons of all degrees from the Prince to the Peasant, to appear agreeably upon the Stage; but the Antients were confined, or kept themselves within a much smaller compass, as appears from their characters enumerated above.

AGAIN, *Plautus* and *Terence*, however capable they might be of inventing their own Subjects, chose rather to borrow them from the *Greek* Stage, where they knew they had already pleased. They have both given proofs of their judgment in the many additions and alterations they made to these borrowed Subjects; and I doubt not had they lived an Age later, when all Arts were in their full glory at *Rome*, and the empire in its highest state of power and splendor, they would have found subjects enough at home to furnish out their Scenes, and would have given more life as well as variety to their Characters; the fewness of which was certainly a great cramp to their Genius, which has thereby appeared to a disadvantage, in having so few subjects to work upon. And this may be some apology for our Poets, who, one would think, would, both for their honour and conveniency, have varied their Characters oftener, had it been either agreeable to the Audience, or indeed possible to be done in that infancy of Arts among them.

Miscellaneous Poets.

BESIDES those Poets, of whose Life and Writings an account has been given at large, there should be some notice taken of several both Dramatic and others, who have been esteemed by the Antients. Though their Works being now chiefly lost, we can form no certain judgment of our own concerning them; yet it is worth our while to know their character as far as we find it given by antient Writers. However, to avoid perplexity, I shall not quote the passages themselves, but content my self with just mentioning the authority I have for what is advanced concerning them.

AND there are some few Poets, whose Works tho' yet partly extant, I thought hardly deserved a particular examination, and therefore left them to be mentioned in this place.

I have ranged them in the order of time as nearly as I could. Only as the Dramatic Writers come first most of them, I chose not to interrrupt their Series. Such among these Poets as have been treated of elsewhere, I shall say nothing of here, but by way of Supplement to the former accounts.

To begin with LIVIUS ANDRONICUS, I have nothing more to say of him, than that I find his Tragedy of *Ulysses* was esteemed the best of all his Works.

NÆVIUS of *Campania* published his first Play five years after *L. Andronicus*. He was banished *Rome* by a faction of the Nobles, and died the same year, of the second *Punic* war, that *Scipio* passed over into *Africa*, in the Consulship of *M. Cornelius Cethegus* and *P. Sempr. Tuditanus*.

ENNIUS of *Tarentum* wrote many Tragedies, as well as Annals and Satires. He survived *Plautus* fourteen years, and died in the Consulship of *Q. Martius Philippus* and *Cn. Serv. Cæpio*.

PORCIUS

Porcius Licinius Tegula, or *Imbrex*, flourished about the same time, and was a celebrated Comic Writer. *Volcatius Sedigitus*, in his list of them, places him in the fourth rank.

Si erit, quod quarto detur, dabitur Licinio.

Statius, at first a Slave, with his Freedom obtained the surname of *Cæcilius*, and became a famous Comic Writer. He is thought to have been an *Insubrian Gaul* by birth, and a native of *Milan*. He was an intimate friend of *Ennius*, whom he survived but one year. *Cicero* does not approve the Harshness of his Stile. *Sedigitus* places him first;

Cæcilio palmam Statio de Comico.

And *Horace* gives him the preference for the gravity of his characters;

Vincere Cæcilius gravitate, Terentius arte.

Varro is of the same opinion with *Horace*. And *Vel. Paterculus*, L. 1. joins him with *Terence* and *Afranius*, whom he reckons the most excellent Comic Writers of *Rome*; *Dulcesque latini leporis facetiæ per Cæcilium, Terentiumque & Afranium sub pari ætate nituerant.*

Pacuvius, *Ennius*'s sister's son, was born the year of *Rome* 533, and 156th *Olympiad*, according to *Eusebius*, and gained a great reputation by many excellent Tragedies which he wrote, as well as by his skill in Painting. He published his last Piece at eighty years of age. Some years before he died he retired to *Tarentum*. He is much commended both by *Pliny* the Naturalist, and *Cicero*, particularly for his *Orestes*, which was revived and acted with applause in the year of *Rome* 624, when *C. Sempr. Tuditanus*, and *M. Aquilius Nepos* were Consuls. But the same *Cicero* condemns his Stile. His Works shewed him a Man of great learning, as *Horace* has observed, where he likewise commends *Attius* for his sublime Manner;

———————*aufert*
Pacuvius docti famam senis, Attius alti.

This *Attius* succeeded *Pacuvius*, and was partly his Cotemporary, for he brought his first Tragedy on the Stage being thirty years old, at the same time that *Pacuvius* wrote his last, which was in the year of *Rome* 614, when *C. Lælius* and *Q. Servilius Cæpio* were Consuls. The Plays were exhibited by the great *P. Licinius Crassus Mucianus*, then Ædile, of whom *Gellius* remarks, that he excelled in five Particulars, being very Rich, of noble Descent, great Eloquence, a profound Lawyer, and High Priest, or *Pontifex Maximus*.

Attius was the son of a Freed-man at *Rome*, and was born the year of *Rome* 583, according to *Eusebius*, when *Martius Philippus* and *Servilius Cæpio* were Consuls, and was sent from *Rome* among others, whilst he was very young, in a Colony to *Pisaurum*. *D. Junius Brutus Callaicus*, who, in the year of *Rome* 616, overcame the *Portuguese* and *Gallicians*, was a great admirer of this Poet, with whose verses he adorned the Temple he had built out of the spoils of that war. See *Val. Maximus*, l. 8. cap. 14. I find no account of *Attius*'s death.

Suetonius speaks of Attilus, a Comic Writer, who is supposed to have lived about this time. *Cicero* condemns his Stile, and observes that he made a bad Translation of the *Electra of Sophocles*. *Licinius*, for the hardness of his Stile, calls him an Iron Writer, but says, he had other good qualities which made him worth reading;

Ferreum scriptorem opinor, verum scriptorem tamen
Ut legendas sit.———

And *Volcatius Sedigitus* has set him a degree above *Terence*. *Marcus Atutius* was Cotemporary with *Plautus*, and a Comic Writer, some of whose Pieces had been ascribed to *Plautus*, but by *Varro* were restored to the right Author. Plautius, another Comic and Cotemporary Writer, suffered in the same manner.

For such was the fondness of the *Romans* for all *Plautus*'s Plays, that they were ready to ascribe all to him that savoured of his manner, unless the true Author was known.

But Cneius Aquilius, another Comic Poet of the same Age, had afterwards the credit of fathering some of *Plautus*'s Plays, 'till the critical enquiry of *Varro* deprived him of it, and ascribed them to *Plautus*.

Ruscius, another Comic Poet, was Cotemporary with *Terence*.

Turpilius and Trabea lived some time after him. These were all Comic Poets of reputation, who are thus ranged by *Sedigitus*.

Turpilius septimum, Trabea octavum obtinet,
Nono loco esse facile facio Luscium.

Turpilius lived to a great age, and died about the time that *Furius Bibaculus* was born, at *Sinuessa* in the 169th *Olympiad*, according to *Eusebius*, about the year of *Rome* 649. *Alexis* and *Menander* are the two *Greek* Poets he is said to have imitated.

C. Titius, a *Roman* Knight, flourished not many years after, both at the Bar by his Eloquence, and on the Stage by his Tragedies.

After him came Afranius, his professed Admirer and Imitator, though in the comic way. But he chose *Roman* subjects, from whence his Comedies were called *Togatæ*. *Horace* has observed his happy Imitation of *Menander*'s manner;

Dicitur Afrani toga convenisse Menandro.

Afranius had so great a value for *Terence*, that he pronounced him almost inimitable, saying, *Terentio non similem dices quempiam*. Both *Quintilian* and *Ausonius* allow his Excellencies, but jointly lament the Lewdness and Immorality of his Writings. I think it is no proof of *Sedigitus*'s judgment, not to have mentioned this polite Writer among his Comic Poets, unless he put him in another Class, because his Comedies were on *Roman* Subjects.

Soon

Soon after him flourished Novius, a writer of *Attellane* Farces, and some time after him Mummius in the same way.

Pomponius Bononiensis is likewise said to have been the author of some *Attellane* Pieces. He was a man of great wit and elegance, according to *Cicero* and *Seneca*, and flourished about the same time with *Mummius*.

C. Julius Cæsar Strabo, who was Ædile in the year of *Rome* 664, wrote many Tragedies according to *Cicero*, who observes, that his stile was smooth and flowing, but wanted strength.

About the same time flourished Titus Quinctius Atta, a comic writer of Plays with *Roman* characters. He died at *Rome* in the 175th *Olympiad*, according to *Eusebius*. *Festus* the Grammarian says, he was surnamed *Atta* from the lameness of his feet; to which *Horace* seems to allude, where he complains, that the *Patricians* would not allow him to examine whether *Atta*, in his Comedies, trod the Stage gracefully; (which used to be strewed with flowers) he means, that they were offended he should presume to doubt the merit of those pieces, in which those excellent Players *Roscius* and *Æsopus* had acted parts.

Recte necne crocum floresque perambulet Attæ
Fabula si dubitem: clament periisse pudorem
Cuncti pene patres, ea cum reprehendere coner
Quæ gravis Æsopus, quæ doctus Roscius egit.

Pomponius Secundus was a man of quality, born at *Bologna*. He flourished about the year of *Rome* 782, and was cotemporary with *Seneca* the Philosopher. He is said to have composed a great many Tragedies. *Pliny*, in the 4th *C*. of *L*. 14. of his natural History, tells us, that he had written an account of his life. *Pliny* the younger relates this remarkable humour of his; that when he read his Plays to a friend, to have his advice, and he proposed some alterations, or to have something omitted, which the Poet, on the contrary, liked, and had a mind to retain as it was, he pleasantly used to say, *I appeal to the People.* *Quintilian*, who says he just remembers to have seen *Secundus*, speaks of him as an excellent critic, and takes notice of a little controversy that happen'd between him and *Seneca* the Philosopher, about the propriety of some expressions of the Poet *Attius*. This Poet was much beloved by *Germanicus*, and the loftiness of his stile got him the surname of the *Tragic Pindar*.

Ovid commends MELISSUS, the freed-man of *Mecænas*, as a comic writer;

Et tua cum Socco Musa, Melisse levis.
De Ponto L. 2. El. 10.

Suetonius says, this *Melissus*'s Comedies were of a different sort from the *Roman Togatæ Fabulæ*, and were called *Trabeatæ*.

TURANIUS was a tragic Poet of some reputation, who flourished about the same time, according to *Ovid*;

Musaque Turani tragicis innixa Cothurnis.

LET us now look a little back to some other Poets whom we omitted, whilst we were willing to present the principal dramatic writers in one view. For to attempt a compleat catalogue of them or the other Poets, if all deserve that name who sometimes diverted themselves with Poetry, would be a tedious as well as a very dull task. *Vossius*, and some others, have been laborious in these Collections, to whom I must refer the Reader, that is curious of such knowledge.

THE first of these Poets we are now to treat of should be CATO the *Censor*, were he acknowledged to be the Author of those moral Distichs which bear his name. This is now given up by all the Critics, but still they are divided in their conjectures about the age and character of the Author. Some imagine him to have been a Heathen of the 4th Century, whilst others more probably suppose it the work of some Christian
writer

writer of the 8th, who, in naming the Book might imitate the Antients, who frequently entitled their Books by the name of some great man that had distinguished himself on the subject which they treated of. *Plato*, *Cicero*, and *Lucian*, furnish us with many examples of this practice. The Book is well adapted to the capacity of children, for whose instruction it seems intended, and the author was a man of good sense and piety at least, though no Poet.

LUTATIUS CATULUS presents himself next. He was Consul the year of *Rome* 650, with *Marius*, when both signalized themselves in defeating and almost destroying the *Cimbri*. Afterwards, in the civil wars between *Marius* and *Sylla*, *Catulus* sided with the latter, and when *Marius*, during *Sylla*'s absence in *Asia*, assisted by *Cinna*'s faction, had made himself Master of *Rome*, where he proscribed and put to death the most illustrious men of the State, who had opposed or not joined with him, *Catulus*, to avoid his fury, having shut himself up in a retired apartment which had been lately plaistered, he was stifled there by the stench of the mortar, and the fumes of the charcoal fire that had been made to dry the walls.

His talent lay at *Epigram*, of which he published many, but his stile was not so correct or elegant as that of *Catullus*, and his versification more irregular. His wit was generally admired, which it would have deserved better, had he not indulged himself in obscene subjects so much. He was an Historian as well as a Poet, and wrote the History of his own Consulship, which he addressed to his friend *Furius Antias*, that is, who was born at *Antium*. *Macrobius*, L. 7. *Saturn* observes, that *Virgil* has been beholden to this Author for many things, which argues that he was a good writer for the age he lived in. But what Poems he wrote I do not find any where mentioned.

D. LABERIUS, a *Roman* Knight, had gained a great Reputation by his comic Pieces called *Mimes*, in the time of *Julius Cæsar*; whom having offended by some of his Railleries, *Cæsar*, in revenge, ordered him,

him, to the disgrace of the *Equestrian* Order, to mount the Stage when he was above sixty years old. *Laberius* very ingeniously complains of this hardship in a fragment which *Macrobius* has preserved, L. 2. *Saturnal*. *Laberius* died the year after *Cæsar*'s assassination, and left the glory of this kind of Dramatic Poetry to be indisputably enjoyed by PUBLIUS SYRUS, whose name should intimate that he was a *Syrian* by birth, and having been made a slave when young and brought to *Rome*, he there obtained his liberty by his merit, and proved so excellent a writer of *Mimes*, that the *Romans* preferred them to the best of their own or the *Greek* Dramatic Writers. *Julius Cæsar* first established his reputation, and gave him the Prize of Poetry against his friend *Laberius*, who contended with *Syrus* for it, who was as yet but a young man. He continued to flourish many years under *Augustus*. *Cassius Severus* was a professed admirer of him, and the two *Seneca*'s speak of him with the highest encomiums, 3 *Controvers*. and *Epist.* 8. Many moderns, and particularly the *Scaligers*, have launched out very much in his praise; they say he stripped *Greece* of all her wit, fine turns, and agreeable raillery, and that his Sentences include the substance of the Doctrine of the wisest Philosophers. They were extracted from his mimic Pieces some time under the *Antonines*, according to the best Editors. They are generally printed with the Fables of *Phædrus*.

FURIUS, surnamed of BIBACULUS, perhaps from his excessive drinking, was born about the year of *Rome* 650. *Quintilian* says, that he wrote Iambics in a very satirical strain, and therefore is censured by *Cremutius Cordus* in *Tacitus* Annal. L. 4. C. 8. as a slandering and invective writer. *Horace* is thought to have ridiculed the false sublime of his stile, L 2. *Sat.* 5. yet, according to *Macrobius Saturnal*. L. 6. C. 1. *Virgil* is said to have imitated him in many places.

Soon after him flourished RABIRIUS, a Poet of a very great character, who is said to have written a
fine

fine Poem on the wars between *Augustus* and *Anthony*. See *Velleius Paterculus*, L. 2. *Ovid* L. 4. *ult*. Eleg. *Quintilian*, L. 10. And *Horace* names him among those genius's of the first rate, whom he desired to please in his writings. The Critics have not been able to collect any fragments of his, sufficient for us to form any judgment of his manner, so that we can only conclude from the joint testimony of his cotemporaries, that he was a fine Critic and a noble Poet, magnificence of expression being his peculiar character, according to *Ovid*,

———*Magnique Rabirius oris.*

VALERIUS CATO, who flourished in *Sylla*'s time, is said by some Critics to be the Author of a little Poem called *Diræ*, that is among the *Juvenilia* of *Virgil*. He was of *Gallic* extraction, and had composed some elegiac Poems under the title of *Lydia* and *Diana*, to which *Suetonius de Gram. Illustr.* is supposed to allude, where he calls this Author the *Syren* of the *Latins*, from the enchanting softness of his Muse.

CORN. LICINIUS CALVUS, cotemporary with, and an intimate friend of *Catullus*, is reckoned by *Cornelius Nepos* as one of the best Poets of the Age. He wrote many Elegies and Epigrams*, in the former he celebrated his passion for *Quintilia*. *Cicero* gives him the character of a very smart Iambic Writer, without regard to Party; for he spared neither *Cæsar* nor *Pompey*. Yet he bore the character of a very good-natur'd man. *Seneca* the Rhetorician, and *Quintilian*, allow him to have been so excellent an Orator, that he contended for some time with *Cicero* for the pre-eminence. He was a man of a low stature, for which he is agreeably rallied by *Catullus*.

The Works of these noble Poets would have ad-

———————————————————————

* *Propertius* takes notice of them as follows:
Hac etiam docti confessa est pagina Calvi,
Cum caneret miseræ funera Quintiliæ.

Lib. 2. El. 25.

mirably

mirably contributed to shew the progress of Poetry from *Ennius* to *Virgil*.

Cornificius flourished soon after *Calvus*, and is celebrated by *Ovid* for a good elegiac Writer. And *Eusebius* says, his sister *Cornificia* was a lady who shewed how capable the fair sex is of conversing with the Muses.

Quintilius Varus, the *Roman* General, whose Army was unfortunately cut in pieces, (for grief of which he killed himself) after several exploits in *Germany*, was one of *Virgil*'s first patrons, and is by him celebrated as such in his *Eclogues*: and *Julius Scaliger* thinks him to be the true Author of *Etna*, a Poem that is commonly ascribed to *Virgil*. This Poem is in good Esteem, and the Critics say even *Virgil* need not blush to own it.

The Two Varro's present themselves next to our consideration. Marcus Terentius Varro, the *Roman*, was born the year of *Rome* 638, and died at 89 years of age. His great Learning made him the Admiration of his Time, which was the most flourishing for Arts and Glory that *Rome* ever knew. There are divers fragments of his works, particularly of his *Menippian* Satires, which were Medleys of Prose and Verse. *Scaliger* has likewise collected some of his Epigrams from among the *Catalecta* of *Virgil*. In general he seems to have been a much greater Critic and Scholar than he was a Poet. He bore many great offices, and among the rest was Tribune of the People. He was an intimate friend of *Cicero*'s, and in the civil wars warmly assisted *Pompey*, but after his defeat soon submitted to *Cæsar*, who was reconciled to him. From hence he applied all his time in the improvement of learning in general, and had the charge of the *Greek* and *Latin* libraries at *Rome*. He was above seventy when *Anthony* proscribed him: however, he found means to escape and save his life, but could not save his library, and some of his works from the fury of the soldiers, which was a great loss to him and to posterity. After this storm was over he peaceably pursued

sued his studies, and in a passage of his quoted by *Gellius*, L. 3. C. 10. *Varro* says, that being seventy eight years old at the time of his writing the book which *Gellius* quotes, he had already composed 490 volumes. *Pliny*, L. 29. C. 4. of his natural History says, that *Varro* continued his studies, and wrote when he was 88 years of age. He was 80 when he published his books of agriculture, which are yet extant. The loss of his several works is doubtless one of the greatest which the Commonwealth could ever suffer, this excellent man having all the talents as well as opportunities requisite to compleat his enquiries, and make his works both instructive and entertaining.

*VARRO ATACINUS was born about the same time as *Cicero*, at a small town near *Narbonne*. Though infinitely inferior to the *Roman* in learning, he was at least as good if not a better poet, which perhaps has made many Critics confound them. His chief Works were a Poem on the war with the *Sequani*, a people of *Gaul*; and the *Astronomics*, that went under the name of *Plauciades* the *Grammarian*. But the *Argonautics* in 4 books, was what gained him the greatest reputation, and is commended by *Quintilian*. And the elder *Seneca* observes, that *Virgil* had so good an opinion of this author, that he sometimes inserted his Verses in his Works, but with some corrections, to give them more strength. Hence we may infer that he was a polite and easy writer.

HELVIUS CINNA, who flourished under the *Triumvirs*, is said to have been author of several Poems on *Achilles*, *Telephus*, *Xerxes*, &c. but his Poem named *Smyrna* got him most reputation, which is said to have spared no pains nor time to deserve, having been nine years about it. His stile was nevertheless so obscure and difficult, that *Crassitius*, a Grammarian

---

* One of the Two *Varro*'s is reckoned among the best Elegiac Poets by *Propertius*;

 Hæc quoque perfecto ludebat Jasone Varro,
 Varro Leucadiæ maxima flamma suæ.
     L. 2. El. 25.

of note, wrote a learned Commentary to explain the Poem; which according to the following Epigram, he was the only person that rightly understood.

Uni Crassitio se credere Smyrna probavit,
Desinite indocti connubio hanc petere.
Soli Crassitio se dixit nubere velle;
Intima cui soli nota sua extiterint.

AUGUSTUS and GERMANICUS were both Poets: The former was so far from admiring his own compositions, that being asked, what he had done with his *Ajax?* a Tragedy he had made of that name, but with which he was dissatisfied, he said pleasantly, *In spongiam incubuit,* he has killed himself with a sponge, intimating, that he had rubbed it out of his tablets.

GERMANICUS, who was one of the greatest men of antiquity, which cost him his life through the jealousy of *Tiberius,* who had been obliged by *Augustus* to adopt him for his Successor, had according to *Quintilian* and *Ovid,* a fine genius to Poetry. *Germanicus Cæsar,* says the *Roman* Critic, if he had not been called away from the Muses by the more important cares of Government, might have rivalled the greatest Poets. Nevertheless, where can we find more learning and excellency in all points than in his juvenile Poems? but who, indeed, better understood to sing of wars than the same person who had behaved so gloriously in them?

PEDO ALBINOVANUS was a writer of great merit in several kinds of Poetry. *Ovid* mentions his *Thesied,* an epic Poem; and *Seneca* commends one on an expedition of *Germanicus. Martial* speaks in praise of his Epigrams, L. 2. *Epigr.* 77. and the Critics are now almost agreed that we have some of his Elegies yet extant, which had been attributed to *Ovid.* That on the death of *Drusus* is reckoned very elegant.

Though we have no particular account of the Works of *Calidius,* he was certainly a Poet of no mean genius; for *Cornelius Nepos,* in the life of *Atticus,* after having observed, that *Catullus* and *Lucretius* were already dead,

dead, gives this *Calidius* the preference to all the Poets of his time.

CAIUS ASINIUS POLLIO had a very sublime genius for Poetry. *Horace* describes him as such, Sat. 10. L. 2. and Od. 1. L. 2. and *Virgil*, in his third Eclogue, celebrates him as a fine Poet. He excelled in writing Tragedies. See *Horace*, L. 2. Od. 1. and *Virgil*, Eclogue 8. verse 6.

Tu mihi seu magni superas jam saxa timavi,
Sive oram Illyrici legis æquoris; en erit unquam
Ille dies, mihi cùm liceat tua dicere facta?
En erit, ut liceat totum mihi ferre per orbem
Sola sophocleo tua carmina digna Cothurno?
A te principium, tibi desinet: accipe jussis
Carmina cœpta tuis, atque hanc sine tempora circum
Inter victrices Hederam tibi serpere Laurus.

He was also a fine Orator and a just Historian. But he could never be reconciled to *Cicero*'s Eloquence, perhaps not only out of Enmity to him but in Friendship to *Marc Anthony*, whom *Cicero* had so bitterly inveighed against in his *Philippics*. He was Consul the year of *Rome* 714, and triumphed the year after. *Julius Cæsar*, some time before his Death, had made him Governour of the farther Provinces of *Spain*. He joined *Anthony* with two Legions before the Triumvirate was established; and when the War broke out between *Anthony* and *Augustus*, he assisted *Lucius Antonius* against *Augustus*, and was afterwards a great Instrument in making the Peace between them at *Puteoli*. After having triumphed over the *Illyrians*, he spent the remainder of his Days in *Italy* in Peace: but still was so far a Friend to *Anthony* that though he would not join with him, yet neither would he side with *Augustus* against him, in regard to the great Obligations which he owed him. He lived to Fourscore, and died towards the End of *Augustus*'s Reign, the year of *Rome* 757.

CASSIUS SEVERUS of *Parma*, who was one of the Conspirators against *Cæsar*, and the last that suffered for that Assassination, was a Writer of great Spirit and Elegance.

Elegance. *Horace* indeed ridicules his ready vein in one place, but in another he thinks he makes a fine Compliment to his Friend *Tibullus*, when he tells that he outdoes even *Cassius* in Elegy:

Scribere quod Cassi Parmensis opuscula vincat.

He also informs us, that *Varrius*, whom *Augustus* had sent to put *Cassius* to death, burnt him in his Study, with all his works. *Quintilian* seems to allow, that *Cassius*'s great Excellency lay in his Versification, but observes at the same time, that if he had lived to finish his Poem on the civil Wars, with the same Spirit that appeared in what was extant of it, he might justly have challenged the second Place among the *Roman* Poets. Perhaps he was busy on this Poem when he was put to Death. He had sided with *Brutus* and *Cassius* against *Anthony* and *Augustus*; *Horace*, who had done the same, being afterwards driven by necessity to turn Poet, by which he had ingratiated himself with *Augustus*, it was Policy in him to speak with Contempt of *Cassius*, and especially since he employed his Genius to celebrate the Exploits of *Brutus* and *Cassius* against the Triumvirs.

CORNELIUS GALLUS, born at *Frejus* in *France*, then called *Forum Julium*, was a person of Distinction as well as a good Poet. He was the particular Favourite of *Augustus*, who made him Governour of *Egypt*, after having conquered it by the Defeat and Death of *Anthony* and *Cleopatra*, but he was guilty of such enormous Oppressions and Male-Administration in his Government, that the Senate was obliged to take cognizance of it; nor could all the Friendship and Interest of *Augustus* save *Gallus* from being condemned to Banishment, and to lose his Estate. He was so grieved at this Disgrace that he put an end to his own Life, being about 43 years old. *Virgil* has complemented him in many Places. The whole tenth Eclogue is on the Subject of his Love to *Lycoris*, the poetical Name of *Gallus*'s Mistress, whose cruel disdain is there lamented. He had written four Books of Elegies or

As for those Elegies that have been published under his Name, the most judicious Critics agree they are not his, but were written by *Maximian*, a more modern Poet, an obscure, trifling, loose Writer, in many Places offending against the common Rules of the quantities of Syllables, and often full of Barbarisms: And in some of them the Poet confesses himself to be an old Man, which was not *Gallus*'s Case, who died at 43. But besides these Six Elegies, *Aldus Manutius* met with some Fragments at *Venice* that were ascribed to *Gallus*, which though written in a better Taste than the former, *Jos. Scaliger* has proved to be spurious. But *Manutius* was guilty of another Mistake, by confounding this *Gallus* with *Asinius Gallus*, the Son of *Pollio*, whom we have mentioned already. Our *Gallus* died the year of *Rome* 728, seven years before *Virgil*. *Pollio*'s Son, *Asinius Gallus*, was cruelly put to Death by the Emperor *Tiberius*, the year of *Rome* 789.

Varius and Tucca, intimate Friends of *Virgil* and *Horace*, are mentioned by the latter in the number of good Poets, and were, with some others, commissioned by *Augustus* to revise and publish the *Æneid* after *Virgil*'s death. *Varius* we find was a noble epic Writer, and *Horace* has intimated, that he was writing a Poem on *Agrippa*'s exploits, in the 6th Ode of Lib 1. addressed to that brave General of *Augustus*:

Scriberis Vario fortis, & hostium
Victor, Mæonii carminis alite.

How much he was beloved by his Prince is testified by the same Poet in his epistle addressed to that Emperor;

Dilecti tibi Virgilius, Variusque poetæ.

The same Writer speaks of him advantageously in other Places, and especially in his Art of Poetry, where it is to be noted, as well as in the former quotation, that he is put next to *Virgil*. And here these two seem to be mentioned as the best Poets of their time, and, as such, justly deserving the highest regard of their Countrymen;

―――*Quid*

VALGIUS was a Poet of the first rank. *Horace* has mentioned him among those excellent Wits, whose approbation he desired: And *Tibullus* compares him to *Homer* in his Poem to *Messalla*———*Æterno propior non alter Homero.*

CORNELIUS SEVERUS, who flourished about the same time with *Valgius*, was likewise a considerable Poet, and some Critics consider him as the Author of the *Ætna*, a Poem among the *Catalecta* of *Virgil*. He had also undertaken to write a Poem of the Wars in *Sicily*, probably between *Augustus* and *Sextus Pompeius*, and though he died before he finished it, is highly commended for it by *Quintilian*. *Ovid* addresses him not only as his Friend, but as a Court Favourite and a great Poet———*O vates magnorum maxime regum,* and a little lower he adds,

*Fertile pectus habes, interque Helicona colentes
   Uberius nulli provenit ista Seges.*
                                     De Ponto. L. 4. El. 2.

RABIRIUS flourished under *Augustus,* and bore the Character of a very sublime Poet, which *Ovid* expresly mentions, De Ponto. L. 4. El. 16.———*Magnique Rabirius oris.* The Reader may consult this Elegy, where he will find many other Poets mentioned, with sometimes a short Character of them, of whom, as we have no other Account, I thought it would be both dull and tedious barely to name them. *Rabirius* is also mentioned by *Horace* as his Friend, and a Person of excellent Merit. *Quintilian* calls him an Author worth being acquainted with, and *Velleius Paterculus* scruples not to place him next to *Virgil,* L. 2. Histor. *Rabirius*'s chief work was a Poem on the War between *Augustus* and *Anthony,* I suppose the *Actian* War, a subject which exercised the Pens of the finest Writers of the *Augustan* Age.

SABINUS was an Elegiac Poet, cotemporary with *Rabirius:* According to *Ovid,* the following Epistles are said to have been published by him: *Ulysses* to *Penelope, Hyppolitus* to *Phædra, Demophoon* to *Phyllis,*

lis, *Jason* to *Hypsipile*, and *Sappho* to *Phaon*, none of which are preserved: Those that are among *Ovid's* under these Titles being esteemed unworthy of him and *Sabinus*. But the general Opinion is, that some, if not all of the six following are *Sabinus's*, though amongst *Ovid's*; namely, *Paris* to *Helen*, *Helen* to *Paris*, *Leander* to *Hero*, *Hero* to *Leander*, *Acontius* to *Cydippe*, and *Cydippe* to *Acontius*. *Ovid* observes, that *Sabinus* was the Author of some other Works, which he did not live to finish.

Quique suam Træzen, imperfectumque Dierum
 Deseruit celeri morte Sabinus opus.
       De Ponto. L. 4. El. 16.

Horace speaks very handsomely of his Friend TITIUS SEPTIMIUS, a Lyric and Tragic Poet.

Quid Titius Romana brevi venturus in ora,
Pindarici fontis qui non expalluit haustus,
Fastidire lacus ac rivos ausus apertos,
Ut valet? Ut meminit nostri? Fidibusne Latinis
Thebanos aptare modos studet auspice Musa
An tragica desævit & ampullatur in arte?
       L. 1. Epist. 3.

And what doth *Titius*, he of growing Fame,
Who doth not fear to drink of *Pindar's* Stream,
Who scorns known Springs and Lakes, that glorious He,
And is he well, and doth he think of me?
Doth he, the Muse propitious, nobly sing,
And fit to *Roman* Harps the *Theban* String?
Or is he writing Plays, and treads the Stage
In murd'ring Verse, and swells with Tragic Rage?
       Creech.

JULIUS FLORUS, to whom this Epistle is addressed, had among other great Qualities, a masterly skill in Poetry according to *Horace*,

——————*Non tibi parvum*
Ingenium, non incultum est, nec turpiter hirtum,
       Seu

Seu linguam caufis acuis, feu civica jura
Refpondere paras, feu condis amabile carmen,
Prima feres hederæ victricis præmia.

GRATIUS, of whom we have part of a Poem on hunting, is fuppofed to have been cotemporary with *Ovid*, and by him pointed out in the laft Elegy of the 4th *L. de Ponto*.

Aptaque venanti Gratius *arma dedit.*

THE Stile of this Poem is reckoned pure, but without elevation; he is cenfured by the Critics for dwelling too long on Fables, and as he is counted much fuperior to *Nemefianus*, who has treated the fame fubject, fo he is reckoned in all points inferior to the *Greek* Poet *Oppian*, who wrote his *Cynegetics* and *Halieutics*, under *Severus* and *Caracalla*, to whom he prefented them, and who is faid to have rewarded the Poet very magnificently.

FLAVIUS ALPHIUS AVITUS flourifhed under *Auguftus* and *Tiberius*, according to *Seneca* the Rhetorician, Controverfy the 15th, he was very famous in his youth for his Eloquence; but is thought by that Critic to have enervated the force of his Stile in Profe, by applying himfelf to Poetry, in which he did not fucceed fo well. *Prifcian* quotes fome Verfes of his out of his *Lives of illuftrious Men*, in two Book in Verfe: and *Terentianus Maurus* mentions him for his Eloquence; which was fo great when he was very young, that all *Rome* followed him with Admiration: but he afterwards neglected the true bent of his genius for Poetry, in which nature feem'd not to defign he fhould fucceed.

CÆSIUS BASSUS, a *Lyric* Poet, flourifhed under the *Vefpafians*. *Quintilian* places him next to *Horace*, and *Pliny* the younger has alfo commended him for his happy talent that way.

TITUS PETRONIUS ARBITER, though more celebrated for that part of his works which is in Profe, may juftly claim our notice among the Poets. He is an admirable Critic and a polite Writer, yet has

nius is generally thought to have been an *Epicurean*, some maintain he was a *Stoic*, and have attempted to prove it from his Works. *Salmasius* and some other Critics are of Opinion, that the present Fragments of *Petronius* are merely *Excerpta* or Passages transcribed by some Student, who noted down what pleased him best in the Course of his reading this Author, and that the Original and entire Copies were destroyed by the rash Zeal of the Monks, which has been more injurious to the learned World in many Respects, than the several Ravages of the barbarous Nations, or the destroying Hand of Time it self. *Petronius* whether through the Favour of *Nero* or his own Merit, was sent Proconsul to *Bithynia*, where this Man of Pleasure, like another *Mecænas*, shewed himself capable of the closest Application to Business, and performed all the Duties of an able Magistrate: He was afterwards, as *Tacitus* says, chosen Consul, perhaps extraordinarily for some Months as was usual, when the Consul died within the year of his Office, which was never left vacant: I mention this because we do not find his Name in any List of the Consuls, and yet the Authority of *Tacitus* is unquestionable, who says he was Consul. The same Historian seems to insinuate that he received the Surname of *Arbiter*, because *Nero* thought none of his Voluptuous Pleasures well fancied, that were not either directed or approved by *Petronius*. This great Favour of *Petronius* could not fail of stirring up *Tigellinus* against him. That jealous and selfish Favourite and Minister of *Nero*'s resolved to ruin this growing Rival, which by false Accusations he effected. Nor was *Petronius* admitted to make his Defence. Some of his Slaves were bribed against him, and the rest carried away to Prison. *Petronius* having (as yet uncertain of his Fate) for some time stayed at *Cumæ*, for the Emperor was gone into *Campania*) resolved to put an End to his Hopes and Fears, by a voluntary Death. He opened his Veins, then closed them again; at Intervals conversing with his Friends,

not

not like *Seneca*, in a solemn Manner on serious Subjects, but in a pleasant and jocose Way, they repeating to him Songs and Verses upon diverting Subjects. In short, he slept, he travelled, rewarded some and punished others of his Domesticks; affecting to do all the ordinary Offices of Life, that his Death might not seem forced but accidental.

When he made his Will, he did not compliment *Nero* or *Tigellinus*, or any of the great Men in Power, as was then the common Practice, with a Legacy; but having described, under the feigned Characters of some vile debauched People, all the infamous Lewdness and obscene pleasures of the Prince, sent the Book sealed up to *Nero*; but broke the Seal in Pieces, that no Use might be made of it afterwards in making Discovery of the Author.

The manner of his Death had a strange Mixture of Constancy and Extravagance, and perhaps not a little Affectation, however *Tacitus* seems to relate it with Applause and Admiration. He died the year of *Rome* 817, and of *Christ* 65, being as we may suppose about 50 Years old.

Aruntius Stella, born at *Apona* in the Territory of *Padua*, is celebrated both by *Statius* and *Martial* as a fine Poet. *Statius* in the Dedication of his *Sylvæ* to *Stella* mentions his Elegies, and a Poem called *Asteris*, but particularly his Poem on the Death of a favourite Dove, which *Martial* prefers to that celebrated one of *Catullus* on *Lesbia*'s Sparrow.

Stellæ Delicium mei Columba,
Verona hæc audiente, dicam,
Vicit maximi passerem Catulli.

Stella was a Person of great Quality and Fortune and bore some of the greatest Offices in *Rome*, having been Prætor and Duumvir, a civil Magistrate of great Authority and Dignity among the *Romans*.

Sentius Augur, is commended by *Pliny* in his Epistles, as a good Epigrammatic Writer. He was a native of *Rome*, and Cotempory with him. The same

same *Pliny* praises his Friend *Spurina*, an illustrious *Roman*, for his happy Talent for *Lyric* Poetry, as he does *Voconius* for his Elegies and Epigrams, and *Passienus* a *Roman* Knight for excelling both in Elegiac and Lyric Poetry; he is also much praised by *Gellius*.

SALEIUS BASSUS is reckoned by *Quintilian* in the Number of the best Epic Poets. He was an intimate Friend of *Lucan*, and grew afterwards much in favour with the Emperor *Vespasian*. *Tacitus* and *Pliny* mention him with Honour, and *Juvenal* has taken notice of his Merit and Poverty.

VOLCATIUS SEDIGITUS, flourished about the Time of the *Vespasians*, and is commended by *Pliny* the younger and *Gellius* for his Learning. We have no Account of any other Work of his, than that in which he makes a Judgment of all the Poets, a Fragment of which relating to the Comic Poets is quoted by *Gellius*.

AULUS SERENUS a Lyric Poet, is much commended by *Maurus Terentianus*, *Diomedes* the Grammarian and *Martianus Capella*. He is said to have published several Poems, some of which are cited by *Nonius* the Grammarian, and particularly that called *Ruralia*: He seems to have lived sometime between *Sedigitus* and *Terentianus*.

SOME Critics make this TERENTIANUS Cotemporary with *Martial*, and suppose him to be the Governor of *Syene*, whom that Poet mentions, L. 1. Epig. 87. He is cited by *Priscian*, *Servius*, and other Grammarians, among what they call the later Writers. He was old as he informs us in the Preface, when he begun his Poem of Letters, Syllables, Feet and Measures, that is, a Prosodia in Verse: He was an *African*, according to many Critics, or a *Carthaginian* by birth, but I should rather think him a noble *Roman*.

SULPITIA, the Poetess, flourished about the same time with *Terentianus*. We have but a Fragment of a Satire that she wrote against *Domitian*, who published a Decree for the Banishment of the Philosophers from *Rome*. But from the Invocation it should seem she

was

was Author of many other Poems, and that she was the first *Roman* Lady who had taught her Sex to vie with the *Greeks* in Poetry.

Cætera quin etiam, quot denique millia lusi.
Primaque Romanas docui contendere Graijs,
Et salibus variare novis constanter omitto.

Her Language is easy and elegant, and she seems to have had a happy Talent for Satire. She is mentioned by *Martial* and *Sidonius Apollinaris*, and is said to have addressed to her husband who was a *Roman* Knight, a Poem on conjugal Love. She was certainly a Lady of a bright Genius, and the Learned World have reason to lament the Loss of her Works.

MARULLUS, a Writer of *Mimes*, distinguished himself by his fine Genius under *Marcus Antoninus* the Philosopher, and was remarkable for making his Reflections with such Liberty, that he spared no Character of Vice or Folly that he met with in those of the first Rank. As a particular Instance of this, it is said, That in the following Verse he expresly named the Empress *Faustina*'s Gallant to the whole Audience;

Ille jam tibi dixi Tertullus dicitur.

His works are all lost. He had the Character of a very strong and elegant Writer, and is often quoted by *Servius* the *Grammarian*.

We meet with no Poets of any Note in the Interval between *Antoninus Philosophus* and *Caracalla*, unless we take PALLADIUS to have lived in this Interval: He has composed a Poem on the Grafting of Trees, which he has executed with some Spirit, but we can find no further Account of him.

Q. SERENUS SAMMONICUS was a celebrated Physician as well as a Poet, under *Caracalla*, who killed him in a Passion one Day as he sate at Table with him, but upon what Provocation is uncertain. He is said to have published many Treatises and Poems, but all that remains of his now is a Poem on Medicines, and this by some Critics, has been attributed rather to his Son
Sammo-

Sammonicus, who was Præceptor to the younger *Gordian*, and was possessed of a fine Library which his Father had begun to collect. The Stile of this Poem of *Sammonicus* is low and dull, but the Expressions are just, and the Language pure.

CALPHURNIUS, a *Bucolic* Poet of *Sicily*, flourished under the Emperors *Carinus* and *Numerianus*. There are seven of his Eclogues addressed to *Nemesianus*, a Man of Quality, and his Patron, and a fellow Poet. Some of the Critics have not scrupled to give *Calphurnius* the next place to *Virgil* among the Pastoral Writers; and *Fontenelle*, in his fine Discourse on Pastoral Poetry, seems to join with them.

NEMESIANUS, abovementioned, was likewise a Writer of Eclogues, of which there are Four extant, which are not in so good a Taste, being neither so well conducted, nor in so lovely a Stile as those of *Calphurnius*. But his Poem on hunting gained him more Reputation, though it is not in so pure a Stile as that of *Gratian*. Such was the Esteem of this Poem in the 8th and 9th Centuries, that it was publickly read in the Schools under the Emperor *Charles* the Great, and some of his Successors. But I fear this may reasonably be taken as an Argument of the bad Taste of the Age, at least as much as of the Excellency of this Poem of *Nemesianus*.

RUFUS FESTUS AVIENUS flourished under *Theodosius* the Great, and was partly Cotemporary with *Claudian*. He has made an elegant Translation of the *Phænomena* of *Aratus*, and the *Periegesis*, or Geographical Description of the World of *Dionysius*. He also turned some Pieces of *Livy* into Iambic Verse, as he did some select Stories from *Virgil*. But there is nothing of these two last extant. We have about Forty Fables of *Æsop* rendered by *Avienus* in Elegiac Verse, and dedicated to *Theodosius*. In general the Critics have a favourable Opinion of this Poet's Writings. His Stile is easy and sometimes elegant, and might pass for the Work of a better Age, had not *Claudian* written about the same Time.

P. RUTILIUS

288 A Chronological TABLE to the

Years of Rome.	Miscellaneous Remarks concerning the Poets, &c.
514	—*Livius Andronicus* brings his first Play on the Stage.
515	—*Ennius* born.
516	
517	
518	
519	—*Nævius* publishes his first Play.
520	
521	
522	
523	
524	
525	
526	
527	—*Plautus* born about this time.
428	
529	
530	
531	
532	
533	*Pacuvius* the Tragic Poet born.
534	
535	
536	
537	
538	
539	
540	
541	
542	
543	

Years of Rome.	A Chronological TABLE to the Miscellaneous Remarks concerning the Poets, &c.
544	
545	
546	
547	
548	
549	—*Nævius* dies. *Scipio* goes into *Africa*.
550	
551	
552	
553	
554	—*Plautus* flourished at *Rome*, and M. *Acuticus*,
555	a *Comic* Poet, and M. *Plautius*, and *Cn. A-*
556	*quilius*, likewise *Comic* Writers.
557	
558	
559	—*Terence* born.
560	
561	
562	
563	
564	—*Porcius Licinius* flourishes, a *Comic* Poet.
565	
566	
567	
568	
569	
570	—*Plautus* dies. *Scipio Æmilianus* born.
571	
572	
573	

Q. Fabius

A Chronological TABLE to the Miscellaneous Remarks concerning the Poets, &c.

Years of Rome.	
574	—*Trebea*, the *Comic* Poet, flourishes about this time, and *Turpilius*, another *Comic* Poet, born.
575	
576	
577	
578	
579	
580	
581	
582	
583	—*Attius*, the *Tragic* Poet born.
584	—*Ennius* dies.
585	—*Statius Cæcilius* the *Comic* Poet dies.
586	
587	—The *Andria* of *Terence* first acted.
588	—The *Hecyra* of *Terence* acted.
589	
590	—The *Heautontimorumenos*.
591	
592	—The *Eunuch* at the beginning, and the *Phormio* at the end of the year.
593	—The *Adelphi*.
594	*Terence* dies.
595	
596	
597	
598	
599	
600	
601	
602	
603	—*Attilius*, the Comic Poet, flourished about this Time, when the 3d *Punic* War began.
604	—*Carthage* taken by *Scipio Æmilianus*.
605	

L. Manlius

CONSULS.

Years before Christ.	
179	L. Manlius Acidinus, Q. Fulvius Flaccus.
178	M. Junius Brutus, A. Manlius Volso.
177	Claudius Pulcher, T. Sempronius Gracchus.
176	Q. Petilius Spurinus, Cn. Cornelius Scipio Hispalus.
175	M. Æmilius Lepidus II. P. Minucius Scævola.
174	Sp. Posthumius Albinus, Q. Mucius Scævola.
173	L. Popilius Albinus, M. Popilius Lænas.
172	C. Popilius Lænas, P. Ælius Ligur.
171	P. Licinius Crassus, C. Cassius Longinus.
170	Q. Martius Philippus II. Q. Servilius Cæpio.
169	Q. Martius Philippus III. Cn. Servilius Cæpio,
168	L. Æmilius Paulus II. P. Licinius Crassus.
167	Q. Ælius Pætus, M. Junius Pennus.
166	M. Claudius Marcellus, P. Sulpitius Gallus.
165	Cn. Octavius, T. Manlius Torquatus.
164	A. Manlius Torquatus, Q. Cassius Longinus.
163	T. Sempronius Gracchus, M. Juventius Talva.
162	P. Scipio Nasica, C. Marcius Figulus.
161	M. Valerius Messalla, C. Fannius Strabo.
160	L. Anicius Gallus, M. Cornelius Cethegus,
159	Cn. Cornelius Dolabella, M. Fulvius Nobilior.
158	M. Æmilius Lepidus, C. Popilius Lænas.
157	Sex. Julius Cæsar, L. Aurelius Orestes.
156	L. Cornelius Lentulus, C. Martius Figulus II.
155	P. Cornelius Scipio II. M. Claudius Marcellus II.
154	Q. Opimius Nepos, L. Posthumius Albinus.
153	Q. Fulvius Nobilior, T. Annius Luscus.
152	M. Claudius Marcellus, L. Valerius Flaccus.
151	L. Licinius Lucullus, A. Posthumius Albinus.
150	L. Quinctius Flaminius, M. Acilius Balbus.
149	L. Martius Censorinus, M. Manlius.
148	Sp. Posthumius Albinus, L. Calpurnius Piso.

A Chronological TABLE to the *Miscellaneous Remarks concerning the Poets, &c.*

Years of Rome.	
606	
607	
608	
609	
610	
611	
612	
613	—*Pacuvius* being 80 years old, published his last Tragedy. *Attius* the Tragic Poet being now 30, wrote his first Play.
614	
615	
616	
617	
618	
619	
620	
621	
622	
623	
624	
625	
626	
627	
628	
629	
630	
631	
632	
633	—About this Time *Afranius* the Comic Poet flourished.
634	
635	

P. Cornelius

296 A Chronological TABLE to the

| Years of Rome. | Miscellaneous Remarks concerning the Poets, &c. |

636
637 —*Novius*, the Writer of *Attellane* Plays, flourish'd about this Time.
638 —*M. Terentius Varro*, the most learn'd *Roman*
639   of his Time born.

640
641
642
643 —*Mummius* flourishes, a Writer of *Attellane* Plays, and *Pomponius* of *Bologna*, a Poet who
644   wrote in the same way.

645
646 —*Cicero* born.
647 —*Varro Atacinus*, an Epic Poet, born about
648   this Time.
649 —*Turpilius*, the Comic Poet, dies. *Furius Bibaculus* the *Lyric* Poet born.
650 *Lutatius Catulus*, the Consul this Year, was a
651   good Epigrammatist.
652
653 —*C. Titius* flourishes. A Tragic Poet and great Orator.
654
655
656
657
658 —*Lucretius* born.
659
660
661
662
663

664 —*C. Julius Cæsar Strabo*, Ædile this Year.
665   He was a fine Tragic Poet.

L. Cæcilius

A Chronological TABLE to the Miscellaneous Remarks concerning the Emperors, &c.

Years of Rome.	
666	
667	—*Catulus* dies.
668	
669	
670	
671	
672	—*Valerius Cato*, the Elegiac Poet flourishes.
673	—*Titus Quinctius Atta*, the Comic Poet dies.
674	—*Bibaculus* flourishes.
675	
676	
677	
678	
679	
680	
681	
682	
683	—*Rabirius* flourishes, an excellent Epic Poet.
684	—*Virgil* born.
685	
686	
687	
688	—*Horace* born.
689	
690	
691	
692	
693	
694	—About this time flourished *Calidius*, an excel-
695	lent Poet, according to the Historian *Corn.*
696	*Nepos.*

Cn. Octavius,

LIVES of the ROMAN POETS.

Years before *Christ*.

CONSULS.

87 Cn. Octavius, L. Cornelius Cinna.
86 Cn. Marius VII. L. Cornelius Cinna II.
85 L. Cornelius Cinna III. Cn. Papyrius Carbo.
84 L. Cornelius Cinna IV. Cn. Papyrius Carbo II.
83 L. Cornelius Scipio Afiaticus, Cn. Norbanus Flaccus.
82 Cn. Papyrius Carbo III. C. Marius, C. Filius.
81 M. Tullus Lecula, Cn. Cornelius Dolabella.
80 L. Cornelius Sulla II. Q. Cæcilius Metellus.

79 P. Servilius Vatia Isauricus. Ap. Claudius Pulcher.
78 M. Æmilius Lepidus, Q. Lutatius Catulus.
77 D. Junius Brutus, M. Æmilius Lepidus.
76 Cn. Octavius, C. Scribonius.
75 L. Octavius, C. Aurelius Cotta.
74 L. Licinius Lucullus, M. Aurelius Cotta.
73 M. Terentius Varro, C. Cassius Varus.
72 L. Gellius Poplicola, Cn. Cornelius Lentulus Clodianus.
71 Cn. Aufidius Orestes, P. Cornelius Lentulus Sura.
70 Cn. Pompeius Magnus, M. Licinius Crassus.

69 Q. Hortensius, Q. Cæcilius Metellus Creticus.
68 L. Cæcilius Metellus, Q. Marcius Rex.
67 C. Calpurnius Piso, M. Acilius Glabrio.
66 M. Æmilius Lepidus, L. Volcatius Tullus.
65 L. Aurelius Cotta, L. Manlius Torquatus.
64 L. Julius Cæsar, C. Martius Figulus.
63 M. Tullius Cicero, C. Antonius Nepos.
62 D. Junius Silanus, L. Licinius Murena.
61 M. Pupius Piso, M. Valerius Messala.
60 Q. Cæcilius Metellus Celer, L. Africanus.

59 C. Julius Cæsar, M. Calpurnius Bibulus.
58 L. Calpurnius Piso, A. Gabinius.
57 P. Cornelius Lentulus Spinther, C. Cæcilius Metellus Nepos.

Lucretius

Years of Rome.	Miscellaneous Remarks concerning the Poets, &c.
697	
698	
699	
700	
701	—*Lucretius* dies.
702	
703	
704	
705	—*Laberius* the Writer of *Mimes* flourishes.
706	—*Phædrus* born about this time.
707	—About this time *Propertius* born.
708	
709	
710	*Laberius* dies. P. *Syrus* flourishes. *Tibullus* and *Ovid* born.
711	
712	
713	—*Virgil* writes his first Eclogue.
714	——*Virgil* writes his 4th Eclogue, *Augustus* and *Antbony* reconcil'd. *Horace*'s Journey to *Brundusium*.
715	——*Pollio* triumphs over the *Illyrians*, *Virgil* writes the 8th Eclogue.
716	——The War renewed between *Sextus Pompey*, and *Augustus*. *Virgil*'s 10th Eclogue.
717	
718	
719	
720	
721	
722	

Cn. Cornelius

CONSULS.

Years before Christ.

56 Cn. Cornelius Lentulus Marcellinus, L. Marcius Philippus.
55 Cn. Pompeiüs Magnus II. M. Licinius Crassus.
54 L. Domitius Ænobarbus, Ap. Claud. Pulcher.
53 Cn. Domitius Calvinus, M. Valerius Messala.
52 Cn. Pompeiüs Magnus, he had no Collegue.
51 Ser. Sulpicius Rufus, M. Claudius Marcellus.
50 L. Æmilius Paulus, C. Claudius Marcellus.

49 C. Claudius Marcellus, L. Cornelius Lentulus.
48 C. Julius Cæsar II. P. Servilius Vatia Isauricus.
47 C. Julius Cæsar Dictator II. Mag. Equitum M. Antonius.
46 C. Julius Cæsar III. M. Æmilius Lepidus.
45 C. Julius Cæsar Dictator IV. Mag. Equitum M. Lepidus.
44 C. Julius Cæsar Dictator V. Mag. Equitum M. Antonius.
43 C. Vibius Pansa A. Hirtius, C. Octavius Cæsar, Q. Pedius.
42 M. Æmilius Lepidus, L. Munatius Plancus.
41 P. Servilius Isauricus II. L. Antonius.
40 Cn. Domitius Calvinus II. C. Asinius Pollio.

39 L. Marius Censorinus, C. Calvisius Sabinus.

38 Appius Claudius Pulcher, C. Norbanus Flaccus.

37 M. Vipsanius Agrippa, L. Caninius Gallus.
36 L. Gellius Poplicola, C. Cocceiüs Nerva.
35 Sex. Pompeiüs, L. Cornificius.
34 M. Antonius II. L. Scribonius Libo.
33 C. Cæsar Octavianus II. L. Volcatius Tullus.
32 Cn. Domitius Ænobarbus, C. Sosius.
31 C. Cæsar III. M. Messala Corvinus—of *Augustus* 13th Year.

The

Years of Rome.	Miscellaneous Remarks concerning the Emperors, &c.
723	——The Battle of *Actium*.
724	——*Virgil* finishes his *Georgics*.
725	——*Augustus* triumphs three times, and shuts
726	the Temple of *Janus*.
727	——*Octavianus* receives the Title of *Augustus* from the Senate.
728	——*Cornellus Galius* the Favourite of *Augustus*,
729	and Governour of *Egypt*, and an *Elegiac* Poet,
730	kills himself.
731	——*Marcellus* dies.
732	
733	——*Augustus*'s Expedition into *Greece* and *Asia*.
734	
735	——*Virgil* dies.
736	
737	
738	
739	——*Pedo Albinovanus* flourished about this Time.
740	
741	
742	——*Tibullus* dies.
743	
744	

AUGUSTUS

AUGUSTUS, after the Battle of *Actium*, and *Anthony* and *Cleopatra*'s Defeat and Death in *Egypt*, became sole Master and Emperor of the *Romans*; from thence therefore I choose to reckon by the Years of the Emperors, the Consuls having now only the Shadow of their former Authority left them.

Years before Christ.	EMPERORS.	
30	*Augustus* Cæsar.	1
29		2
28		3
27		4
26		5
25		6
24		7
23		8
22		9
21		10
20		11
19		12
18		13
17		14
16		15
15		16
14		17
13		18
12		19
11		20
10		21
9		22

Horace

Years of Rome.	A Chronological TABLE to the Miscellaneous Remarks concerning the Poets, &c.
745	——*Horace*
746	
747	
748	
749	
750	
751	——*Tiberius* retires to *Rhodes*.
752	
753	——*Seneca* the Philosopher and Tragic Poet born.
754	——*Melissus* the Comic Poet flourishes, and
755	*Turanius* a Tragic Poet.
756	
757	
758	
759	
760	——*Ovid* banished to *Tomi*.
761	——*Quintilius Varrus* with his Legions cut off
762	in *Germany*. About this Time *Mamilius* had written part of his *Astronomics*, which he lived
763	not to finish; he died before *Augustus*.
764	
765	
766	
767	——*Ovid* dies.
768	
769	
770	
771	
772	
773	
774	
775	
776	

Augustus

EMPERORS.

Years before Christ.			
8	——Augustus.	23	
7		24	
6		25	
5		26	
4		27	
3		28	
2		29	
1		30	

Years after Christ.			
1		31	
2		32	
3		33	
4		34	
5		35	
6		36	
7		37	
8		38	
9		39	
10		40	
11		41	
12		42	
13	——Augustus dies.	43	——Tiberius succeeds.
14	——Tiberius.	2	
15		3	
16		4	
17		5	
18		6	
19		7	
20		8	
21		9	
22		10	
23		11	
24		12	

Pomponius

A Chronological TABLE to the Miscellaneous Remarks concerning the Poets, &c.

Years of Rome.	
777	
778	
779	
780	
781	
782	——*Pomponius Secundus* the Tragic Poet flourishes.
783	——*Phædrus* dies about this Time.
784	
785	
786	——*Silius Italicus* born about this Time.
787	——*Persius* born.
788	
789	——*Lucan* born. *Saleius Bassus* born about
790	the same Time.
791	
792	
793	——*Statius* born about this Time.
794	——*Seneca* banished to *Corsica*.
795	
796	
797	——*Juvenal* born.
798	
799	
800	*Martial* born.
801	
802	——*Seneca* recalled from Banishment.
803	
804	
805	
806	
807	
808	
809	
810	

Tiberius

LIVES of the ROMAN POETS.

EMPERORS.

Years after Christ.		
25		13
26		14
27		15
28		16
29		17
30		18
31		19
32		20
33		21
34		22
35	—*Tiberius* dies.	23
36	—*Caligula*.	1
37		2
38		3
39	—*Caligula* dies.	4
40	—*Claudius*.	1
41		2
42		3
43		4
44		5
45		6
46		7
47		8
48		9
49		10
50		11
51		12
52		13
53		14
54	—*Nero*	1
55		2
56		3
57		4
58		5

Ballus

A Chronological TABLE to the Miscellaneous Remarks on the Roman Poets, &c.

Years of Rome.

811
812 ———*Saleius Bassus* flourishes.

813
814
815
816 *Lucan* and *Seneca* die by *Nero*'s Order, and *Persius* the *Satirist* dies about this Time.
817 ———*Petronius Arbiter* dies.
818
819 ———This Year *Silius Italicus* was Consul.
820
821
822 ———*Martial* comes to *Rome*.

823
824
825 ———*Valerius Flaccus* flourished about this time.
826
827
828 ———*Volcatius Sedigitus* flourishes.
829
830
831
832

833 ———*Aulus Serenus* flourishes
834
835
836
837
838 ———*Stella* flourishes.
839
840 ———*Maurus Terentianus*.
841
842 ———*Sulpitia* the Poetess.

Nero

Years after Christ.		EMPERORS.	
59		6	
60		7	
61		8	
62		9	
63		10	
64		11	
65		12	
66		13	
67	—Nero dies.	14	Galba succeeds. (Vitell.
68	—Galba dies.	1	Otho succeeds, and then
69	—Vitellius dies.	1	Vespasian succeeds.
70	—Vespasian.	1	
71		2	
72		3	
73		4	
74		5	
75		6	
76		7	
77		8	
78		9	
79	—Vespasian dies.	10	Titus his Son succeeds.
80	—Titus.	1	
81		2	
82	—Titus dies.	3	Domitian his Brother suc-
83	—Domitian.	2	(ceeds.
84		3	
85		4	
86		5	
87		6	
88		7	
89		8	
90		9	

Juvenal

Years of Rome	A Chronological TABLE to the Miscellaneous Remarks concerning the Poets, &c.
843	
844	
845	—*Juvenal* published his Satire for which he was
846	banished into *Ægypt* by *Domitian*.
847	
848	
849	—*Juvenal* returns to *Rome*.
850	
851	
852	
853	
854	—About this time *Statius* dies, and *Silius Ita-*
855	*licus.*
856	—*Martial* retires to his native City *Bilbilis* in
857	*Spain.*
858	
859	
860	
861	—About this time *Martial* dies.
862	
863	—*Voconius* and *Passienus* flourish.
864	
865	
866	
867	
868	
869	
870	
871	—*Juvenal* writes his 13th Satire.
872	
873	
874	
875	
876	

Years after Christ.	EMPERORS.	
91	10	
92	11	
93	12	
94	13	
95	14	
96 —Domitian dies.	15	
97 —Nerva.	1	
98 Nerva dies.	2	Trajan succeeds.
99 Trajan.	2	
100	3	
101	4	
102	5	
103	6	
104	7	
105	8	
106	9	
107	10	
108	11	
109	12	
110	13	
111	14	
112	15	
113	16	
114	17	
115	18	
116	19	
117 —Trajan dies.	20	—Adrian succeeds.
118 —Adrian.	2	
119	3	
120	4	
121	5	
122	6	
123	7	
124	8	

Juvenal

Years of Rome.	A Chronological TABLE to the Miscellaneous Remarks concerning the Poets, &c.
877	
878	
879	—*Juvenal* dies.
880	
881	
882	
883	
884	
885	
886	
887	
888	
889	
890	
891	
892	
893	
894	
895	
896	
897	
898	
899	
900	
901	
902	—*Palladius* flourishes about this time.
903	
904	
905	
906	
907	
908	
909	
910	

EMPERORS.

Years after Christ.		
125		9
126		10
127		11
128		12
129		13
130		14
131		15
132		16
133		17
134		18
135		19
136		20
137	—*Adrian* dies.	21 *Antoninus Pius* succeeds.
138	—*Antoninus Pius.*	1
139		2
140		3
141		4
142		5
143		6
144		7
145		8
146		9
147		10
148		11
149		12
150		13
151		14
152		15
153		16
154		17
155		18
156		19
157		20
158		21

Marullus

Years of Rome.	A Chronological TABLE to the Miscellaneous Remarks concerning the Poets, &c.
911	
912	
913	
914	
915	
916	
917	
918	
919	
920	
921	
922	—*Marullus* the Writer of *Mimes* flourishes.
923	
924	
925	
926	
927	
928	
929	
930	
931	
932	
933	
934	
935	
936	
937	
938	
939	
940	
941	
942	
943	*Antoninus*

Years after Christ.	EMPERORS.	
159	*Antoninus Pius* dies. 22	*Marcus* succeeds.
160	*Marcus Aurelius Antoninus Philosophus.*	1
161		2
162		3
163		4
164		5
165		6
166		7
167		8
168		9
169		10
170		11
171		12
172		13
173		14
174		15
175		16
176		17
177		18
178		19
179	*Marcus Aurelius* dies 20	*Commodus* succeeds.
180	*Commodus* the son of *M. Aurelius.*	1
181		2
182		3
183		4
184		5
185		6
186		7
187		8
188		9
189		10
190		11
191		12

Q. Serenus

A Chronological TABLE to the *Miscellaneous Remarks concerning the Poets, &c.*

Years of Rome.	
944	
945	
946	
947	
948	
949	
950	
951	
952	
953	
954	
955	
956	
957	
958	
959	
960	
961	
962	
963	
964	—2. *Serenus Sammonicus.*
965	
966	
967	
968	
969	
970	
971	
972	
973	
974	
975	
976	
977	*Commodus*

EMPERORS.

Years after Christ.			
192	—Commodus dies.	13	
193			Pertinax reigned 87
194	—Severus.	1	Days. Didius Julianus
195		2	succeeded, and reign'd
196		3	66 Days, and Severus
197		4	succeeded.
198		5	
199		6	
200		7	
201		8	
202		9	
203		10	
204		11	
205		12	
206		13	
207		14	
208		15	
209		16	
210		17	
211	—Severus dies.	18	Caracalla succeeds with
212	—Caracalla his	1	his Brother whom he
213	Son.	2	kills in his Mother's
214		3	Arms.
215		4	
216		5	
217		6	
218	—Caracalla dies.	7	Heliogabalus succeeds.
219	—Heliogabalus.	2	
220		3	
221		4	
222	—Heliogabalus dies.	5	Alexander Severus suc-
223	—Alexander Severus.	1	ceeds.
224		2	
225		3	

P 3   *Alexander*

A Chronological TABLE to the Miscellaneous Remarks concerning the Poets, &c.

Years of Rome.

978
979
980
981
982

983
984
985
986
987
988
989
990
991
992

993
994
995
996
997
998
999
1000
1001
1002

1003
1004
1005

1006
1007
1008
1009
1010

Alexander.

EMPERORS.

Years after Christ.			
226		4	
227		5	
228		6	
229		7	
230		8	
231		9	
232		10	
233		11	
234		12	
235	—*Alexander* dies.	13	—*Maximin* succeeds.
236	—*Maximin.*	2	
237		3	
238	—*Maximin* dies.	4	—*Gordian* the younger succeeds in conjunction with *Balbinus* and *Pupienus.*
239	—*Gordian.*	2	
240	—*Gordian* alone.	3	
241		4	
242		5	
243	—*Gordian* dies.	6	—*Philippus Arabs* succeeds.
244	*Philippus.*	2	
245		3	
246		4	
247		5	
248	—*Philippus* dies	6	
249	—*Decius.*	1	
250	—*Decius* dies.	2	—*Gallus* succeeds.
251	—*Gallus.*	1	—*Æmilianus* succeeds, and soon after him *Valerianus*, who associates his Son *Gallienus.*
252	—*Gallus* dies.	2	
253	—*Valerianus.*	1	
254	—*Gallienus.*	2	—The 30 Tyrants almost dismember the *Roman* Empire at this time.
255		3	
256		4	
257		5	
258		6	

P 4 *Calpurnius*

Years of Rome.	Miscellaneous Remarks concerning the Poets, &c.
1011	
1012	
1013	
1014	
1015	
1016	
1017	
1018	
1019	
1020	
1021	
1022	
1023	
1024	
1025	
1026	
1027	
1028	
1029	
1030	
1031	
1032	
1033	
1034	
1035	—*Calpurnius* and *Nemesianus* flourish about this
1036	time.
1037	
1038	
1039	
1040	
1041	
1042	
1043	*Gallienus*

Years after Christ.	EMPERORS.		
259		7	
260		8	
261		9	
262		10	
263		11	
264		12	
265		13	
266		14	
267		15	
268		16	
269	———*Gallienus* dies.	17	———*Claudius* succeeds.
270	———*Claudius*.		
271	———*Claudius* dies.	3	———*Aurelian* succeeds.
272	———*Aurelian*.	2	
273		3	
274		4	
275	———*Aurelian* dies.	5	———*Tacitus* succeeds.
276	———*Tacitus* dies.	2	—*Florianus* his Brother
277	———*Probus*.	1	succeeds and dies.
278		2	
979		3	
280		4	
281		5	
282		6	
283	———*Probus* dies.	7	—*Carus* succeeds and as-
284	———*Carus*.	2	sociates his sons *Cari-*
285	———*Dioclesian*.	1	*nus* and *Numerianus*,
286		2	who associates *Maxi-*
287		3	*mian* next Year.
288		4	
289		5	
290		6	
891		7	

P 5   *Constantine*

Years of Rome.	Miscellaneous Remarks concerning the Poets, &c.
1044	
1045	
1046	
1047	
1048	
1049	
1050	
1051	
1052	
1053	
1054	
1055	
1056	
1057	
1058	
1059	
1060	
1061	
1062	
1063	
1064	—*Constantine* takes *Rome*, and defeats the Tyrant *Maxentius*.
1065	
1066	
1067	
1068	
1069	
1070	
1071	
1072	——*Ausonius* born.
1073	
1074	
1075	

Dioclesian

Years after Christ.	EMPERORS.	
292		8
293		9
294		10
295		11
296		12
297		13
298		14
299		15
300		16
301		17
302		18
303		19
304		20
305	——*Dioclesian* and *Maximian* renounce the Empire.	21 ——*Constantius* and *Galerius* declared Emperors; *Constantius* dying,
306	——*Constantine* the Great.	2 his Son *Constantine* succeeds him.
307		3
308		4
309		5
310		
311		6
312		7
313		8
314		9
315		10
316		11
317		12
318		13
319		14
320		15
321		16
322		17
323		18

Constantine

A Chronological TABLE to the Miscellaneous Remarks concerning the Emperors, &c.

Years of Rome.

1076
1077
1078
1079
1080
1081
1082

1083
1084
1085
1086
1087
1088
1089
1090

1091
1092

1093
1094
1095
1096
1097
1098
1099
1100
1101
1102

1103
1104
1105
1106
1107
1108

Years after Christ.	EMPERORS.		
324	—*Constantine* sole Em-	19	by the Death of *Gale-*
325	peror	20	*rius.*
326		21	
327		22	
328		23	
329		24	
330		25	
331		26	
332		27	
333		28	
334		29	
335		30	
336		31	
337		32	
338	—*Constantine* the Great dies.	33	his Sons *Constantine, Constans* and *Constan-*
339	—*Constantius.*	2	*tius* divide the Empire.
340		3	
341	—*Constantine* the	4	
342	younger kill'd.	5	
343		6	
344		7	
345		8	
346		9	
347		10	
348		11	
349		12	
350		13	
351		14	
352		15	
353	—*Constantius* sole	16	
354	Emperor.	17	
355		18	
356		19	

Claudian

A Chronological TABLE to the
Miscellaneous Remarks concerning the
Poets, &c.

Years of Rome.

1109
1110
1111
1112

1113
1114
1115
1116
1117———*Claudian* born.
1118
1119
1120
1121
1122

1123
1124
1125
1126
1127
1128———*Ausonius* made Præfect of Gaul.
1129
1130
1131———*Rufus Festus Avienus* flourishes.
1132

1133———*Ausonius* Consul this Year.
1134
1135

1136
1137
1138
1139———*Ausonius* dies about this time.
1140
1141

Constantius

EMPERORS.

Years after Christ.		
357		20
358		21
359		22
360		23
361	—*Constantinus* dies.	24—*Julian* the Apostate succeeds.
362	—*Julian*.	2
363	—*Julian* dies.	3—*Jovian* succeeds.
364	—*Jovian* dies.	1—*Valentinian* succeeds, and associates his Brother *Valens*, to whom he gives the Government of the Eastern Empire.
365	—*Valentinian*.	2
366		3
367		4
368		5
369		6
370		7
371		8
372		9
373		10
374		11
375	—*Valentinian* dies	12——*Gratian* and *Valentinian* the IId, whom he had before associated, succeed.
376	—*Gratian* and *Valentinian*.	2
377		3
378		4
379	—*Theodosius* the Great associated by *Gratian*, who yields him the East.	5
380		6
381		7
382		8
383	——*Gratian* killed by *Maximus*.	9
384	—*Valentinian* alone.	10
385		11
386		12
387		13
388		14
389		15

R. Rutilius

328 A Chronological TABLE to the Miscellaneous Remarks concerning the Poets, &c.

Years of Rome.

1142

1143
1144

1145

1146

1147—*P. Rutilius Numatianus*——*Claudian* comes first to *Rome* about 30 Years of Age.

1148
1149
1150
1151
1152

1153
1154
1155
1156
1157
1158
1159
1160
1161
1162

N. B. I have not insisted on all the particular Events relating to each Poet, because that would have swell'd this TABLE to an immoderate Size, and because many remarkable Events often fell out the same Year, of which several Poets that were Cotemporary might take Notice: So that I might have filled a Page sometimes with the Events of one Year. And the Reader will find this partly done to his Hand in the *Chronologia Virgiliana, Horatiana,* &c. *Valentinian*

Years after *Christ*. **EMPERORS.**

390   16

391   17
392—*Valentinian* killed 18
       by *Arbogaſtus*.
393—*Theodoſius* alone, in both Eaſtern and Weſtern
       Empires.
394—*Eugenius* proclaim'd Emperor and acknowledg'd
       by *Theodoſius*, but both dying ſoon after,
       Honorius ſucceeds.
395—*Honorius*.   2

396   3
397   4
398   5
399   6
400   7

401   8
402   9
403   10
404   11
405   12
406   13
407   14
408   15
409   16
410—*Rome* taken by *Ala-* 17
      ric, King of the *Goths*.

INDEX.

Athamas, his Story   5, 6
Afta, Titus Quinctius, a Comic Poet, when flourished, 265——his Character   *ibid.*
Attic Wit and Urbanity, what   255
Attilius, a Comic Poet, when flourished, 263——his Character   *ibid.*
Attius, the Tragic Poet, when born, 263——his Character, and by whom admired   *ibid.*
Attellane Plays, their Character, 161 ——whence first derived, 162——Privileges of their Actors. *ibid.*
Augustus, his Poetry   272
Ausonius, Time and Place of his Birth, 96——Prediction of his future Greatness, 97——his Favour with *Gratian*, 98——proved to have been a Christian, 99——his Friendship with *Paulinus*, *ibid.*——*Theodosius*'s Letter to him, 100——his Answer, 102——*Symmachus*'s Character of his Poem on the *Moselle*, 103——his Letter to *Paulinus*, 106——Character of his *Cento*, *ibid.*——of his other Poems   108, 109, 110
Avienus, Rufus Festus, when flourish'd and his Character   286

B.

Bacchides, a Comedy of *Plautus*, its Character   230
Bassus, Cæsius, when flourished, 280 ———his Character   *ibid.*
Bassus, Saleius, his Character   284
Bathyllus, the Pantomime, his Character, 163——his Answer to *Augustus Cæsar*   *ibid.*
Buskin, of what use in Tragedy   164

C.

Cæcilius, Statius, when flourished, 262———his Character   *ibid.*
Cæsar, Julius, his Character of *Terence*   223

Calidius,

INDEX.

Calidius, when flourished, 272——his Character *ibid.*
Calphurnius the Bucolic Poet when flourished, 286——his Character *ibid.*
Calvus, Corn. Licinius, when flourished, 209——his Character *ibid.*
Captivi, a Comedy of *Plautus*, its Character 229
Casina, a Comedy of *Plautus*, its Character *ibid.*
Cato, the Censor, why he opposed the Progress of Learning among the *Romans*, 226——whether Author of the Distichs extant in his Name, 266——Character of that Book 267
Catulus, Lutatius, when Consul, 267——his Exploits, *ibid.*————proscribed by *Marius*, 277——his Death, *ibid.*———his Character as a Poet *ibid.*
Chorus's, their use in Tragedy, 167——their Office laid down by *Horace*, *ibid.*————in Comedy, 168————soon laid aside, and why *ibid.*
Cistellaria, a Comedy of *Plautus*, its Character 230
Claudian, Time and Place of his Birth, 112——first coming to *Rome*, 113——Favour with *Stilicho*, *ibid.*————his Statue erected at *Rome*, why, 115————Character from the Critics, *ibid.*————some account of it from the Inscription, 116——to which of his Poems his Honour's owing, *ibid.*————Favour with the Princess *Serena*, 117——his Marriage, *ibid.*———account of his Stile, 118——of the Rape of *Proserpine*, 119———of his other Poems, 136——of his Invectives, *ibid.*——of his Panegyrics. 138
Comedy, how improved among the *Greeks*, 156——Liberty of the old *Greek* Comedy, *ibid.*——restrained by the thirty Tyrants, *ibid.*——Rise of the middle Comedy, 157——of the new, *ibid.*——parts of Comedy what, 175——defined by *Aristotle*, 190————its first Inventors, 191————how improved among the *Romans*, 219——Difficulty of writing a good Comedy 241
Comparisons,————of *Jason* to a Horse roused by Sound of the Trumpet, 25————of *Hercules*'s Anxiety to a Bird's for her young, 27————of the

Valour

INDEX.

Valour of *Colaxes* to a Torrent, 30 ———— of a Traveller at Sea, 48 ———— The Fall of *Chryses* to a Pile cast into the Sea, 50 ———— of a raw Sailor to a young Poet, 119 ———— of *Lachesis* and *Æolus*, 129 ———— of a young Hero to a Lion's Whelp, 139 ———— *Honorius* and *Arcadius* compared to *Castor and Pollux* 141

D.

Dancing, among the Ancients, how comprehensive, 172 ———— reckoned a part of Music 173
Dionysia, the Feasts of *Bacchus*, how first celebrated 151 ———— and when 152
Drama, its first Rise, 149 ———— among the *Greeks*, 150 ———— among the *Romans*, 158, &c. divided into three Sorts 160
Dramatic Fiction, what 182, &c.

DESCRIPTIONS.

In *Claudian*.

Of *Jupiter* calling a Council of the Gods 121
Of the Joy in *Hell* on *Pluto*'s Marriage 124, &c.
Of *Sicily* and Mount *Ætna* 139. &c.
Of *Ceres*'s Anxiety for her Daughter 133, &c.
Of a signal Victory gained by Favour of a Storm 139
Of the Apotheosis of *Theodosius* 140
Of the *Cytherean* Grove 142, &c.

In *Flaccus*.

Of the Seat of the Winds 15
Of *Alcimede*'s Imprecation 17, &c.
Of the Gates of *Hell*, and Seat of the Blessed 20, &c.
Of Fame 22, &c.
Of growing Love 24, &c.
Of the Soul's Immortality 26

INDEX.

Of the Harpies   48

In *Ovid.*

Of the Gods assembling in Council   122

In *Silius Italicus,*

Description of the *Alps*   47, &c.
Of the Soldiers Surprize there   48
Of the River *Ticinus*   49

In *Juvenal.*

Of Moderation in the Desire of Riches   84
Of the absurd Oaths of the *Romans*   86
Of their Debauchery and Luxury   88
Of the Divine Goodness   90
Of the Fall of *Sejanus*   91, &c.
Of the Ambition of *Annibal* and *Alexander*   92, &c.
Of the Force of ill Habits   94, &c.

In *Virgil.*

Of the Seat of the Winds   16
Of *Dido*'s Imprecation   19
Of *Hell* and *Elyzium*   21
Of Fame   23, &c.
Of growing Love   25
Of the Harpies   29
Of a Torrent   31
Of the Council of the Gods   122

E.

Ennius, when flourished   161
Eloquence, why so much studied by the Ancients   182
Epic Poetry, some Reflections upon it   135

Epicharmus,

INDEX.

Epicharmus, the Comic Poet, when flourished, 191
———his Birth, *ibid.*———and Character *ibid.*
Epidicus, a Comedy of *Plautus*, its Character 230
Epigram, defined, 57———how distinguished, *ibid.*
———Epigram on *Pætus* and *Arria*, 69———how faulty, 68———on *Anthony* and *Cicero, ibid*———another on the same, 60———the latter how faulty, *ibid.*———Instance of a Turn in one on a false Thought, 61———that on *Brutus* and *Portia*, 62———how faulty, *ibid.*———on *Mucius Scævola*, 63———in what blameable, *ibid.*———one concluding with a moral Sentence, 64———upon a rehearsing Poet, 65———on *Decianus*, 66———Epigram of one Distich, *ibid.*———on *Rufus, ibid.* one without a Turn, 67———one consisting only of Antitheses, *ibid.*———a fine one of *Virgil's* of this Sort *ibid.*
Eunuch, a Comedy of *Terence*, when first acted, 245
———what Sum he received for it 246
Eupolis, a Comic Poet, when flourished, 192———his Character *ibid.*
Euripides, when born, 155———his Character and Death 156
Exodia, a kind of Farce among the *Romans* 162

F.

Fables. *Strabo's* account of their Usefulness 183
Fiction, the Soul of Poetry, 184—its great use in Dramatic Poetry 185
Flaccus, Valerius, when and where born, 1———his Character from *Martial*, 2———compared with *Virgil* and other Poets, 3, &c.———his Poem, by whom continued, 14———compared with the Æneid 15, &c.
Floralia. Games. *Cato* ridiculed by *Martial* for coming on the Theatre whilst these Games were performing there, 71———absurd conduct of the *Romans* on this occasion censur'd *ibid.*

Florus,

INDEX.

Florus, Julius, his Character 279
Flutes, Tibiæ of what use on the ancient theatres, according to *Horace*, 169——according to *Donatus*, 170—how distinguished, *ibid.*——Madam *Dacier* mistaken about them, 171——how distinguished by *Diomedes* the Grammarian 172
Furius Antias, flourished when, 267——his Character *ibid.*
Furius Bibaculus, his Birth and Character 268

G.

Gallus Cornelius, when and where born, 274——his Character and Favour with *Augustus, ibid.*——his Misbehaviour, Condemnation and Death, and Account of his Works, 275——Character of him and them from *Virgil, ibid.*——of his Elegies 276
Germanicus Cæsar, his Character, 272——Account of his Poetry from *Quintilian* *ibid.*
Getulicus, when flourished 277
Gratius, when flourished, 280——Character of his works *ibid.*

H.

Hadrian discovers *Stilicho*'s Plot against *Honorius*, 114——his Favour with that Prince and Enmity to *Claudian, ibid.*——compared to *Mallius Theodorus, ibid.*——his Severity to *Claudian* 115
Heautontimoreumenos, a Comedy of *Terence* when first acted 245
Hecyra, a Comedy of *Terence*, when first acted *ibid.*
Helvius Cinna, when flourished, 271——account of his *Smyrna* 272
Hercules, his Adventure with *Laomedon*, &c. 8
Homer, his Works preferred by *Horace* to those of the Philosophers for Instruction 185
Hypsipile, her Story 7 & 8

INDEX

I.

Iambics, why preferable to other Measures in Dramatic Poetry, 189——by whom invented, *ibid.*——*Aristotle's* Remark upon it   190
Jason, his Adventures   5 to 14
Imitation, Man naturally inclined to it   183
Italicus, Silius, Time and Place of his Birth, 33——His Death, 35——His Character from *Pliny* and *Martial*, 35 and 36——Character of his Poem, 37——Character as a Poet   52
Jupiter, his Speech to *Venus* in *Sil. Italicus*. 40, &c. His Speech to *Venus* in *Virgil*   43, &c.
Jupiter Ammon, Origin of his Temple   46, &c.
Juvenal, Time and Place of his Birth, 73——His Banishment where and by whom, 74——The Passage that occasioned it, 75——When return'd, *ibid.* his Death, 77——compared to *Horace* and *Persius*, 80, &c.——his stile, 81——the freedom of his expressions how far justified   82, &c.

L.

Labirius, Decius, when flourished, 267——Character of his *Mimes*, 268——how affronted by *Julius Cæsar*, *ibid.*——his Death   *ibid.*
Lavinius the Poet, his Character and Enmity to *Terence*   250
Livius Andronicus, when flourished, 159——how he acted his Plays   160
Love in Dramatic Poetry, differently treated by the Antients and Moderns   259
Lucilius the Satirist, his Character   80
Luscius the Comic Poet, when flourished, 264——how far he imitated the *Greek* Comic Poets   83

M.

Macer, when flourished, 297——his Works   *ibid.*
Martial, Time and Place of his Birth, 54——his Character in Life, 55——his Death, 56——Character of

INDEX.

of his Epigrams from himself, 68—of his Stile and Poetry, *ibid.*—*Pliny*'s Account of him, 69 Epigram of *Martial* to him, *ibid.*——*Martial's* Looser Works censur'd, 70——his ludicrous Epigram on *Cato*   71

Marullus the Poet, when flourished, and the Character of his Writings   285

Measures, what used in Comedy, difficult to ascertain   181

Medea, her Adventures with *Jason* 12, &c.

Medea, Tragedy of, its Character, 205——examined   206, &c.

Mask, its Use among the Antients, 164—how different from ours, *ibid.*——A Fable of *Phædrus* explained on this Occasion, *ibid.*——how useful to the Voice   165

Melissus, a Comic Poet, his Character 266

Menander, his Character, 157—when flourished, 192—*Terence* how beholden to him, 251—how much admired   255

Menæchmi, a Comedy of *Plautus*, its Character 231

Mercator, a Comedy of *Plautus*, its Character *ibid.*

Miles Gloriosus, a Comedy of *Plautus*, its Character   *ibid*

Mimes, a Species of Dramatic Poetry among the *Romans*, an Account of them   162

Mostellaria, a Comedy of *Plautus*   231

Mummius, a Writer of *Attellane* Plays, when flourished   265

Music of the Antients, account of it as relating to the Drama, 172, &c——how divided by them, 174 Hypocritical Music, what, *ibid*—Metrical, *ibid.*—how applied to the Drama   175, &c.

N.

Nævius, when flourished, 261 published his first Play   *ibid.*

Novius, a Writer of *Attellane* Plays when flourished 265

Nomesianus, when flourish'd and his Character 286

INDEX.

O.

Octavia, a Tragedy, its Character 215
Oedipus, his Story, 210——*Oedipus*, a Tragedy, examin'd, 212————Stile of it 215

P.

Pacuvius, Birth and Character, 262—Death, *ibid.*— his Stile censur'd *ibid.*
Palladius the Poet, when flourish'd and his Character 285
Pantomimes, their Character 163
Paulina, Wife to *Seneca*, her Affection and Constancy 202
Persa, a Comedy of *Plautus* 233
Petronius, Titus, Arbiter, when flourished, 282—his Favour with *Nero*, *ibid.*—Account of his Work, 281—Account of him from *Tacitus*, 282, &c.—Manner of his Death censured 283
Philemon, the Comic poet, when flourished, and his Character, 192—often gain'd the Prize from *Menander* *ibid*
Phormio, a Comedy of *Terence*, when first acted 245
Phormys, the Comic Poet, when flourished, and his Character 192
Plautus, when and where born, 240——how many Plays of his according to *Varro*, 217—his Epitaph, 218—his Character, 220, &c.—his Numbers and Wit condemn'd by *Horace*, 221—how far to be excused, *ibid.*—his Character from *Quintilian*, 223 Conduct of the Drama, 224—in what blam'd, 225—his Numbers on what Account censured by *Horace*, 221—compared with *Terence* 227
Plautius a Comic Poet, when flourished 263
Plato, his Objections to Dramatic Poetry, 194——answered 195, &c.
Plays, those of *Plautus* and *Terence* compared, from 234 to 241
Pluto, his Speech to *Proserpine* 126, &c.
Poetry, how far superior to History 184, &c.

Pœnulus,

INDEX.

Pœnulus, a Comedy of *Plautus*, Character of it 233
Pollio, Caius Asinius, when flourished, 273———his Character, *ibid.*———Enmity to *Cicero*, *ibid.*——— Conduct, Exploits, and Death *ibid.*
Pomponius Secundus, a Tragic Poet, when flourished, 265———his Character 266
Pomponius, a Writer of *Attellane* Plays, 265———his Character 266
Ponticus, when flourished, 277———his Character *ibid.*
Porcius Licinius Tegula, when flourished, 262———his Character *ibid.*
Prologues, how used by *Plautus*, 232———and by *Terence* 249, &c.

Q.

Quintilius Varus, when flourished, 270———his Employments and Character *ibid.*

R.

Rabirius, when flourished, 278—his Character *ibid.*
Rape of *Proserpine*, a Poem, Account of it 119, &c.
Roscius, the Comedian, when flourished, 180———his Contention with *Cicero* *ibid.*
Rudens, a Comedy of *Plautus* 233
Rutilius Numatianus Gallus, when flourish'd and his Character 287

S.

Sabinus, when flourished, 278————Account of his Works *ibid.* & 279
Satire perfected by *Juvenal*, 78————its Original Signification, *ibid.*————Beginning and Progress, 79, &c. imitated the old *Greek* Comedy, 83——its Subjects 89 & 90
Satirical Pieces, by whom first brought to some perfection, 157—whether the *Romans* had any 161
Scenic Games, when first instituted at *Rome* 158
Sedigitus Volcatius, when flourish'd and his Character 284

Seneca,

INDEX.

Seneca, Lucius Annæus, the Philosopher and Tragic Poet, when and where born, 201——his Banishment, *ibid*—Favour with *Agrippina* and *Nero*, 285—his Disgrace, 202—Manner of his Death, 203—Character as a Dramatic Poet, 209, &c.—his Stile 210

Seneca the younger, a Tragic Poet, his Character 215

Sentius Augur, his Character 283

Septimius Titius, his Character 393

Severus, Cassius, when flourished, 273—his Character, Death and Conduct 274

Severus, Cornelius, when flourished, 278—his Character *ibid*.

Serenus, Aulus, his Character 284

Serenus Sammonicus, his Character 285

Sock, its use in Comedy 164

Sophocles, when flourished, 155—his Character *ibid*.

Spurina, his Character 284

Stage, if well regulated, a School of Virtue 199

Stella, Aruntius, when flourished, 383—his Character *ibid*.

Stichus, a Comedy of *Plautus* 233

Stile, how far depends on the different Genius of Nations, 356—an Author's Stile, why difficult to be shewn in the best Translations *ibid*.

Stilicho, his Character, 113——Favour and Alliance with *Theodosius*, 114—with *Honorius, ibid*.—his Fall *ibid*.

Strabo, Cæsar, a Tragic Poet, when flourished 265

Sulpitia, the Poetess, when flourished, 284—Character of her Works *ibid*. & 285

Syrus, Publius, when flourished, and Character of his Mimes 268

T

Taste of the Moderns, why different from that of the Romans 258

Terence, when and where born, 242—made a Slave, 243—by whom made free, *ibid*—his Intimacy with *Scipio* and *Lælius, ibid*.—assisted by them in writing his

INDEX

his Plays, *ibid.*—*Suetonius's* Account of it, 244—
what *Valgius* said of it, *ibid.*—reads his first Play to
Cæcilius, *ibid.*—his Character in general among the
Antients, *ibid.*—how he treated *Terence*, *ibid.*—
Terence sets out for *Greece*, *ibid.*—*Suetonius's* mistake about the true Number of his Plays, *ibid.* &
246—his Character as a Dramatic Poet, 247—his
excellency in describing the Manners, *ibid.* &c.—
in the Disposition of his Plays, 248—in the Decorum
of the Stage, 249—in managing a double Plot, *ibid.*
—why he always copied from the *Greeks*, 252—
his Character from *Varro* and *Velleius Paterculus*,
253—Politeness of his Dialogue, 254——*Terence*
more a *Roman* in his Genius than *Plautus*, 255—his
Rule of writing his Plays, 257—wherein he failed
                                                              259

Terentianus, Maurus, when flourished, and his Character   284
Theatre of the Antients, Account of it   177
Thespis, when flourished, 152——Improvements he
made in the *Greek* Drama.   153
Titius, Caius, a Tragic Poet, when flourished   264
Tragedy, defined by *Aristotle*, 187—its usefulness
illustrated, 193, &c.—some Reflections on the
Conduct of the Antients in it   204, &c.
Trinummus, a Comedy of *Plautus*   233, &c.
Truculentus, a Comedy of *Plautus*   234
Turanius, a Tragic Poet, when flourished   266
Turpilius and *Trabea*, Comic Poets, when flourished
                                                               264

V.

Valerius Cato, when flourished, and his Character
                                                               269
Valgius, when flourished, and his Character   278
Variety of Characters, the Antients deficient in their
Plays as to this, 259—how excusable, *ibid.* and 260
Varius and *Tucca*, when flourished, 276—Character
                                                            of

INDEX.

of *Varius*, and of his Writings, *ibid.*—his Favour
with *Augustus*. *ibid.*

Varro, Marcus Terentius, when and where born, 270
—his Death and Character, *ibid.*—Account of his
Works, Employments, Behaviour in the Civil
Wars, by whom proscribed *ibid.* & 271

Varro Atacinus, his Birth, and Account of his Works,
271—his Character *ibid.*

W.

Wit, whose Province, 57—how hard to attain, 222
—false Wit, where allow'd 57—by many mistaken
for the true 222

FINIS.

Lightning Source UK Ltd.
Milton Keynes UK
29 March 2010

152055UK00001BA/9/P